# A Teacher's Introduction to Reader-Response Theories

## College Section Committee

Tilly Warnock, Chair
University of Wyoming

Lil Brannon
SUNY at Albany

Doris O. Ginn, CCCC Representative
Jackson State University

Brenda M. Greene
Medgar Evers College, CUNY

Linda H. Peterson
Yale University

James F. Slevin
Georgetown University

Joseph F. Trimmer
Ball State University

Art Young
Clemson University

James Raymond, ex officio
University of Alabama

H. Thomas McCracken, CEE Representative
Youngstown State University

Janet Emig, Executive Committee Liaison
Rutgers University

# A Teacher's Introduction to Reader-Response Theories

Richard Beach
University of Minnesota

NCTE Teacher's
Introduction Series

National Council of Teachers of English
1111 West Kenyon Road, Urbana, Illinois 61801-1096

Staff Editor: David A. Hamburg

Interior Design: Tom Kovacs for TGK Design

Cover Design: Barbara Yale-Read

NCTE Stock Number 50187-3050

**Library of Congress Cataloging-in-Publication Data**

Beach, Richard.
    A teacher's introduction to reader-response theories / Richard Beach.
        p.    cm. — (NCTE teacher's introduction series)
    Includes bibliographical references and index.
    ISBN 0-8141-5018-7
    1. Reader-response criticism.  2. Literature—Study and teaching (Secondary)  3. Literature—Study and teaching (Higher)  I. Title. II. Series.
PN98.R3B43   1993
801'.95—dc20                                                    92–38891
                                                                    CIP

# Contents

*Acknowledgments* ................................................... vii

*Foreword* ........................................................ .ix

1. Introduction ..................................................... 1

2. Textual Theories of Response ................................... 15

3. Experiential Theories of Response ............................. 49

4. Psychological Theories of Response ........................... 71

5. Social Theories of Response.................................. 103

6. Cultural Theories of Response .............................. 125

7. Applying Theory to Practice: Making Decisions
   about Eliciting Response ..................................... 153

*Glossary* ....................................................... 163

*Bibliography* ................................................... 167

*Index* .......................................................... 201

*Author* ......................................................... 209

# Acknowledgments

I wish to acknowledge the following people for their helpful comments and suggestions: Philip Anderson, Karen Ebert Armstrong, Patrick Dias, Michael Hancher, Susan Hynds, and Alan Purves. I also want to thank my original coauthor, Russell Hunt, for his contributions prior to his withdrawal from the project to become an academic vice president.

# Foreword

*A Teacher's Introduction to Reader-Response Theories* is the third in a series of books that are especially useful to teachers of English and language arts at all levels. Ours is a wide-ranging discipline, and important scholarly developments in various aspects of our field can be highly complex, not to mention voluminous. We often wish we had the time to take courses or do extended personal reading in topics such as deconstruction, psycholinguistics, rhetorical theory, and the like. Realistically, each of us can read intensively and extensively only in those areas that are of special interest to us or that are most closely related to our work. The Teacher's Introduction Series, then, is geared toward the intellectually curious teacher who would like to get an initial, lucid glance into rich areas of scholarship in our discipline.

Let me stress three things that are *not* intended in *A Teacher's Introduction to Reader-Response Theories* and in other books in this series. First, the books are in no way shortcuts to in-depth knowledge of any field. Rather, these straightforward treatments are intended to provide introductions to major ideas in the field and to whet the appetite for further reading. Second, the books do not aim to "dumb down" complicated ideas, sanitizing them for an imagined "average reader." Many of the ideas are quite challenging, and we don't seek to patronize the reader by watering them down. Third, we don't want to send the message that every subject which is important to English and language arts teachers should be taught directly in the classroom. The personal enrichment of the teacher is paramount here. A great deal of misery might have been avoided in the 1960s if teachers had been doubly urged to learn about grammars new and old—that's part of being a well-rounded teacher—but to *avoid* bringing their new insights, tree diagrams and all, directly into the classroom.

We are grateful to Richard Beach for taking on the formidable work of writing so lucidly about the complexities of reader-response theories. We welcome your comments on the *Teacher's Introduction* concept.

Charles Suhor
Deputy Executive Director, NCTE

# 1 Introduction

Some revolutions occur quietly: no manifestoes, no marching and singing, no tumult in the streets; simply a shift in perspective, a new way of seeing what had always been there. [We] have been witnessing just such a change in the field of literary theory and criticism. The words "reader" and "audience," once relegated to the status of the unproblematic and obvious have acceded to a starring role.

> —Susan Suleiman, *The Reader in the Text*

Among many dramatic changes in literary theory over the past thirty years, one of the most striking has been the growing prominence of what has come to be called reader-response criticism. Building on M. H. Abrams's well-known "triangle" of author, work, and reader, Terry Eagleton has in fact characterized the history of modern literary theory as occurring in three stages: a Romantic "preoccupation with the author," a New Critical "exclusive concern with the text," and finally, "a marked shift of attention to the reader over recent years" (1983, 74). The various theories of reader response to be surveyed in this book could be somewhat loosely characterized as sharing a concern with how readers make meaning from their experience with the text. While literary criticism is equally concerned with making meaning, the focus is generally more on extracting meaning *from* the text rather than making explicit the processes by which readers, or the critic, make meaning. In some cases, they refer to, or characterize, a hypothetical reader's responses; less commonly, the responses of actual readers are cited as evidence for claims about the reader/text transaction. These theories therefore assume that the text *cannot* be understood or analyzed as an isolated entity.

It is often assumed that reader-response criticism represents a relatively unified position. It is particularly tempting to slip into this assumption when the reader-response position is contrasted to the limitations of the New Critical orientation which dominated much theory—and virtually all instruction—through the middle third of the twentieth century. However, writers who have been called "reader-response critics" embrace an extremely wide range of attitudes toward, and assumptions about, the roles of the reader, the text, and the social/ cultural context shaping the transaction between reader and text. One particularly contentious issue has centered on the relative influence of the reader, the text, and the reading situation on how the reading transaction is shaped. Steven Mailloux (39–53) has charged, on the one hand, that some reader-response critics who privilege the influence of the text on readers' responses are no more than New Critics in disguise, assuming that at bottom, the text determines (or ought to determine) everything else. On the other hand, some critics have come very close to insisting that the text is no more than an inkblot, whose meaning is created entirely by the reader. And, more recently, still others have argued that to focus exclusively on the reader/text transaction is to ignore the crucial influence of social, cultural, or situational contexts on the nature of this transaction.

It is also necessary to bear in mind that many theorists who might not identify themselves as reader-response critics have, in recent years, expressed increasing interest in the meaning and conduct of the reader/ text transaction. Such critics and scholars come from as wide a range of different disciplinary perspectives as feminism, Marxism, phenomenology, rhetoric, perceptual and cognitive psychology, psychoanalysis, pragmatics, and aesthetics. Moreover, many of these theorists have been increasingly interested in how response theories shape classroom instruction.

## How Theory Shapes Practice

Theories of how texts mean shape practice in a number of different ways. For example, New Criticism continues to influence undergraduate and high school literature instruction. Despite the dramatic shifts in interest in literary theory in the past thirty years, secondary and postsecondary literature teachers in general continue to employ methods reflecting New Critical orientations. Applebee's recent nationwide survey of literature instruction practices found that little has changed since a previous survey in the 1960s. Teachers continue to focus primarily on "close reading" of literary texts, on the assumption that such texts are invariably integrated or organic wholes. Or, in the "formalist" approach found in traditional textbooks, students focus on how the specific aspects of texts—setting, character, plot, language, and theme—fit together to form a coherent whole. Such approaches are often assumed by their practitioners to be merely "commonsense" (as John Mayher calls it) methods of literary study, and to be untouched by "theory."

Teachers' own theories of how texts mean influence their daily practice. For example, an analysis by Newell, MacAdams, and Spears-Burton (1987) of three high school teachers' theories of literature instruction found markedly different ways of teaching, each corresponding to the individual teacher's beliefs about the role of literature. The teacher whose theoretical stance emphasized imparting knowledge about literature was more likely to focus on the text and employ written formal analysis of the text. In contrast, the two other teachers, who asserted that they believed in using literature to write about experience, were more likely to focus on the student response and to emphasize expression of personal responses. While these teachers' theories do shape practice, teachers may not always reflect systematically on how their practice is driven by certain theories. In contrast, teachers often note the ways in which their writing instruction is shaped by contemporary theories of the composing process. An increased theoretical emphasis on the composing process has resulted in focus on revision, peer evaluation, student-centered writing workshop approaches, and social dimensions of writing in a wide range of classrooms. (It is important to remember that, as Applebee's study of writing instruction shows, such process-centered approaches are no threat to the hegemony of more traditional methods. Still, contemporary theory has certainly had more influence on the practice of composition teaching than on that of literature.)

Contemporary theories of writing may exert such influence because they specify the processes, both cognitive and social, that teachers could then adopt for use in the classroom. In the 1970s and 1980s, numerous publications translated the theory and research on composing into practical implications for teaching. Moreover, the descriptive research extracted from composing theory of students' use of these processes in the classroom—by Donald Graves, Sondra Perl, Lucy McCormick Calkins, and many others—provided teachers with vivid illustrations of concrete ways to translate theory into practice. In contrast, reader-response theories may have had less influence on practice because, with the exception of Rosenblatt, Purves, Probst, Bleich, McCormick, and a few others, there has been little systematic attempt to translate theory into practice.

Another problem, of course, is that teachers need to do more than simply "apply theory." No theory—not even New Criticism—has within itself a clear set of instructions for how one might teach in a classroom. Simply "applying" a theory often entails no more than a reification of the traditional knowledge-transmission model, in which the teacher draws on theory to impart knowledge. The theory does not by itself promote the creation of classroom situations in which students may create their own knowledge through active sharing of ideas (Salvatori). In order to recognize how their own theories shape practice, teachers may find it useful to make explicit the response theories underlying how they themselves respond to texts. In such a process, knowledge or theory construction takes center stage in the classroom. And as Joseph Harris notes, "the theory of reading driving the work of the course gets foregrounded as a theory, as one possible view among others, rather than submerged as an unstated and invisible part of the teacher's method" (176).

In a study of five junior high school teachers, Don Zancanella found that the teachers' own theories of reading influence their teaching. For example, one teacher, Mr. Davidson (a pseudonym), believes that understanding literature involves treating the text as a constructed object. He therefore focuses the students' attention on understanding the literary techniques or elements constituting the constructed object. And he believes that the text is a puzzle or problem to be solved by unpacking the " 'levels' or 'layers' "(11) of the text. He values knowledge of literary techniques, a value he wants to pass on to his students. As he notes, "If students come to learn what is meant by theme or plot, and they see these elements interacting as they must in a good story—that joy of discovery—they'll be reading a story and see the theme emerging and they'll say, 'Look how he's doing that' "(15–16).

This emphasis on knowledge of techniques influenced Mr. Davidson's teaching style. As Zancanella notes:

> His teaching consists primarily of asking questions about characters and events in the work, some of which required simple recall to answers and others which required inference, analysis, and interpretation. When a student answered, Mr. Davidson continued, adjusting or extending the student's answer, or asking for evidence to support it. At some point during the lesson, he turned his questions toward a literary term such as "mood" or "theme" or a literary technique such as characterization. The term or technique was then defined or demonstrated, partly through brief periods of lecture and partly through examples found in the text at hand. (12)

In contrast to Mr. Davidson's text-centered theory of reading, Ms. Kelly believes in the value of readers' vicarious participation in the world of the text. As a nonreader in secondary school, she discovered the value of reading literature in college in providing insights into her life. From the literary experience, she hopes that her students will learn "to know about other people and how they think" (18). She values " 'being' a character when she reads," leading to "her practice in the classroom or asking students to see things from a character's point of view, to 'feel' what a character feels" (22). In her teaching, she therefore encourages students to talk about their own experiences with texts, as well as their own life experiences related to their experience with a text. For example, in talking about a poem about families, she asks the students to talk about their own experiences with family reunions. Much of her focus therefore centers on the value of the literary experience for the reader.

It may therefore be the case that teachers with a more "text-based" theoretical orientation focus more on the text, while those with a more "reader-based" orientation focus more on students' responses. In a recent study of beginning teachers, Pamela Grossman found that teachers who espoused a "transactional" theory of reading were more likely to elicit students' responses in discussions or in writing activities than those teachers who espoused a more "text-centered" orientation. While the difference between a "text-centered" and a "reader-based" theory of reading is more of a continuum than an either/or distinction, these studies suggest that teachers who adopt a "reader-centered" theory may be more likely to consider individual differences in students' responses than teachers with a more "text-centered" theory. Rather than assuming that students will respond in any predetermined, composite manner, "reader-centered" teachers may therefore anticipate a variety of quite different responses.

## Conceptions of Roles, Purposes, Texts, and Contexts

Even within a "reader-based" orientation, theorists and teachers may adopt quite different conceptions of readers' roles, purposes, texts, and contexts, suggesting that there is no single "reader-response" theory.

Reader-response theories suggest that readers adopt a range of different roles. Many theorists, including traditional literary critics, refer vaguely to a hypothetical, impersonal being known as "the reader." (In most cases, of course, "the reader" is an imagined extension of these theorists' own reading experience. In this rhetorical move, the writer or critic proposes an interpretation and then presumes that "the reader" will make the same interpretation. Other theorists, as Elizabeth Freund catalogs in her survey of response theories, specify personifications of "the reader": "the mock reader (Gibson); the implied reader

(Booth, Iser); the model reader (Eco); the super reader (Riffaterre); the inscribed or encoded reader (Brooke-Rose); the narratee/reader (Prince); the "competent" reader (Culler); the literate reader (Holland); or the informed reader in the interpretive community (Fish)" (7).

Few of these conceptions arise from investigations of actual readers. Rather than exploring the ways in which actual readers may respond, these different conceptions reflect assumptions about the hypothetical nature of the text/reader transaction. Conceiving of the reader as "implied" reflects a more text-based orientation; in contrast, conceiving of the reader as resisting, as does feminist Judith Fetterley, reflects a more reader-based orientation. Or, a liberal humanist perspective conceives of the reader as a coherent, autonomous being whose response reflects determined moral certainties (Goodheart).

At the same time, the very notion of "actual" readers as autonomous, independent "individuals" has been challenged by poststructuralist theories whose proponents conceive of "actual" readers as themselves constructed by various institutional discourses. Similarly, they may argue that the postmodern literature of writers like Barthelme and Coover serves to undermine and decenter the reader's responses, thereby undercutting his or her attempt to respond as a coherent self (Barthes). By calling into question traditional forms of representation, postmodern literature questions the idea of established moral and institutional norms defining a reader's self (Hebdige).

Theorists also argue that readers respond for a range of different purposes. Readers may respond to express their emotional reactions, to explore difficulties in understanding, to corroborate or verify their opinions with others, to build a social relationship through sharing responses, or to clarify their attitudes.

These different purposes imply an equally wide range of response strategies—engaging, conceiving, connecting, explaining, interpreting, and judging—that can serve as the basis for devising various response activities (Beach and Marshall). Equally important, students do not simply use these strategies one at a time; they learn to employ a range of strategies simultaneously, moving from one to the next. An understanding of these various strategies thus serves as a theoretical basis for devising and organizing classroom activities.

Responding in the classroom is not limited to written or discussion responses. Reader-response theory also gives us grounds to acknowledge a steadily widening range of response media, including, for example, oral interpretation, role-playing, artwork, rewriting texts, or creating new ones (Corcoran and Evans; McCormick, Waller, and Flower; Protherough; Purves, Rogers, and Soter).

In addition to interest in defining a range of different roles and purposes, reader-response theorists have been increasingly interested in responses to a range of different types of texts. Traditional literary theory usually focused exclusively on "literary" or canonical texts— novels, stories, poems, essays, or drama. Recently, theorists such as Robert Scholes have broadened our conceptions of texts to include a range of modes, genres, and media forms (advertisements, history books, movies, television programs, bumper stickers, editorials, computer hypertext, etc.). For example, rather than assume that literature is "fiction" and history is "fact," both Hayden White and Paul Ricoeur have argued that historical writing could be perceived as narratives. In applying a literary perspective to historical texts, readers may conceive of the text as shaped by writers' use of various literary techniques.

Reader-response theory also calls into question the idea of the literary canon as a means to simply position readers as potential members in an elite, cultural club. Traditional notions of the canon presuppose that readers will evaluate works judged to be "classics" differently from works perceived to be of lesser literary quality. However, as Tompkins and many others (including I. A. Richards in his very early work) have demonstrated, judgment of texts as "classics" was often due to promotions of select, influential critics whose responses were perceived to be more valid than those of readers.

Furthermore, reader-response theorists recognize that the meaning of responses varies considerably according to differences in specific social, historical, or cultural contexts. As any teacher knows, the responses of a period-one class will differ dramatically from the responses of a period-four class to the same text. And these specific social or rhetorical contexts are embedded in larger, and quite different historical and cultural contexts. The members of medieval religious sects responded to "sacred" icons in quite a different manner than do contemporary believers (Greenberg).

## Five Theoretical Perspectives on Response

Given these multiple roles, purposes, text types, and contexts, reader-response theorists tend to focus on different aspects of these components. I have therefore organized this survey of different response theories according to a theorist's primary theoretical perspective. While each theorist may represent a range of different perspectives, he or she has been somewhat arbitrarily categorized as falling within one of five primary theoretical perspectives: the "textual," "experiential," "psychological," "social," and "cultural."

As illustrated in the following figure, these five perspectives represent different angles or lenses that illuminate or highlight particular aspects of the reader/text/context transaction. For example, while the textual perspective illuminates the reader's knowledge of text conventions, the social perspective illuminates the social context.

*Textual* theorists focus on how readers draw on and deploy their knowledge of text or genre conventions to respond to specific text features. For example, in responding to a mystery story, a reader applies her knowledge of mystery genre conventions to predict the story outcomes. *Experiential* theorists focus on the nature of readers' engagement or experiences with texts—the ways in which, for example, readers identify with characters, visualize images, relate personal experiences to the text, or construct the world of the text. *Psychological* theorists focus on readers' cognitive or subconscious processes and how those processes vary according to both unique individual personality and developmental level. *Social* theorists focus on the influence of the social context on the reader/text transaction—the ways, for

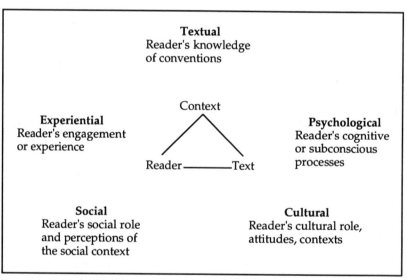

Five perspectives representing different lenses that illuminate particular aspects of the reader/text/context transaction.

example, that a book club context serves to encourage a lot of open-ended responses. Finally, *cultural* theorists focus on how readers' cultural roles, attitudes, and values, as well as the larger cultural, historical context, shape responses. For example, members of a religious sect are socialized to respond to sacred texts according to the cultural values of that sect.

Each of these perspectives is limited by the fact that it illuminates only a particular facet of the reader/text transaction. At the same time, they are all focusing on the same process: how readers create meaning. Given their disciplinary perspectives and philosophical bias, each conceives of meaning in quite different terms. While a cognitive psychologist associates meaning-making with applying cognitive strategies, a social theorist finds meaning as inherent in the social dynamics of sharing responses.

These five perspectives could be conceived of as moving from the specific to the global, from the textual and experiential theorists' focus on the immediate text/reader transaction to the psychologist's concern with cognitive and subconscious forces shaping the reader's transaction to the social and cultural theorists' interest in how social and cultural phenomena shape meaning.

The order in which I discuss these five perspectives is based somewhat on the historical development within reader-response criticism since the work of I. A. Richards and Louise Rosenblatt in the 1920s and 1930s. The early theorists, drawing on structuralist linguistics, narrative theory, and aesthetic theory, focused more on the reader's knowledge of text conventions and/or the reader's experience. With the increased interest in psychoanalytical and cognitive psychological perspectives in the 1960s and 1970s, theorists attempted, with mixed success, to apply these approaches to understand response. Then, in the 1980s and early 1990s, the rise of social constructivist, poststructuralist, feminist, and cultural/media studies perspectives led to an increased interest in the transaction as embedded in social and cultural contexts. As suggested by my discussion of the limitations of each of these perspectives, the later perspectives, in challenging the assumptions of earlier perspectives, often built on the limitations of those perspectives.

At the same time, while all of these theoretical perspectives rest on different assumptions about meaning, they ultimately intersect and overlap. The local—the focus on readers' textual knowledge and experience—is embedded within the global, larger social and cultural contexts (Beach and Hynds). I invite the reader, using these five perspectives as a set of heuristic categories, to entertain the possible ways in which these perspectives inform each other, for example, how the quality of the social context influences readers' shared textual conventions or how the readers' acts of "doing gender" in a cultural context influence the quality of a reader's experience.

How do these theories apply to the classroom? Teachers could use my brief summaries of these theories to reflect on the assumptions driving their literature teaching. In asking students to respond to a text, we may assume that some responses are of greater value than others. We assume that certain kinds of activities may be more appropriate than others. And, we also assume that certain kinds of students with certain kinds of backgrounds will respond in certain ways. Each of these theoretical perspectives serves to challenge these assumptions. Hence, a second invitation to reflect. Teachers could consider which of these perspectives they are most likely to value or subscribe to (e.g., that from a textual perspective, responding requires knowledge of genre conventions) and weigh that assumption against the assumptions inherent in the other perspectives. By using the other perspectives to challenge one's own assumptions, teachers may examine their basic goals for teaching literature.

In discussing each of these five theoretical perspectives, I will make references to my own and some students' responses to the following poem, Sylvia Plath's "Mushrooms." I cite these responses to illustrate the idea that the same responses can be analyzed according to each of the different perspectives. Given a particular reader responding to a particular text in a particular social and cultural context, it may then be possible to describe differences in the meanings of their responses in terms of these different perspectives. (I suggest that readers write out their own responses to the poem and then apply each of the perspectives to those responses.)

Mushrooms

Overnight, very
Whitely, discreetly,
Very quietly

Our toes, our noses
Take hold on the loam,
Acquire the air.

Nobody sees us,
Stops us, betrays us;
The small grains make room.

Soft fists insist on
Heaving the needles,
The leafy bedding,

Even the paving.
Our hammers, our rams,
Earless and eyeless,

Perfectly voiceless,
Widen the crannies,
Shoulder through holes. We

Diet on water,
On crumbs of shadow,
Bland-mannered, asking

Little or nothing.
So many of us!
So many of us!

We are shelves, we are
Tables, we are meek,
We are edible,

Nudgers and shovers
In spite of ourselves.
Our kind multiplies:

We shall by morning
Inherit the earth.
Our foot's in the door.

## A Student's Responses to the Poem

The following responses of a 15-year-old student (whom I will call
"Jill") at Comberton Village College, a high school outside of Cambridge, England, were elicited by Patrick Dias of McGill University,
who has done extensive research on students' responses to poetry.
After spending ten days in small-group discussion work, the students
wrote their "stream-of-consciousness" responses to as many rereadings
as they believed were necessary.

1. Loam? Top, on soil; Bland-mannered? Good things are never
   nasty.

2. The mushrooms only seem to grow at night because it says
   "overnight" in the first verse, they are white in color and grow
   very quiet, and nobody sees them grow because it is nighttime
   and they are not noticed.

3. When their toes and noses take hold of the loam it suggests to
   me that they are coming out of the soil and they feel the air for
   the first time. The soft fists insist on heaving the needles could

be the soft top of the mushroom as it grows out of the soil pushing away fallen pine needles and dead leaves as it grows upward.

4. Nobody sees them because they grow at night and so nobody can stop them, nobody can betray us, may mean that nobody saw them grow there and so they wouldn't be perceived before they had finished growing that night. What sort of person wrote this poem? Would he be a nature man? Did he actually see a mushroom grow at night?

5. The small grains make room. Would that mean the grains of soil part and move away as the mushroom breaks through the soil or as it is growing up underneath the soil?

6. What did it mean by "even the paving"? Are "our hammers, our rams" supposed to be the tops of the mushrooms pushing? Or is it the mushrooms imagining they have hammers and rams? Earless and eyeless obviously tells us mushrooms have no ears and eyes, as we already know.

7. The mushrooms don't talk, no plant can, they are very silent when they are growing. Does widening the crannies, shouldering through holes, mean the mushrooms widen the hole in the soil as they grow bigger and the shoulder is the top of the mushroom?

8. They diet on water because plants don't eat food or do they? A plant like a mushroom needs water to grow and crumbs of shadow mean maybe that mushrooms grow in the shadows of trees and bushes. They try to find any little bit of shadow they can to grow in.

9. Mushrooms in fairy tales were always used as tables for little creatures and according to the poem the poet seems to think the mushrooms refer to themselves as tables and shelves and don't mind being used as such things because they are meek, harmless, friendly, quiet sorts of plants and are also edible, and much loved as edible plants.

10. Mushrooms grow very quietly and they grow everywhere. The poet obviously believes that given the change, mushrooms would take over the world.

11. The poet likes plants and things and may have spent a night in the woods watching mushrooms grow or seeing how silent mushrooms grow.

*My Responses to the Poem*

1. I'm caught up in flow of the slow, silent growth of mushrooms as they become more and more numerous. They seem to grow more and more powerful so that by the end of the poem they think that they can take over the world. The poem seems to pick up speed as the mushrooms grow in numbers and intensity and then suddenly there's a pause prior to the final pronouncement that "We shall by morning/Inherit the earth." The very fact that they made such a bold announcement means that they've assumed a lot of power by the end of the poem. I'm reminded of the way a whole bunch of mushrooms will suddenly appear in the backyard, pretentiously unannounced, as if they owned the place.

2. I hear a repetition of sounds—the "s's" in "toes," "noses," "sees us/Stops us, betrays us;/The small grains make room./Soft fists insist on/Heaving the needles . . . hammers, out rams,/earless and eyeless, etc. And the mushrooms engage in a ritual chant: "So many of us!/So many of us!" that suggest that on the one hand, they are zombie-like, but, on the other hand, that they are very human, very much caught up in a human emotion of feeling betrayed and tasting the power of revenge. I'm intrigued by these competing feelings of feeling powerless ("We are shelves, we are/Tables") and powerful, something I experience often in my own life. And, they seem to grow louder and louder as their "kind multiplies," as if a mob of people, become more and more boisterous. I'm reminded of the story "The Locusts," in which millions of swarming locusts wipe out entire farmlands, and, I recall a number of horror films—*Night of the Living Dead* (1968) and *Invasion of the Body Snatchers* (1956, 1978)—in which zombie-like creatures increase in numbers to the point that they start to take over a society. As I envision them taking over the world, I'm growing increasingly more apprehensive and fascinated by their very audacity.

3. Now that I sense that the poem's not about mushrooms, I'm envisioning all sorts of meanings for the mushrooms. The biblical allusion suggests that it's about power and the powerless "inheriting the earth." I'm thinking that the mushrooms represent the downtrodden in society, possibly the poor or the homeless. Or, given Plath's interest in the role of women in a patriarchal world, the poem could be about women. Often, the downtrodden are those who are silenced by society—out of sight, out of mind.

However, as their numbers grow, which was certainly the case in the 1980s, they collectively assume more power. Is this an allegory of a revolution? I'm apprehensive again about the romanticizing or idealization of a revolution given the potential backlash of the system, once challenged, to simply step all over the "mushrooms" as embarrassing blemishes on the landscape. The romantics of the French Revolution didn't last long.

4. In reflecting on my own response, maybe I'm playing out my own desires for a political or cultural upheaval. Maybe all those who've been on the short end of the stick since the early '80s will finally combine forces and make some changes. In looking back over my earlier readings, I'm also struck by how I'm just distancing myself from worrying about the messy reality of whatever these mushrooms represent—a very safe, analytical, middle-class stance. So, there's a tension here between caring and distancing, between really pondering realities and cynically drawing back.

Jill and I obviously responded in quite different ways to "Mushrooms." She focused more on describing the growth of the mushrooms, while I focused more on the symbolic meanings of the mushrooms. She also did not talk much about her own experiences, while I self-consciously referred to my own responses. Each of the five theoretical perspectives summarized in this book serves to explain reasons for differences in our responses in terms of readers:

- Knowledge of text conventions (textual theories)
- Modes of experience (experiential theories)
- Psychological perspective (psychological theories)
- Social context (social theories)
- Cultural identities (cultural theories)

# 2 Textual Theories of Response

Reader-response theory is typically described as a reaction to the New Criticism that achieved prominence in the 1940s and 1950s. The New Critics—John Crowe Ransom, Rene Wellek, Austin Warren, William Wimsatt, Monroe Beardsley, and others—were themselves reacting against "Old Criticism," which embraced literary history, literary biography, impressionistic/appreciative criticism, and moral/didactic criticism. In reaction to the Old Criticism concern with matters "outside" the text, they assumed that the meaning was primarily "in" the text. They dismissed consideration of the author's role in shaping meaning as the "intentional fallacy"—a violation of the idea that the meaning was in the text, rendering attempts to impute authorial intentions or even to seek out an author's statements of intention as wrongheaded. (They relished D. H. Lawrence's quip, "Trust the tale, not the teller.") They labeled as the "affective fallacy" any consideration of the idea of the reader's emotional reactions as constituting the meaning. They advocated precise, technical, objective analysis of the language of the text, particularly figurative language. As Steven Mailloux argues in *Rhetorical Power,* this appeal to technical precision and objectivity served to legitimate literary studies within the political arena of the university as a "scientific" endeavor of knowledge production worthy of equal recognition to the emerging fields of the natural and social sciences. He quotes John Crowe Ransom as advocating that " 'criticism must become more scientific, or precise and systematic, and this means that it must be developed by the collective and sustained effort of learned persons—which means that its proper seat is in the universities' " (329). Ransom's appeal to a scientific approach was also a reaction to ascendancy of behaviorist psychology, whose proponents were skeptical of "internal" or "subjective" phenomena they associated with work in the humanities.

These ideas served as a set of often unacknowledged assumptions guiding literature instruction since the 1940s. Teachers assumed that texts were central; that they were best regarded as well-wrought urns, artistic objects that were endlessly rich and self-consistent; that students should appreciate their complexity; and that therefore the teacher's job was to teach the skills of close, concise, attentive analysis. Encouraging expression of and attending to differences in students' own responses was considered less important.

The early reader-response theorists, I. A. Richards, Louise Rosenblatt, D. W. Harding, James Britton, Walter Slatoff, Norman Holland, and others, rejected these assumptions as failing to consider the role of the reader in constituting meaning. These theorists argued for the need to consider the responses of actual readers creating their own unique meaning. For example, during the 1920s, I. A. Richards had asked his Cambridge students to "respond freely" to poetry read in his classes (17–22). He then categorized a range of different difficulties students experienced in understanding poetry, particularly in terms of students' failure to explore or extend their thinking beyond "stock responses." While Richards's study reflected text-centered assumptions about the role of the text, the fact that he contended that "the personal situation of the reader inevitably (and within limits rightly) affects his reading" (277) added credibility to valuing the role of the reader. Richards was also aware, back in 1929, that literary critics are often expected to talk about the text—not about the effects of texts on readers:

> We are often compelled, for example, to say things about the poem, or the words in it, which are only true of the effects of the poem on the minds of its readers. . . . We speak of the poem's beauty instead of entering upon elaborate and speculative analyses of its effect upon us . . . we come temporarily to think that the virtues of a poem lie not in its power over us, but in its own structure and conformation as an assemblage of verbal sounds. (1929, 23)

At the 1967 Dartmouth Conference, these early theories were translated in some influential pedagogical statements (Squire). Participants at that conference, particularly the British educators James Britton and John Dixon, were reacting against academic New Critical literature instruction. Drawing on theorists such as D. W. Harding, they posited the need for a broader theory of literacy development that encompassed students' creative, reflective, and oral uses of language. They argued that active expression of response in the classroom contributed to students' literacy development.

However, it is difficult to pinpoint any specific date when theorists moved away from thinking about the literary experience as purely a textual matter and began thinking of the experience as involving readers. Even the most uncompromising of the New Critics had never denied that readers were involved. They had merely asserted that to be concerned with the vagaries of actual individual acts of reading was not to attend to literature. Studies of "the reader," Rene Wellek and Austin Warren stated, would lead to "complete skepticism and anarchy" and eventually to "the definite end to all teaching of literature" (146). In their essay, "The Affective Fallacy," William Wimsatt and Monroe Beardsley concurred. They were simply less interested in reading. For them, the word tended to be more a noun (as in "a reading" of a text) than a verb (as in the student "is reading" the text). If they were interested in different "readings," they wanted to evaluate the legitimacy of these "readings" against the "work itself" in terms of which "reading" best approximated the work's verbal artistry. All of this served to legitimate the central role of teacher as master explicator who, as mediator between students and critics, held the keys to unlocking the text before the admiring eyes of the students, serving to center the authority for knowledge construction in the hands of the teacher.

The New Critical approach was eventually challenged. During the 1960s and 1970s, with the increasing interest in structuralist and transformational linguistics, the "new rhetoric" of Kenneth Burke's dramatism, speech-act theory, and popular cultural analysis of media, there was an increased interest in the role of the reader/viewer. Response theorists drawing on these fields were interested in how readers' knowledge of language and text/genre conventions influenced their responses to texts. I categorize these theorists as adopting a "textual" perspective because they focused primarily on readers' application of knowledge of *text* conventions to infer meaning. Contrary to New Critical orthodoxy, the meaning was now perceived to be constituted by the transaction between the knowledgeable reader and the text. Theorists drawing on structuralist linguists posited that readers understand texts according to the conventions constituting text structures. Given the rhetoricians' interest in the audience's response to the rhetorical appeals of texts, attention also shifted to interest in audiences. All of this led to increasing attention to how readers or viewers used their knowledge of text conventions and rhetorical strategies to understand texts.

Textual theorists posit that text conventions are "constitutive" rather than "regulative," i.e., they constitute rather than regulate a form or genre. As with the rules of baseball, without the conventions there would be no form or genre. Without baseball rules, there would be no game. Without the conventions of the musical, there would be no musical in which actors suddenly and inexplicably break into song, something an audience accepts as constituting the musical genre.

Readers acquire a tacit, "knowing-how" knowledge of these conventions from years of reading certain types of texts. Having read hundreds of mystery stories, they intuitively know, along with the detective hero, how to sort out clues and spot red herrings. Just as somebody learning to ride a bike may not be able to explain the process, students, as "beginners," may not be able to readily abstract about their theoretical "knowing-how" knowledge (Ryle). Similarly, teachers know that simply teaching theoretical "knowing-that" knowledge of conventions will not necessarily transfer to a "knowing-how" capacity to respond. From a "knowing-that" perspective, teachers can teach conventions of comedy to students; but with a rich experience with comic plays, students will not acquire a "knowing-how" ability to respond to comedy. All of this means that students best "learn" literature simply from spending time reading, something they seem to devote little of their limited leisure time to doing (Applebee).

In responding to the poem "Mushrooms" both Jill and I are drawing on my own "knowing-how" knowledge of conventions constituting poetry. We both know that reading poems requires multiple rereadings, knowing that with each new reading, we will extract new and different meanings. On her fourth rereading, Jill asks the questions, "What sort of person wrote this poem? Would he be a nature man?" The very fact that she asks these questions suggests that she has some sense of the poem as an expression of the poet's own experiences. At the conclusion of her rereadings, she infers that "The poet likes plants and things and may have spent a night in the woods watching mushrooms grow or seeing how silent mushrooms grow." She is speculating about how the poet transformed her observations into a poem, which suggests that she has some sense of the process by which writers construct texts—that poets draw on their experience. At the same time, she conceives of the poem as a sort of biology lab report, a conception that reflects the difference between her knowledge and my knowledge of conventions constituting poetry. I know that a poet's particular style often reflects certain recurring interests and themes (Kintgen). Having read Sylvia Plath's other quite serious, often dark, brooding poetry, I respond to "Mushrooms" as a poem about something more than simply mushrooms. I therefore perceive the mushrooms as representing a host of possible symbolic meanings.

I attempt to personify the mushrooms because I know that having made "Mushrooms" the title, Plath was signaling to me that the poem is about a lot more than mushrooms. I also know that *sound* is important in poetry. I therefore notice Plath's repetition of the "s" sound in almost every line: "discreetly," "toes," "noses," "sees us, stops us, betrays us," "small grains," "soft fists," etc., sounds that contribute to my sense of the mushrooms as living, moving persons. I also know that *repetition* itself conveys meaning. The repetition of the "s" sound creates in me a sense of a slowly building background noise that grows louder and louder, much as the eerie synthesizer noise in David Lynch's movies or his "Twin Peaks" television program.

And, given my experience with poetry, I know that *pauses* and *white space* also convey meaning by interrupting the continuous flow of language. In responding to the pauses and white space after each of the short stanzas in the poem, I sense that Plath is punctuating the actions to give the impression of the mushrooms as persistent battering rams. I thus infer that Plath is inviting me to read her text not simply as a nature poem, but as a portrayal of the attempt of the downtrodden to assume power and recognition. Textual theorists tend to endow the text with considerable force in inviting or shaping readers' responses. Jonathan Culler, whose early work, as represented in *Structuralist Poetics: Structuralism, Linguistics and the Study of Literature*, drew on structuralist linguistics, argues that "interpretation is always interpretation of something, and that something functions as the object in a subject-object relation, even though it can be regarded as the product of prior interpretations" (5). Culler is therefore critical of the tendency of reader-response theorists to focus solely on the reader, noting that there will always be some dualism inherent in the reader/text transaction.

## Phenomenological Theories of Response

Phenomenological response theorists such as Georges Poulet and Roman Ingarden represent the textual theorists' interest in how the text shapes meaning. They are primarily interested in the relationship between the consciousness of the perceiver/reader and the perceived text, in how an object itself "intends" to be perceived to describe the ways readers apprehend texts by losing themselves to the writer's or speaker's own ways of perceiving reality.

Poulet's phenomenological theories of response suggest that readers "bracket out" their preconceptions and assumptions in order to achieve an intense engagement with these ways of perceiving. Poulet argues that the reader is passively dependent on the work, which assumes a life of its own. As he notes, "Because of the strange invasion of my person by the thoughts of another, I am a self who is granted the experience of thinking thoughts foreign to him. I am the subject of thoughts other than my own" (56). The "work" as a "subjectified" object then becomes the "other" consciousness to which the reader surrenders. The "work" is "intended" by an author for the reader to absorb and surrender to the writer's or speaker's consciousness.

In contrast to Poulet, Roman Ingarden argues that the reader assumes a more active role in order to "concretize" the text (17). Like a musician performing a musical text, a reader performs the text as a set of possibilities. For Ingarden, the text is composed of strata, or layers, of various schemata. In order to synthesize the indeterminacy of these various schemata, readers create "concretizations," which are distinct from the work itself. Readers draw on their own prior knowledge of ways of perceiving and imaging to make sense of the text, a more active role than that assumed by Poulet's passive surrender. Given the gaps of indeterminacy in the work's schematic, a reader may create an infinite number of what Poulet defined as "concretizations."

All of this served as the groundwork for Wolfgang Iser's response theories described in *The Implied Reader* and *The Act of Reading*, theories central to the Constance School of Reception Theory (Holub, 53–106). Drawing on the idea of gap-filling, Iser describes the text as a set of incomplete instructions to be completed by the reader. Applying knowledge of text conventions, the reader fills in the gaps by employing such strategies as predicting outcomes or constructing characters. To determine how to fill these gaps, in Iser's model, the reader adopts a "wandering viewpoint" within the text. In adopting this "wandering viewpoint," a reader "travels along inside that which it has to apprehend" (108). Rather than adopt a single perspective, a reader is vaguely aware of the competing perspectives that serve to challenge their initial perspectives. In Iser's model, readers are therefore consciously aware of their own strategic processing of texts.

Iser's model is exemplified by my response to "Mushrooms," in which I engage in gap-filling by linking the disparate words on the page to construct a sense of coherence. I seek a sense of coherence by drawing on my prior knowledge to create a narrative about how the mushrooms build in numbers and strength during the night. In creating this narrative, I predict what may be happening to the mushrooms. In my own "concretization" of their story, I imagine that they are building their own force during the night. When Plath refers to the fact that "we are shelves, we are/Tables, we are meek," I sense a gap between what I thought the poem was about—mushrooms— and a new possibility that the mushrooms could be about almost anything. Because I am seeking some sense of coherence that works for me, I am the one who is creating the gaps to be filled.

In adopting a "wandering viewpoint," I entertain a range of possible perspectives within the text. For example, the words "bland-mannered, asking little or nothing" invite me to infer that the mushrooms are reserved, humble, unassuming beings. Then, later in the poem, I read that they are "nudgers and shovers," images that challenge my earlier inference. While I may initially adopt the perspective of mushrooms as meek nonentities, I later adopt the perspective of mushrooms as a powerful mass movement. I am therefore continually revising my perspectives, leading me to recognize the limitations of initial, premature perspectives.

A reader who embraces these different perspectives, however, never achieves a final sense of the overall text. In what Iser defines as a journey through these perspectives, a reader seeks to establish "a pattern of consistency, the nature and reliability of which will depend partly on the degree of attention he has paid during each phase of the journey" (16). The different perspectives in a text reflect larger social, cultural, or historical ideas that help a reader recognize larger thematic perspectives. In the process, a reader "combines all that he sees within his memory and establishes a pattern of consistency, the nature and reliability of which will depend partly on the degree of attention he has paid during each phase of the journey. At no time, however, can he have a total view of that journey" (144). In this way, textual response theorists differ from New Critics in recognizing the reader's dynamic, strategic role in continually defying attempts to achieve a final, fixed "total view" of a text.

In my consistency-building, I am also able to distinguish between important information that belongs in what Iser describes as the "theme" or foreground and what information I need to leave in the background, or "horizon." For example, I recognize that the fact that the mushrooms are "voiceless" implies that they are quietly growing in strength without a lot of self-serving fanfare. As I move through the poem, what's less important to me is the idea that nothing, not even something concrete, can stop them. Later in the poem, when their "foot's in the door," I infer that they have already moved beyond any barriers to achieve a new level of power. What was a "horizon" now assumes a foreground position of "theme." Thus in shifting my "wandering viewpoint," I also keep shifting the "themes" and "horizons."

Steven Mailloux's earlier model of response, as explicated in *Interpretive Conventions*, revolves around this idea that the text invites me to continually reexamine shifting perspectives. Mailloux argues that reader-response theory, as well as much literature instruction, often focuses on the reader's holistic response to the overall text rather than to the ongoing experience with the text. Drawing on both Iser and Stanley Fish, Mailloux argues that an author uses various strategies "to control the reader's temporal interaction with the text" (71). As readers move through a text, their expectations are either fulfilled or frustrated, requiring a continual shifting and revising of perceptions which may cause readers to become uncertain as to whom or what to believe.

In an analysis of how a hypothetical reader might respond to Hawthorne's "Rappaccini's Daughter," Mailloux demonstrates that in the process of trying to determine whom to believe about the death by poison of Rappaccini's daughter, readers recognize that their own initial judgments may have been misguided. In the beginning of the story, readers are presented with a series of enigmas (Who is Rappaccini's daughter? What is the garden?) dramatized by a number of different sources of information. Readers must then judge which of these sources to trust. While they may initially believe the narrator's perceptions, they may later begin to doubt those perceptions. All of this serves to encourage readers to distrust their own judgments, creating a sense of ethical concern. As Mailloux notes, "The reader arrives at this point only by passing through a succession of different concerns pressed on him by the discourse. From a worrying over external facts, the discourse moves the reader to judge first internal motivation and then moral responsibility" (88). The meaning of the textual response therefore derives not from a one-shot "instant-interpretation" about the overall theme but from the unfolding experience with Hawthorne's complex discourse strategies. In the process, readers become aware of how their own beliefs and attitudes are shaping their experience.

Although readers assume a highly active role in constructing meaning, from a "textual" perspective, their activities are continually constrained by what is perceived to be a text functioning independent of their activity. The numerous criticisms of Ingarden's and Iser's gap-filling models center on the paradox of readers who create meaning and a text that simultaneously limits meaning. Elizabeth Freund charges that the theory presumes both an actively engaged reader employing cognitive strategies to create coherence, while, at the same time, the text's schemata is also considered to be independent of the readers' meaning-making (143–51). Her argument assumes both a text that instructs readers and readers who construct their own text—a seeming contradiction. (This contradiction often occurs in literature instruction in which students are encouraged to relate their own experience to a text but must then adopt a particular interpretation. As Peter Griffith notes, "Great stress is laid on the pupil's experience . . . but the ultimate goal will be phrased as something like 'understanding what the poem has to say to us.' " [32].)

Critics also charge that Iser's idea of consistency-building reflects a need to achieve some synthesis in the face of a perplexing indeterminacy. As Mailloux argues, Iser's need to cope with this indeterminacy reflects a New Critical propensity to achieve a definitive interpretation. The ability to admit to indeterminacy requires an awareness of "a meaninglessness which is at the same time a rich meaningfulness, indeterminable by any single interpretation or analysis" (Martin, 381). Iser also presupposes a confident, unified, knowledgeable reader who can synthesize meanings into a coherent totality. However, as William Spurlin (737–38) argues, this optimistic, humanistic conception of the reader flies in the face of experiences in which readers may entertain a sense of multiple, conflicting, problematic perspectives that undermine a sense of a unified self.

Another germinal textual theorist is Hans Robert Jauss, whose work examines readers' responses as constituted by meanings inherent in particular historical contexts. To reconstruct these historical meanings, readers compare their own responses with those of historical persons in the past. By exploring the disparities between their own and past "horizons of expectations," readers can examine how their own "horizons of expectations" shape their experience. These horizons include knowledge of the literary conventions or norms operating in a certain period, conventions or norms that are distinct from social or cultural norms. For example, sixteenth-century readers brought considerable knowledge of classical allusions and religious symbolism to their response to texts of the period (Greenberg). They were therefore uneasy about placing pictures of people in their bedrooms because they assumed that, given their religious beliefs, they would "possess" the people in the pictures.

Gunnar Hansson argues that literary history needs to focus on the particular strategies readers employed during certain historical periods. In his own study, he analyzed Swedish high school students' exam essays written in response to similar prompts from 1865 to 1968. The students' predominant response orientation in their essays consistently reflected shifts in literary instructional approach employed in Swedish schools: During the 1900s and through the 1920s, students used an "idealistic" approach, in which texts were appreciated for their depiction of ideal values and inner truths; from the twenties to the forties, a "historical-empirical" approach in which they focused on the author's craftsmanship in portraying the world; from the forties to the sixties, a "psychological-symbolic" approach that focused on the author's own psychological insights into inner experiences. For Hansson, these approaches reflect relatively traditional literary critical approaches employed in universities that shape, in a top-down manner, secondary school curricula.

Historical analyses also reveal that writers are concerned about the kinds of text-reading strategies they apply to their texts. For example, the Romantic poets were quite concerned about their readers' newfound authority in shaping the meaning of the text (Klancher). In some cases, they were so concerned about how their readers would respond to their poems that they provided, as did Wordsworth in his preface to *Lyrical Ballads,* a set of instructions on how to read his poems. As Scott Simpkins points out, "He testifies to the veracity of accounts given in the poems, relates pertinent elements of landscape or historical facts, or stresses personal experience with the subjects described," notes that "significantly alter the ways that readers construct an image of the poet and his work" (46). Understanding Wordsworth's need to provide these notes requires an understanding of conceptions of audience roles operating within certain historical periods.

The work by Ingarden, Iser, and Jauss suggests the value of focusing on how students' responses are invited by texts. By having students express freewriting or "think-aloud" responses, students could discuss how specific aspects of texts evoke specific responses. In the process, students may intuitively recognize how their own "knowing-how" competence shapes their responses.

## Theories of Readers' Knowledge of Narrative Conventions

In order for readers to interpret the meaning of the text's language, they apply their knowledge of narrative conventions. The theorist who has formulated the most elaborate model of readers' knowledge of narrative conventions is Peter Rabinowitz. In his book *Before Reading* Rabinowitz posits that readers adopt the roles of the "authorial audience," whom the author assumes will be responding to the text. By making assumptions about their "authorial audience's" knowledge of narrative conventions, the authors can then develop their narrative with that audience in mind. Similarly, readers sense that an author is making a certain appeal or pitch to an assumed "authorial audience," even though they may not identify with that audience.

In adopting the role of the "authorial audience," according to Rabinowitz, a reader is accepting "the author's invitation to read in a particularly socially constituted way that is shared by the author and his or her expected readers" (22). If, for example, I infer that in "Mushroom's," Plath is inviting me to sympathize with a scenario of the downtrodden assuming power, then I am adopting the role of Plath's authorial audience. Plath and I are then sharing the same conventional ways of understanding, ways that even precede experience with a text. Hence, the significance of the title, *Before Reading*. As Rabinowitz notes, "A reader who picks up Ellery Queen's *Tragedy of X* for the first time knows to eliminate obvious suspects, not because of some *systematic* understanding of possible literary types, but rather because it is the *conventional* thing to do in that kind of a book" (28). Had I not known the conventions constituting ways of reading "Mushrooms," I would not have been able to construct my sense of the "authorial audience."

In a similar typology of readers, W. Daniel Wilson (850–55) proposes four types of readers: the "real reader," the "implied reader," the "characterized reader," and the "intended reader." In contrast to the actual, flesh-and-blood "real reader," the "implied reader" is a stance or set of behaviors and attitudes presupposed by the text. The "implied reader" of "Mushrooms" is based on a set of presuppositions—that the reader understands the symbolic meaning of the mushrooms and adopts a sympathetic stance toward them. The "characterized reader" is directly addressed by the text's speaker and therefore is a "character" or is "characterized." While there is no explicitly identified "characterized" audience in the poem, the mushrooms directly address an unknown audience which can be considered a "characterized audience." The fourth type, "intended reader," is the writers' conception of their audience. "Actual readers" attempt to define a relationship with the presuppositions associated with the "implied reader" by drawing on their prior knowledge and experience with the conventions of reading and experiences with other texts. According to Rabinowitz, readers acquire this knowledge of conventions primarily from their experience of reading. Having read a lot of poetry, I acquire a "knowing-how" sense of how images in poems function symbolically.

Rabinowitz (*Before*) proposes four types of conventions or rules that assist readers in defining their relationship to the implied stance:

1. *Rules of notice*—for giving priority to or privileging certain aspects of texts (titles, first and last sentences, opening scenes, etc.).

2. *Rules of signification*—for inferring the significance of specific aspects of a text, for example, to assume that characters are motivated by psychological motives.

3. *Rules of configuration*—for inferring patterns in order to predict outcomes so that in the beginning of a novel, a reader knows how the novel will end.

4. *Rules of coherence*—for conceiving of how the disparate parts of the work fit together as a "completed totality" (112).

## Rules of Notice

In responding to "Mushrooms," I have to determine which information is most, and which is least, relevant to or significant for understanding a text. To do so, I apply rules of notice. I know that I need to give primary attention to particular text features—titles, beginnings, endings, etc. Knowing that the information in the beginning of a chapter often sets the scene in a manner that anticipates potential problems, readers attend to the details of the opening scenes. Or, using their knowledge of what Rabinowitz (*Before*) calls "rules of rupture," readers notice disruptions, violations of norms, or inappropriate behavior as signaling the fact that something unusual or extraordinary is happening. In responding to the adverbs, "whitely, discreetly, very quietly," I know that something unusual or extraordinary is going on right from the start.

On the basis of his research on narratives William Labov posits that storytellers invite their audience's notice by dramatizing the unusual, extraordinary aspects of an event in order to make that event worth telling, what Labov calls "tellability" (112–15). If, for example, a friend tells me in a matter-of-fact way that he drove home from work today, I begin to wonder about why he is telling me about something that is so inconsequential. In contrast, if he breathlessly recounts that on his drive home from work, he almost crashed into an "enormous" truck, then the event is unusual enough to merit telling. To dramatize the unusualness of the event, a teller uses linguistics deviations, asides, comments, or repetitions such as "You wouldn't believe what happened to me on the way home from work." All of this explains why I take notice of the repetition in "very/ whitely, discreetly,/very quietly" of the first stanza, as well as the unusual use of "whitely." I also pay attention to the poem's speaker's later uses of the repetition, "So many of us!/So many of us!" that further dramatizes the emerging power of the mushrooms.

Or, tellers convey tellability by shifting tense. Rather than stating that "I sat on the park bench," a teller says, "I was sitting on the park bench," in order to create a sense of the passing of time that may be disrupted by an unexpected event—"and suddenly there was this loud explosion right near me." In his own research, Jerome Bruner (*Actual,* 75–83) found that in retelling texts, students would shift to a subjective tense to imply that they were experiencing the story from their own perspective in present time.

## Rules of Significance

In applying rules of significance, readers are able to recognize that characters' actions are representative of larger social or psychological meanings. For example, they may infer that Willy Loman's behaviors represent a consistent psychological blindness to the realities of his life. They learn to infer or interpret the *significance* of behaviors as symbolic actions. In responding to "Mushrooms," I interpret the mushrooms' actions as implying that they are representative of the downtrodden, women, minorities, or disenfranchised workers, who, by banding together, assert power.

What intrigues Rabinowitz (*Before*) is the question of *how* readers infer significance. For example, to judge a character's moral stance as "good" or "bad," readers apply a rule of appearance. They judge characters "by their exterior, until the text gives us sufficient reason to judge them in some other way" (86).

In order to infer the significance, readers also need to be able to suspend their disbelief and accept the text as a pretense. Part of that involves adopting the role of what Rabinowitz (*Before*) defines as the "narrative audience." The "narrative audience," as distinct from the "authorial audience," is "a role which the text forces the reader to take on" (95). To assume the role of the narrative audience, readers pretend that they accept the text world as real. They therefore ask themselves, " 'What sort of reader would I have to pretend to be— what would I have to know and believe—if I wanted to take this work of fiction as real?' " I therefore construct a world in which the mushrooms are real human beings.

As teachers know, the ability to become engaged in Coleridge's "willing suspension of disbelief that constitutes poetic faith" is difficult for many students, particularly those that are "reality bound"— students who are reluctant to envision alternative versions of reality. Willingness to suspend disbelief is related to students' stance—how they approach the text. In a series of studies, Russell Hunt and Douglas Vipond found that students typically adopt one of three different types of stances: "information-driven," "story-driven," and "point-driven" (27–28). In adopting an "information-driven" stance, readers are reading primarily for the information. In reading a story about Paris, they are reading to determine which sites to visit in Paris. To some degree, Jill's responses to "Mushrooms" reflect an "information-driven" stance: she is, to an extent, reading the poem to extract and clarify information about how mushrooms grow. As she notes in her eighth rereading, "they diet on water because plants don't eat food or do they? a plant like a mushroom needs water to grow and crumbs of shadow mean maybe that mushrooms grow in the shadows of trees and bushes."

In adopting a "story-driven" stance, readers are responding primarily in terms of enjoying the story and are less concerned about inferring the story's significance. In adopting a "point-driven" stance, they are responding in terms of interpreting the text's meaning, requiring them to construct the text as a text world.

The differences among these stances are evident in Hunt and Vipond's ("First," 72–73) study of college students' responses to John Updike's "A&P," a story about a grocery-store checkout boy, Sammy. Most of the students did not like the story. Many of these students did not understand the purpose of Sammy's extensive, detailed descriptions of the customers in the grocery store. Hunt and Vipond argue that these students may have read the story in terms of a "story-driven" orientation rather than a "point-driven" orientation. The students who adopted a "point-driven" orientation were more likely to define the intentional use of descriptive details or characters' actions as contributing to understanding the larger significance or point of the story. They were also able to suspend their disbelief and accept the world of a grocery store as real and fraught with significance. In contrast, the "story-driven" students, who perceived the details as "pointless," had difficulty inferring the symbolic function of these details.

In attempting to construct a fictional world, as Michael Smith discusses in his book on responding to unreliable narrators, readers also learn that within the confines of this world, speakers are not always to be trusted. In adopting the role of the "narrative audience," a reader accepts what the speaker is saying as the truth. At the same time, a reader may sense that the speaker is not reliable and in doing so, may self-consciously reflect on how they are applying narrative conventions to respond to a story. Jo Keroes (5–8) cites the example of Hawthorne's "Wakefield," in which a man leaves his wife and lives for twenty years in a nearby house, undetected by his wife, only to return home one day. The narrator creates his own version of the story from a newspaper account, promising that the story will have a moral. He welcomes readers' participation in trying to explain Wakefield's bizarre behavior. While the narrator continually moralizes about Wakefield's behavior, he provides little or no details about Wakefield as a character. Readers, aware that the narrator withholds this information, and applying rules of significance, sense that something is amiss and may begin to suspect the narrator. By distrusting the narrator, readers realize that the very form of the story itself calls into question the veracity of all stories and all narrators, inviting them to entertain larger questions about the conventions of storytelling and the difficulty of understanding or interpreting the world.

## Rules of Configuration

As they are moving through a text, readers employ rules of configuration to predict outcomes. For example, readers typically expect that something unusual will happen. When nothing happens, they become suspicious. They then sense that given the inertia, something will eventually happen, but it may take awhile. As Rabinowitz notes, "If the course of action seems smooth, then anything that looks like a potential obstacle has a likelihood of turning into one" (124). Readers may also become suspicious in responding to characters who concoct unrealistic plans or get-rich-quick schemes, predicting that such plans or schemes will fail. From my storehouse of literary know-how, I know that typically the downtrodden tempt fate by challenging "the system." Hence, I predict an ominous future for the mushrooms.

## Rules of Coherence

Readers apply rules of coherence to understand how the elements serve to create an overall whole. In contrast to applying rules of configuration during their reading, readers typically apply rules of coherence after completing the text, including "rules of balance" to determine how diverse strands of action will cohere. Or, a reader applies "the other-shoe rule," that "when one shoe drops, you should expect the other" (Rabinowitz, 132). Readers may also apply the "rule of conclusive endings" by which readers assume that the text's ending will be the conclusion. Thus, as Rabinowitz demonstrates, when readers encounter texts with open, inconclusive endings such as *The French Lieutenant's Woman*, they recognize that openness itself is important to the meaning of the text. Or, as Barbara Herrnstein Smith demonstrates in *Poetic Closure*, by being frustrated in their attempts to seek closure in responding to poems, readers recognize the limitations of their own attempts to impose closure.

The differences between applying "rules of configuration" and "rules of coherence" have implications for the classroom, as Rabinowitz argues. Having reread and taught a text many times, teachers become so familiar with a text that they are more likely to apply rules of coherence to each rereading. They may therefore be more likely to focus their instruction on responding to how specific parts contribute to the overall text. In contrast, students are experiencing the text for the first time and may be more likely to be applying rules of contingencies, responding to the unfolding sequence of events. Thus, while the teachers are responding according to one set of rules, students may be applying quite a different set of rules. In teaching a text, teachers may therefore need to recapture the perspective of the first-time reader and recognize that students may not be as able as they are to infer overall coherence.

## Knowledge of Genre Conventions

In addition to applying Rabinowitz's narrative conventions, readers also learn to apply knowledge of conventions constituting specific genres—the mystery, comedy, romance, adventure story, science fiction, western, horror, spy thriller, fantasy, gangster, sports, historical novel, etc. From their experience with these genres, readers acquire knowledge of conventions constituting typical roles, settings, and story lines. For example, Jill draws on her knowledge of the conventions of fairy tales, noting that "mushrooms in fairy tales were always used as tables for little creatures." In conceiving of "Mushrooms" as a horror story, I apply my knowledge of a host of prototypical character types, settings, and story lines to the poem, transforming the mushrooms into the typical nature-gone-berserk scenario found in movies such as *The Birds*. Or I may read the poem as a science fiction story, in which the mushrooms are visitors from a foreign planet who mysteriously begin to pop up on earth. In this case, I draw on my knowledge of the prototypical science fiction plot that revolves around the threat of a foreign/alien invader, disease, nuclear/technological disaster, destructive animal, etc., all of which represent a society's underlying fears (Sontag).

In applying knowledge of these genre conventions, I also evaluate the ways in which an author or filmmaker deliberately uses stock genre techniques to appeal to a reader or viewer. In discussing this awareness of technique, Umberto Eco distinguishes between two levels of response: semantic and critical. Semantic interpretation entails understanding the text according to the implied instructions. For Eco, this entails adopting the stance of the naive "Model Reader," who simply infers the unfolding meaning (18–42). In contrast, responding at the level of critical interpretation is "a metalinguistic activity—a semiotic approach—which aims at describing and explaining for which formal reason a given text produces a given response" (54). In reflecting on interpretations, this critical Model Reader stands back and appreciates the ways in which a text employs verbal strategies to produce the naive Model Reader. As someone who is familiar with Hitchcock's techniques—as the critical Model Reader—I can appreciate the ways he builds anticipation, suspense, and fear in the naive Model Reader.

As readers become more familiar with the conventions of a certain genre, they are more aware of how their experience with the genre is shaped by the text. They also develop a growing sense of their own expertise, perceiving themselves as "mystery" or "science fiction" buffs or as fans of a certain television genre series. For Eco, the fact that a reader recognizes the deliberate use of repetition of the book/movie sequels or comic strip/television series serves to create this sense of expertise in a reader/viewer. Part of that expertise entails recognizing that in a series such as "Superman," certain aspects of a character are rediscovered and reworked in order to create a new story line, a phenomenon Eco describes as a "loop" (86). As Eco notes, "in the stories of Charlie Brown, apparently nothing happens; each character is obsessively repeating his/her standard performance. And yet in every strip the character of Charlie Brown or Snoopy is enriched or deepened" (87).

Readers who are more knowledgeable about a range of different text conventions therefore may respond differently to texts than those who are less knowledgeable. For example, in one study (Beach), I compared the responses of college and high school students to a Dorothy Parker comic, one-act play about a squabbling honeymoon couple traveling on the train to their hotel in New York. Given their superior knowledge of the conventions of comedy constituting written drama, the college students were more likely than the high school students to perceive the couple's acts as humorous. Thus the college students were more likely than the high school students to infer that the couple's arguments, disagreements, and challenges to each other's integrity were all serving to create comic effects.

Students are most likely to be aware of their own use of both Rabinowitz's narrative and genre conventions through writing and sharing stories. For example, in writing adventure, mystery, or romance stories (Hubert; Willis), students are consciously applying their tacit knowledge of the conventions of these genres to create stories. They perceive their characterization and story development as tools for intentionally inviting readers to apply knowledge of appropriate text conventions. They know, for example, that when they plant some misleading clues in a mystery story, they are counting on their peers to apply their knowledge of mystery stories. When in responding to a draft of the story, a peer recognizes that the writer is deliberately using the misleading clues to "put me on the wrong track," the writer appreciates how both writer and reader share knowledge of genre conventions. All of this points to the value of integrating reading and writing. Students are then reading texts from the perspective of being writers and, in giving feedback to each other, they are responding as readers who draw on their knowledge of shared conventions.

## Rhetorical Theories of Response

In responding to "Mushrooms," I am also reacting to the speaker's rhetorical appeal to gain my sympathy for whatever causes or ideals are being espoused. I cannot help but be caught up with the appeal of the mushrooms to the idea of the little person on the street attempting to gain some recognition and power. Theorists such as Wayne Booth, Steven Mailloux, Robert Scholes, and Peter Rabinowitz draw on rhetorical theory to examine the complex relationships among writer, narrator, intended or narrative audience, and reader (see also Brock, Scott, and Chesebro for a review of different schools of rhetorical theory). As Kenneth Burke (*Rhetoric,* 5–23) argues, a contemporary "dramatistic" or "dramaturgical" rhetorical approach examines the ways in which audiences *identify* with a speaker's or author's role, position, or attitudes. In identifying with the text's people, ideas, or institutions, an audience is seeking social unity according to a certain symbolic hierarchy of values. In responding positively to the speaker of the "Mushrooms" poem, I am identifying with the speaker's appeal for an alternative social order in which the meek assume power. Or, in responding to a television beer ad featuring young, attractive "good-time people" frolicking on the beach and drinking beer, viewers identify with these people and equate membership in the "good-time people" group with drinking a certain brand of beer. Critical viewers recognize this as an attempt to falsely associate being popular with beer drinking. At this point, as Robert Scholes demonstrates in his discussion of response to ads, viewers' own attitudes kick in. They may then, given their attitudes about beer drinking or the shallowness of "good-time people," disassociate themselves from the intended audience so that the ad fails to gain their identification.

In responding to such ads, students could critically examine the ways in which ads seek to create identification with intended audiences. They could then discuss whether they identify with those audiences. (For strategies on critical response to ads, see Len Masterman, *Teaching about Television*; Hugh Rank, *The Pitch: How to Analyze Ads*; and Robert Scholes, Nancy Comley, and Greg Ulmer, *Text Book*.)

In their writing, students are seeking their audience's identification. To assess whether they achieved that identification, they adopt an audience perspective, responding to their writing as "their own best reader" (Murray). For example, students may consider whether their description of a character serves to convey the idea of a character as nervous. They then assess their texts according to what they are *doing* to readers rather than simply what they are saying, noting that they are using the character's twitching eyes to invite readers to infer that the character is nervous. Students, in adopting the stance of readers who have the know-how to use a behavior to convey a trait, then note that the twitching eyes do not fulfill their intentions. Writers then revise their descriptions of the twitching eyes to add twitching hands to bolster the sense of nervousness. Thus students learn to apply their rhetorical know-how to create hypothetical audience's responses in order to assess and revise their writing.

## Responding to Form

Burke (*Counter-Statement*) also posits that readers respond to texts according to a subjective sense of arousal and fulfillment: "Form in literature is an arousing and fulfillment of desires. A work has form in so far as one part of it leads a reader to anticipate another part, to be gratified by the sequence" (124). Burke's conception of form or organization differs sharply from the idea of text organization being "in" the text. As Richard Haswell (34–39) argues, this equates "organization" with a formalist notion of "structured" according to text structure models (e.g., the five-paragraph theme). Haswell proposes a more "reader-based" definition of "organization" by which individual readers' own sense of organization may vary according to readers' own subjective sense of arousal and fulfillment. He cites his own research on college students' freewritings, which are often assumed to be "unorganized" when compared to more "organized" essay writing. However, as Haswell found, from a "reader-based" perspective, most of the students' seemingly unorganized freewritings were highly organized around their creation of arousal, which was then eventually fulfilled. For example, in one entry, a student wrote about not being able to concentrate on his work and sleeping in class, followed by a scene in which, were he at home, his parents would be nagging him, followed by a description of his sense of freedom in being away from home. On the surface, this writing would seem to follow a "What next?" pattern of writing down whatever comes to the student's mind. However, from a "reader-based" perspective, it is organized around sequences of emotions—a sense of sin leading to guilt leading to self-atonement associated with a sense of freedom from parental control, a sequence of emotions shaping the student's organization of his writing.

Haswell's "reader-based" conception of organization has profound implications for writing instruction. Rather than assume that students' writing should conform to external and often highly arbitrary models of text structure, teachers could emphasize students' own "felt-sense" perceptions of organization of their own writing, or, as peers, their "reader-based" reactions to other students' writing. In responding to another student's description of his hometown girlfriend, a student could talk about her experience of arousal—of wanting to know what attracted him to her, followed by a sense of fulfillment—of finding out the reasons for the attraction.

Audiences also respond to what Ernest Bormann defines as a text's "fantasy theme" or "group fantasy vision"—those idealized heroes, villains, plot lines, or attitudes that appeal to the wish fulfillments of a certain group (211). Hitler, for example, created a fantasy vision for the German people by portraying them as a superior race who could only maintain their power by destroying their enemies, enemies who were continually threatening their legitimacy (213). Similarly, the Puritan minister's fantasy vision of hard work, sacrifice, and good deeds as a means of achieving salvation and escape from God's punishment served as a fantasy theme for the Puritans. Contemporary evangelical TV programs convey the fantasy vision that being "born again" through belief in Jesus will lead to salvation. In an impersonal society, individuals identify with these group visions as a means of coping with their sense of anonymity and need for group membership.

In responding to formulaic adventure, romance, or sports novels, students could explore the ways in which they identify with the fantasy visions inherent in these novels' story lines. For example, in the romance novel, students may identify with the idea that "love conquers all," associated with a female's willingness to sacrifice her own autonomy "for a man." In responding to a sports novel, students may discern the theme of "hard work pays off" in that the hard-working, self-sacrificing hero triumphs in the end. Students could then discuss the potential appeal of these fantasy visions for Eco's Model Reader and, adopting the stance of the "critical reader," cite counter-evidence from their own experience that refutes these visions.

Many of these rhetorical appeals are familiar to readers and audiences because they have learned to associate certain appeals with certain social contexts, contexts such as courtroom trials, therapy sessions, radio talk shows, religious ceremonies, or classrooms (MacGregor and White). For example, in responding to black Pentecostal preaching, members of a congregation actively engage with the preacher in "talk-backs" and positive affirmations (Callender and Cameron). Analysis of listeners' responses to the sermons indicates that they react according to rhetorical devices of two-part contrasts (*Preacher:* "Jesus did not come to make life easy, but he has come to make champions out of difficulties"; *Congregation:* "Amen" [166]) and three-part lists (*Preacher:* "They can't see the goodness of God"; *Congregation:* "Praise him"; *Preacher:* "And the joy in the presence of the Lord"; *Congregation:* "Amen, praise him"; *Preacher:* "And the pleasures at his right hand"; *Congregation:* "Amen" [167–68]). Thus the very act of response serves to shape the direction of the speaker's presentation.

## Semiotic Theories of Response

Surveys of adolescents' use of leisure time indicate that they devote far more time to mass media—watching television or movies, listening to the radio, and reading magazines—than to reading literature (Beach, Appleman, and Dorsey). They readily learn the text conventions of mass media form because, as Eco notes, mass media are based largely on the repetition of familiar forms and images. The television series or saga ("Dallas," "Star Trek," or "Upstairs, Downstairs"), the remake of movies, the popular novel genre, or the comic strip all involve a recurrence of the same narrative forms and images.

Semiotic theories of response explicate the ways in which these forms and images assume meaning. As originally formulated by Charles Peirce and Ferdinand de Saussure, and later applied to the media by Eco, John Ellis, Terence Hawkes, Christian Metz, and Teresa de Lauretis, semiotics defines the ways in which signs mean (for a concise review, see Ellen Seiter). In Saussure's model, the *sign* is an image or object that serves as a *signifier* of meaning. For example, the image or picture of Martin Luther King, Jr., as *sign* is a *signifier* for the concept or meaning conveyed, the *signified*. The signified meanings may include "leader of the civil rights movement." Viewers learn the conventions by which meanings are signified through the various signs or images of film and television. These signs may be *symbolic* (colors, sounds, camera techniques as representative of certain meanings—slow motion as representative of dream), *iconic* (a similar structural resemblance—an image of a basketball hoop conveying the meaning of the game, basketball), and *indexical* (one image is likened to another related image in time or proximity, as smoke is linked to fire). In watching television news, viewers learn, for example, to accept the fact that background pictures behind the anchorpersons are indexical signs for the verbal stories being read.

Another important distinction in semiotics is the differences between *denotation* and *connotation*. The denotation is simply the image as signifier, and the signified is the type of image shown. The connotation entails an additional signified that serves to limit the meaning of the original denotation. For example, when the image on a television screen fades to black, the sign of the black screen has acquired the connotated signified, "the end." However, on a "quality" prime-time soap opera, the fade to black may last a few seconds longer than on other programs, with the connotated signified of " 'serious drama,' 'high class show' " (Seiter, 30). In broadcasting the images of the explosion of the space shuttle *Challenger*, the television networks had to cope with the fact that the usual connotations for the sign, space shuttle—"scientific progress, manifest destiny in space, U.S. superiority over the U.S.S.R." (Seiter, 30)—were undermined by the disaster. As a result, the networks had to quickly create a new alternative set of connotations consistent with a positive public relations image for the government. They therefore used a graphic in newscasts, "an image of the space shuttle with a U.S. flag at half-mast in the left foreground. Television fixed the connotation 'tragic loss for a noble and patriotic cause' to the sign 'space shuttle' " (Seiter, 31). Viewers are therefore socialized to limit the potential range of possible connotations to one that most benefits the producer of the image.

Readers and viewers also learn to define the meaning of certain techniques. In responding to film, viewers are placed by the camera in relation to the object, placement which itself carries meaning. Being close up to a face creates a sense of intimacy, while being far away from the same face creates a sense of distance or alienation. In contrast, in viewing a stage, theatergoers select their own perspective, focusing on whatever stage action they wish. In responding to the language of a literary text, a reader infers metaphorical meanings not available to a viewer. Louis Giannetti gives the example of a line in Wallace Stevens's poem, an image of "barbaric ice" to describe the appearance of frozen ice on a window. While moviemakers could show ice on a window, they could not communicate the same metaphoric meaning inherent in Stevens's metaphor. Thus a reader may imagine various meanings that viewers never experience in adaptations of literary texts.

In some cases, experiences with the form of one media influence response to other media. This is most evident in the ongoing competition between television and film. In order to lure people away from their home TV, during the past forty years, filmmakers have created a number of technical innovations: wide-screens, Dolby sound, 3-D, and even, in the 1950s, scents released in the theater that wafted out over the audiences. However, as Mark Miller argues, viewers have grown increasingly accustomed to the conventions of form associated with television viewing—short, focused scenes sandwiched between continuous ads. As a result, current Hollywood movies employ more of the flashy "look" of television advertisements conveyed through self-contained scenes and quick edits. And despite the experimentation in film and video that violates viewers' acquired traditional conventions of realist portrayal—seamless editing, use of establishing shots, and organization of events around familiar plots—most Hollywood films and commercial television programs avoid experimentation out of fear of alienating the viewer.

To understand differences in their response to printed texts, film, television, theater, and radio, students could compare meaning of the same content or story as portrayed through these different forms (e.g., comparing their responses to reading *Hamlet* versus viewing the play on stage versus seeing the movie). In making these comparisons, it is important that students focus on differences inherent in the media as opposed to simply evaluating whether one form is "better" than another.

### Intertextuality and Response

In organizing their units or courses, teachers are continually interested in how the students' experience with one text is related to their experience with another text, or with all the other texts in their reading history. Another essential aspect of semiotic theory, particularly in the work of Roland Barthes, is the idea of "intertextuality." While literary critics interested in intertextuality typically examine an author's use of derivative material from other texts, response theorists such as Eco, Barthes, or Julia Kristeva are more interested in the reader's own creation of intertextual links (Morgan; O'Donnell and Davis; Valdes and Miller; Worton and Still).

These theorists argue that readers experience each new text in terms of their experiences with previous texts. Barthes (*S/Z*) distinguishes between the "work" as an object that has its own closed meaning and the "text" whose meaning is constituted by readers' application of a range of intertextual links: "Every text, being itself the intertext of another text, belongs to the intertextual . . . the quotations from which a text is constructed are anonymous, irrecoverable, as yet *already read*" (443). As Barthes argues in *S/Z* (1974), the reader "rewrites" the text based on his or her intertextual knowledge, suggesting that the "I," the reader, is himself or herself constituted by a plurality of textual connections. He illustrates this concept in his autobiography, *Roland Barthes* (1977), in which he demonstrates how his own "self" is constituted by a range of cartoons, writings, photos, art, and music.

Educators such as David Bloome, Douglas Hartman, Dennie Wolf, Kathy Short, and Kathryn Pierce are particularly interested in understanding the process by which readers make intertextual links between current and past texts. Unfortunately, as Wolf argues, students often experience texts as autonomous entities with no sense of how they are related to other previous texts. They study a text and then move on to the next one with no reference to previous texts and their knowledge of conventions constituting those texts. In contrast, by exploring possible links between the current and past texts, students are learning to draw on their experience with prior texts to evoke knowledge of conventions relevant to responding to the current text.

In organizing units and courses, teachers encourage students to define links between texts. Students may be more likely to recall past texts if they elaborate on their responses to the current text. They then discover specific aspects of texts that may evoke recollections of other related aspects. For example, by completing a freewrite and then mapping various aspects of a short story, eighth-grade students elaborated on a range of different features of the story, features which they then used to recall other texts. They then completed a freewrite and map for the related text. By connecting the nodes on the maps for the current and past texts, students defined the similarities between the stories, similarities they then used to further respond to the current story (Beach, Appleman, and Dorsey).

Readers also use intertextual links to continually revise their prior knowledge. Employing what Hoesterey describes as the "intertextual loop" (325), readers retrospectively revise their knowledge of text conventions by incorporating each new experience into their literary databank of conventions. Having read a spy-thriller novel in which the writer experiments with alternative ways of organizing events, readers may then revise their conception of the spy-thriller novel conventions.

One reason for the increased interest in intertextuality and response is the emergence of computer-generated "hypertext" or "hypermedia" (Bolter; Landow; McAleese; Nix and Spiro; Schneiderman and Kearsley; Slatin). "Hypertext" is a complex computer database program that contains a wide range of different types of texts organized according to categories or features. In "hypertext" programs, readers click on categories that open up information associated with a text. For example, in responding to a hypertext program built around "Mushrooms," I would access information from a number of different categories of potential intertextual links: "Sylvia Plath," "labor/women's movements," "horror films," "the Bible," or even categories containing other readers' responses. By simultaneously connecting these various bits of information, I am constructing my own text based on intertextual links. In responding to an "online environment" (Slatin, 874), users operate either as browsers simply in search of specific information, or, more dynamically, as coauthors who define "links" between "nodes"— documents, images, or materials—in whatever way that suits their own needs. By encouraging students to make their own links, these programs may foster more learning than does traditional literature instruction.

In developing a pedagogy of hypertext consistent with a response approach, educators want to do more than simply overwhelm students with a lot of information. They also want to incorporate students' own and others' responses so that students can link back to a whole class databank of previous responses. In some cases, a program also records the decisions students are making in forming their links, fostering an awareness of their own response process. For example, Thurber, Macy, and Pope of the University of San Diego created a software program *NewBook Editor* designed to help students organize information in preparation for writing. In one of their texts, *Warsaw, 1939*, students are presented with three levels of information. At the first level, they read about events in Poland prior to 1939. By clicking on boldface words in the text, such as **World War I,** they gain more information about various related topics. At the second level, readers are placed inside the Warsaw ghetto in 1939 and asked to enter in decisions about what they would do as members of the ghetto. At the third level, the students compose "interactive essays" based on their own responses compiled from level two, as well as questions designed to foster reflection on issues and comments by the instructor.

Similarly, interactive computer literature and encyclopedia, CD-ROM databases, and computer-driven video discs actively involve readers in constructing their own plot lines. In some cases, readers' own dialogue reactions become incorporated into the text. In *The Writing Space*, a book that most directly relates response theory to response to hypertext, Jay David Bolter cites the example of a combination inter-action fictional text and computer video game, "Afternoon," by Michael Joyce: "Readers respond to a series of windows on the screen by typing in replies. The nature of readers' responses determines the direction of the experience. Readers experience the story as they read: their actions in calling forth the story, their desire to make the story happen and to make sense of what happens, are inevitably reflected in the story itself" (Bolter, 126). Moreover, readers forego traditional assumptions about text structure. As Bolter notes:

> The electronic reader is encouraged to think of the text as a collection of interrelated units floating in a space of at least two dimensions. The reader's movement among units does not require flipping pages or consulting the table of contents: instead the reader passes instantly and effortlessly from one place to an-other. . . . A printed book's natural order provides the foundation for the architecture of the text, but an electronic text is all architecture, all reference. (122)

The text, as is often the case with hypertext, is always decentering itself because there is always a sense of something missing, a sense of the need for supplementary material. As George Landow describes hypertext or intermedia: "they are bodies of linked texts that have no primary axis of organization. In other words, Intermedia has no center. [This] means that anyone who uses Intermedia makes his or her own interests the de facto organizing principle (or center) for the investi-gation at the moment" (150).

On the other hand, much of the attention given to hypertext raises a fundamental question—whether or not hypertext, in providing students with vast amounts of information, is inviting an active, as opposed to a passive, stance. Simply because a reader is given an endless number of options does not necessarily mean that that reader will respond in a manner that could be described as any more "creative" or "active" than responding to old-fashioned books. On a continuum from passive to active stances, if readers are simply gap-fillers, filling in the missing information as they combine text segments, then readers may be adopting a relatively passive role or stance.

In a critique of Landow's hypertext program, James Sosnoski charges that focusing primarily on making intertextual links may limit the extent to which readers critically explore the social and cultural categories that shape their own responses. As he notes, "An asocial, apolitical, ahistorical neo-formalism dominates the students' activities in English 32 . . . the study of literature is prone to devolve into a computer game which revolves around a series of formulae (structures) or rules" (276). In Sosnoski's classes, students construct their own anthologies of literature in which they justify their selections and categories according to their own social and cultural values, a self-reflexive theorizing lacking in the hypertext program.

## The Poststructuralist Critique of Textual Theories

The text theorists reviewed up to this point adopt a predominantly structuralist or formalist orientation. They also presuppose a reader who is relatively fixed and unified according to seemingly stable categories of knowledge. Poststructuralist theories challenge these structuralist, formalist perspectives, arguing that traditional, "realist" conventions reflect a misguided, ideological "modernist" belief in social order and traditional morality. In his attack on modernism, Jurgen Habermas noted that the conventions associated with the modernist tradition rested on a set of social and cultural beliefs in scientific truth, morality, and "high art" that were "dominant but dead" (8). While I will discuss poststructuralist theories again within the context of "cultural" theories, I examine their critique of textual theories at this stage because it points to the limitations of textual theories.

Poststructuralist theories (Baudrillard; Habermas; Hassan; Lyotard; Foucault; Jameson; Weedon), particularly when applied to education (Aronowitz and Giroux; Britzman, Brodkey; Cherryholmes), posit that language and categories are unruly, slippery, and therefore always suspect. They investigate the ways in which underlying power relationships and discourses shape and limit readers' knowledge. The very notion of a reader applying definitive knowledge of literary conventions to extract appropriate interpretations is challenged by poststructuralists. They posit that the identity of the reader is subjected to multiple, competing discourses that shape identity. Thus the discourses of education, humanism, and practical criticism condition and limit the relationships between self and texts. As Deborah Britzman notes:

> The primary category of analysis is the discourse of experience rather than the experience itself . . . we are the tellers of experi-ence. . . . How one understands experience depends upon what it is that structures one's capacity to name something as experience in the first place. And in naming something as an experience, the "I" of that experience must also be constructed. A poststructuralist

approach to identity, then, is concerned with tracing identity as
subjected to the constraints of social structure and to the practices
of discourse. (4)

Thus, rather than responding to "Mushrooms" as a singularly unified
self, I bring multiple, competing identities and perspectives constituted
by a number of different discourses. The fact that I deconstruct my
own categories of the downtrodden engaged in a political revolution
and my own "very safe, analytical, middle-class stance" reflects my
awareness of the multiple sensibilities in myself.

*Responding to Postmodern Literature*

This poststructuralist perspective also posits that knowledge of "realist"
literary conventions constituting coherent, internally consistent, modernist literature is no longer relevant for responding to postmodern
texts. Contemporary postmodern, experimental texts violate or parody
these "realist" conventions, often leaving readers or viewers in a state
of engrossed perplexity. For example, in responding to experimental
contemporary literature or film, readers may expect a consistent development of story line or character or, as viewers, may expect the
continuity of traditional realist editing. More indeterminate contemporary texts lack consistency and continuity as established by traditional
conventions. For example, Henry Green's novels often explicitly address
the reader, contain random stretches of dialogue, and build on indeterminate events. In his theorizing about his novels, Green notes that
"all my books were written as if they hadn't ended and as if they'd
start again the next morning." (Lambourne interview, 64; Carlson,
183). In responding to these texts, readers experience a sense of
disinheritance from their knowledge of modernist, realist literature. In
the process, they become self-consciously aware of how they apply
realist text conventions and the attitudes associated with a realist,
modernist worldview.

Postmodern texts or metafiction invite readers to reflexively examine
their own processes of reading. For example, in responding to Gilbert
Sorrentino's *Mulligan Stew*, a reader responds to a series of letters
written by a novelist, another "new-wave mystery" novel, Sorrentino's
own commentary about the novel, and rejection letters received from
actual publishers regarding *Mulligan Stew*. As Sharon Buzzard argues,
the distinction between the real and fiction that is presupposed by
conventions of "realist" narratives is blurred, encouraging readers to
recognize the limitations of categories such as the novel: "The metafiction of *Mulligan Stew* places a reader in a position to watch the very

process of the illusion of reading fiction . . . we are shown the perpetual choices we make between inner and outer as we create our own texts" (75).

The postmodern theorists celebrate the reader's own independence from conformity to externally dictated text conventions associated with the "work" as the physical book and the "text," which the reader creates. Barthes ("Work") posits that the text does not simply have "several meanings, but rather that it achieves plurality of meanings, an *irreducible* plurality. . . . The Text's plurality does not depend on the ambiguity of its contents, but rather on which could be called the stereographic plurality of the signifiers that weave it. . . ." (75). From this experience of plurality, readers gain a sense of pleasure derived from the perversion of any deluded attempt to establish sense of unified meaning associated with moral unity. Adopting the language of semiotics, Raman Selden notes that for Barthes, "readers are free to open and close the text's signifying process without respect for the signified. They are free to take their pleasure of the text, to follow at will the defiles of the signifier as it slips and slides evading the grasp of the signified" (79).

Barthes's celebration of the reader's own pleasurable freedom serves to challenge Culler's idea of the "competent reader" who dutifully acquires appropriate literary conventions. In his book *Contingent Meanings: Postmodern Fiction, Mimesis, and the Reader* Jerry Varsava notes that if readers have difficulty understanding a postmodern text, they are therefore deemed "incompetent." Or, if writers fail to invite "competent" interpretation, they are judged to be failures, judgments that assume that there are normative conventions for responding to texts.

Varsava argues that postmodern literature implicates readers to recognize their relationship to the world through their experience with the text. "Such literature enables the reader to make the text his or her own, to relate the text to the lived-world that he or she shares with peers" (56). Readers "appropriate" a text through their experience of tensions between present and past, the individual and the collective; a tolerance for lack of closure or resolution; an awareness of how political and ethical meanings are shaped by institutions; and an openness to parody of traditional forms.

Postmodern literature therefore implies a different mode of responding according to what could be called "postmodern conventions." For example, from their experience of responding to the more visually oriented magazines currently popular with adolescents, younger readers may be acquiring a mode of responding quite different from that of their more "logocentric" elders. In his analysis of the British magazine, THE FACE, which consists primarily of advertising images, Dick Hebdige notes: "THE FACE is not read so much as wandered through. It is first and foremost a text to be 'cruised' as Barthes . . . used to say. The 'reader,' s/he is invited to wander through this environment picking up whatever s/he finds attractive, useful or appealing" (267).

In adopting the stance of "cruising," readers are responding primarily to what is most appealing in the visual images without critically analyzing the presumed truth element inherent in the image. Hebdige quotes a leading poststructuralist critic, Jean Baudrillard, who argues that it is impossible to judge the truth value of images according to some underlying reality: "One is no longer in a state to judge, one no longer has the potential to reflect . . . Each event is immediately ecstatic and is pushed by the media to a degree of superlative existence" (Baudrillard quoted in Frankovits, 45). This raises the difficult question as to whether, in adopting a "cruising" response mode, students are acquiring a stance that bears little relationship to the more "logocentric" interpretive orientation favored by their teachers. If students do not read literature, but rather experience primarily visual media, teachers are faced with a fundamental pedagogical question of how students acquire knowledge of literary conventions. Can they, for example, be taught the conventions of literature if they do not read literature?

Educators are quite divided in their answer to this question. Some argue that students need explicit, direct instruction in text conventions, while others argue that these conventions are acquired primarily from reading. Much of this debate revolves around the previously cited distinction between theoretical "knowing-that" knowledge and "knowing-how" knowledge. For example, in the current debate over the inclusion of direct instruction of genre forms in the Australian curriculum, some educators argue that students need abstract knowledge of text forms and conventions. Proponents of this position argue that unless students are taught to recognize the use of these conventions, they otherwise would not know how to interpret texts. On the other hand, educators who align themselves with the Whole Language Movement argue that students acquire these conventions intuitively from reading and writing texts, rendering as redundant a lot of direct instruction in text or genre conventions. Students, for example, do not need to be told that titles function symbolically to summarize text content; it is assumed that they simply know that intuitively from their reading. Whole language advocates also argue that devoting a lot of class time imparting and testing for "knowing-that" abstract knowledge of conventions interferes with students' reading and writing time, and does not necessarily translate to a "knowing-how" capacity to respond to or create texts.

In my more idealistic moments, I tend to side more with the latter in this debate. Cai Svensson compared the responses to poetry of secondary students who had had extensive versus little background experience in reading literature. Those students with extensive reading backgrounds were more likely to interpret the poems and poets' uses of conventional devices than those students with less extensive backgrounds. Students with extensive backgrounds were also better able to perceive the symbolic function of the poems' titles or the function of the arrangement of lines on the page than those with less background.

At the same time, I believe that students should be taught to appreciate their own knowing-how capacity to respond to literature. They may gain a metacognitive awareness of their knowing-how ability by conducting "slow motion," think-aloud responses to a dialogue exchange between characters (Beach and Marshall). Take, for example, the following exchange between characters John and Mary that occurs in the beginning of a hypothetical story:

> *John:* "There's a good movie coming to town this Friday."
> *Mary:* "That's nice."

Students could discuss *how* they made inferences about this dialogue exchange. For example, students may differ in their inferences as to whether John is simply describing the fact that a movie is coming to town, praising the movie as "good," or inviting Mary to come to the movie, or whether Mary is simply concurring with John's perceptions of the movie or, assuming that John is issuing an invitation, accepting or rejecting the invitation. Students could discuss reasons for their inferences by inventing character traits for John and Mary having to do with their power, status, ability, sincerity, or gender. Students could also reflect on their use of genre conventions—whether they were conceiving of this exchange as being part of a romance story, a comedy, or a realistic conflict story.

## The Limitations of Textual Perspectives

In addition to those limitations suggested by the poststructuralist critique, there are a number of limitations to the textual theorists' perspectives surveyed in this chapter. For one, most of these theorists focus on readers' use of these conventions to understand and interpret texts. In focusing on understanding and interpreting, they underestimate the role of subjective experiences in shaping meaning. Secondly, in focusing on knowing text conventions, they privilege "formalist" instruction in which students learn to classify the functions of setting, titles, imagery, figurative language, etc., to demonstrate their knowledge of text conventions. Emphasizing the need to be "competent" presumes a normative ideal whereby, having achieved the prerequisite knowledge, all students are expected to generate the same or similar interpretations, dampening the value of the unique, subjective response. As a result, students lose interest in expressing what Louise Rosenblatt described as a reader's aesthetic response—his or her experience of "living through" engagement with the text—the fact that a reader can be fascinated, engrossed, angered, or even moved to tears through his or her experience with texts, a perspective to be discussed in the next chapter. In thinking back over my own responses to "Mushrooms" from a textual perspective, I miss any sense of my own aesthetic engagement with the poem.

Another limitation of these theories is that they are often solipsistic. As Elizabeth Freund argues, Culler's position (representative of his early work, in contrast to his more recent deconstructive approach) that responding to poetry is a rule-governed system may itself be a product of his own interpretive system. As a result, textual theorists may not adequately acknowledge the ideological assumptions regarding the nature of forms and conventions, assumptions that often stem from structuralist linguistics. As Terry Eagleton notes:

> Having characterized the underlying rule-system of a literary text, all the structuralist could do was sit back and wonder what to do next. There was no question of relating the work to the realities of which it treated, or to the conditions which produced it, or to actual readers who studied it, since the founding gesture of structuralism had been to bracket off such realities. (109)

Moreover, some textual theories may be used to imply that there exists a distinct "knowledge of literary conventions" that exists "out there," distinct from students' own construction of knowledge. Assuming that there is a "body of knowledge" that students either know or do not know also assumes that students simply absorb prepackaged bits of information as transmitted by the teacher. Thus a teacher tells the student that comedies have happy endings, has the student apply that convention to some texts, and then tests to determine if the student knows that comedies have happy endings. This transmission/testing model of teaching fails to recognize that knowledge is not simply absorbed by students' preformulated chunks of information.

Rather, knowledge that leads to true understanding is constructed through experience with texts. Students may be able to mimic the teacher's language on a test, i.e., that "comedies have happy endings," but in order to truly understand the nature of comedy, they need to have read and responded to a number of different examples of comedy.

At the same time, the poststructuralist critique has its own limitations. By critically examining the role and value of responses, the poststructuralists may not adequately address the question as to what it is that readers do with their responses. In comparing his own responses to a poem with those of some colleagues with poststructuralist leanings, Norman Holland and his more psychoanalytical peers used their responses to reflect back on their responses and themselves. "We threaded our associations and interpretations back through the text and thereby evoked further associations and themes from the poem . . . we gave the poem a human significance" (102). In contrast, the poststructuralists "moved away from the poem and stayed away . . . the aftertext became an end in itself . . . [they] favored philosophical and intellectual associations. For them, a text led to other *texts*, not to persons or experiences" (103). Thus for Holland, the sense of the psychological, "human I" is left behind by poststructuralists' uses of responses to link into a vast, intertextual network of texts and ideas.

Missing, also, in structuralist and some poststructuralist accounts is a consideration of the readers' act of responding as an exploration of ideology. In her discussion of the relationship between narrative conventions and ideology, Elizabeth Wright notes that the increased interest in ideological aspects of form involves "the replacement of Saussurean synchronic fixity by Derridean diachronic slippage" (438) as well as "the fear that a would-be scientific objectivity about structures is no more than a self-concealing device of ideology" (438). For example, textual theorists may have difficulty looking beyond the reader's knowledge or deconstruction of text conventions to consider the fact that, for example, as Lennard Davis argues, the conventions of the novel form reflect certain ideological values. In her critique of structuralist theories of narrative, Barbara Herrnstein Smith cited the example of a range of different variations of the Cinderella story, variations due to differences in cultural attitudes and values. While the basic story structure itself remains constant, readers of these variations experience quite different meanings because of differences in cultural contexts. This points to a major flaw in the structuralist assumption that the meanings of text features or structures are consistent for different readers. Smith, adopting a pragmatist's perspective, argues the meaning of texts such as the Cinderella story, despite the fact that it has the same basic structure, vary considerably across different social and cultural contexts. Thus textual theories fail to account for the meaning of response as shaped by readers' own subjective experiences and the social and cultural forces shaping their responses. It is to these alternative perspectives that we now turn.

# 3 Experiential Theories of Response

In responding to "Mushrooms," Jill was intrigued by and even entranced with the vision of the mushrooms taking over the world. She creates images of the mushrooms quietly growing at night and pushing up through the soil. In my responses, I envision masses of these creepy, little mushrooms taking over people's lawns during the night. In the beginning of the poem, from the "o" and "s" sounds and pace of the words, I sense a calm quietness. Then, the noise and pace begins to increase as the mushrooms become more boisterous and vociferous. I become caught up in their sense of mission and destiny. In responding in this more experiential mode, I am no longer singularly concerned with applying literary knowledge to interpret the poem. I am responding more in terms of my experience with the poem. At the same time, while I am shifting my attention to my own subjective experience, I know that the words and sounds of the poem are evoking that experience. Thus, rather than contradicting a textual perspective, the experiential perspective serves to complement and extend the textual perspective.

By "experiential theories" of response, I am referring to the work of theorists who are primarily interested in describing readers' processes of engagement and involvement in composing their own "envisionments" (Langer, J.). In examining responding as an experiential experience, theorists are primarily interested in describing those specific processes of a reader's experience, a focus best summed up by Emily Dickinson's description of reading poetry: "If I read a book and it makes my whole body so cold no fire can ever warm me, I know that it is poetry. If I feel physically as if the top of my head were taken off, I know that it is poetry" (95).

Central to experiential theories of response is Louise Rosenblatt. First formulated in the 1938 publication *Literature as Exploration,* Rosenblatt's ideas did not have a strong pedagogical impact until the sixties. Carolyn Allen attributes this to the fact that Rosenblatt was primarily interested in education (she was a professor of English education at New York University), that she drew on largely American, as opposed to European, thinkers—John Dewey and William James—

and that as a woman perceived to be dealing primarily with feelings, she was not given the credibility in the literary critical establishment that even male response theorists were afforded. It is important to note that Rosenblatt's theories involve more than simply expressing feelings. In advocating a focus on the experience itself, she is including a range of different response strategies, including those traditionally labeled cognitive. In focusing on responding as an "event" (5), she is also suggesting the need to consider the importance of the social context, and, reflecting her debt to Dewey's social progressivism, the liberalizing force of the literary experience. In describing responding as an "event," Rosenblatt wrote in 1938:

> The special meanings, and, more particularly, the submerged associations that these words and images have for the individual reader will largely determine what the work communicates to *him*. The reader brings to the work personality traits, memories of past events, present needs and preoccupations, a particular mood of the moment, and a particular physical condition. These and many other elements in a never-to-be-duplicated combination determine his response to the peculiar contribution of the text. (30–31)

In 1978, with the publication of *The Reader, The Text, The Poem*, Rosenblatt focused more specifically on a pedagogical program for the classroom. She was highly critical of the narrow focus of much literature instruction on inferring "correct answers." This led to her familiar distinction between two opposing modes of experiencing a text—the "efferent" and the "aesthetic." In responding in an *efferent* mode, readers are driven by specific pragmatic needs to acquire information; they simply want to comprehend what the text is saying. In reading "Mushrooms" from an efferent perspective, I would simply be interested in determining what and who the mushrooms were. In contrast, in responding in the *aesthetic* mode, readers are responding according to their own unique lived-through experience or engagement with a text. While Jill spends much of her response attempting to describe the growth of the mushrooms, she does adopt an aesthetic orientation in that she is more engaged by the experience with the language of the poem than in simply extracting information about mushrooms.

Rosenblatt recognizes that readers may shift back and forth along a continuum between efferent and aesthetic modes of reading. In adopting an aesthetic mode, a reader may focus on defining the techniques employed in a text. Or, in an efferent mode, a reader may refer to a related experience ("Writing and Readers," 14). Unfortunately, teachers often use activities that entail only efferent responses: short-answer or multiple-choice test questions that presuppose a "correct answer," discussion questions that are limited to "literal recall" questions about "known information" (Mehan), or discussions that are "recitations" (Dillon and Searle) in which "procedural display" of "mock participation" (Bloome) undermines any genuine, mutual sharing of experience. Thus, in reading a text in preparation for a class, students anticipate responding in an efferent mode, limiting their experience to getting the facts: "The student reading *A Tale of Two Cities* who knows that there will be a test on facts about characters and plot may be led to adopt a predominately efferent stance, screening out all of the relevant data" ("Writing and Readers," 14). By setting an interpretive agenda in advance of a class, which leads "the student" toward a particular meaning, a teacher undermines the potential for the surprising, unusual response. Based on his research on preferred ways of responding in the classroom, Alan Purves believes that "the penchant for experiential reading . . . is driven out of the heads of readers by instruction" (72). He finds that in contrast to secondary students in a number of different countries, American students prefer to respond in ways that focus on the "surface and symbolic meaning of the text and with the moral to be derived from it," preferences that are shared by their teachers. Focusing on extracting moral messages may discourage students from expressing their unique responses.

Consistent with her interest in the particulars of responding as an event, Rosenblatt argues that teachers need "to help specific human beings—not some generalized fiction called the student—to discover the pleasures and satisfactions of literature" (*Literature*, 34). In contrast to the textual theorists, who are interested in the "competent" or "ideal" readers' knowledge *in general*, Rosenblatt focuses on the uniqueness of a particular, momentary transaction. While the textual theorists are concerned with achieving interpretation consistent with knowledge of appropriate literary conventions, theorists adopting Rosenblatt's transactional model are open to exploring their responses as reflecting the particulars of their emotions, attitudes, beliefs, interests, etc. In thinking about the effects of Rosenblatt's model on his own teaching, John Clifford notes a sense of relief from having to focus on and achieve a final interpretive closure:

> I realized that I did not have to split my inner life and my work, my sociopolitical values and my professional ethos. I could simply read the text as I read the world, with the same personal commitment, the same desire and need to understand, but without the certainty that it all needs to make sense, that there must be eventually coherence, that there is an ultimate intentionality one needs to uncover. (3)

For Probst, this means that "students must be free to deal with their own reactions to the text," which in turn means that teachers "ask students what they see, feel, think, and remember as they read, encouraging them to attend to their own experience of the text" (31). And, as Patrick Dias (*Developing*) argues in his application of Rosenblatt to the classroom, students may describe their experiences of responding through free-association think-alouds, which encourage expression of their own ongoing thoughts and feelings.

According to John Willinsky, Rosenblatt narrowed her social vision of 1938 to the more specific pedagogical focus of 1978 in *The Reader, The Text, The Poem.* He misses the social and critical aspects of her 1938 theory in her more current theory. While he notes that the implementation of her transactional theory has contributed to a less authoritarian approach to teaching literature, Willinsky finds that "the development of a larger literary transaction with the world of authority and meaning has not been pursued" (143). On the other hand, the very practicality of her later work has had a profound impact on teaching literature in the past fifteen years.

## The Processes of the Experiential Response

On the basis of Rosenblatt's transactional theory, theorists have delineated a number of specific response processes (Purves and Beach; Beach and Marshall):

- *Engaging*—becoming emotionally involved, empathizing or identifying with the text
- *Constructing*—entering into and creating alternative worlds, conceptualizing characters, events, settings
- *Imaging*—creating visual images
- *Connecting*—relating one's autobiographical experience to the current text
- *Evaluating/reflecting*—judging the quality of one's experience with a text

### Engaging

Engaging with a text involves a range of different subjective experiences—emotional reactions and associations, involvement, empathy, identification. Readers gain a heightened sense of these emotions by attending to their own "felt-sense" experience with texts (Bleich, 15).

They may be aware of a welling-up of a lump in the throat or a sense of apprehension over a character's impending doom. In *With Respect to Readers,* Walter Slatoff notes that readers simultaneously experience a range of different emotions: "We can share the experience of Gulliver, say, feel the experience, and at the same time view him with detachment and view with detachment the part of us that is identifying" (39). For Slatoff, readers achieve a "full response" by being totally engrossed in a text while simultaneously being aware of their engrossment (29–56).

The theorist who has contributed the most to promoting the value of the emotional in responding is David Bleich. Bleich (*Readings*) criticizes the New Critical orientation that attempts to objectify the reader/text transaction by dismissing readers' emotional responses under the guise of the "affective fallacy." To the contrary, he argues that the subjective response leads to cognitive understanding. In *Subjective Criticism,* he describes the "subjective paradigm" in which readers define knowledge by how they are continually responding to and collectively negotiating meaning in specific circumstances with others. Readers enter into an inner dialogue between their experience with the text and their own conceptual framework, creating a dialectical tension between private experience and shared public knowledge which leads to a change in perceptions. This dialectical negotiation occurs best with others. Students proffer response statements, thereby transforming private experience into shared, collectively negotiated knowledge. For Bleich, these response statements attempt "to objectify, to ourselves and then to our community, the affective-perceptual experience" (147).

Critics of Bleich's *Subjective Criticism* (Ray, Goldstein) point to the interesting irony of the idea of a specific program of pedagogical strategies, including objective "response statements" which involve "the putting into practice of willful subjectivism [that] ultimately promotes its objective counterpart" (Ray, 87). If, for example, a group of readers in Bleich's classroom need to negotiate which response statement is the more satisfying for the group, then the majority must decide on what best pleases the majority. For Ray, this is the "hallmark of objective paradigms of knowledge—which once again proves that the subjectivist paradigm of negotiation, the assumption that facts are facts by virtue of satisfying a plurality of subjects, leads naturally to the procedures of objectivism" (88).

Despite this implied objectivism of his methodology, Bleich's argument for the value of publicly sharing emotional responses is much needed in classrooms in which students rarely discuss their subjective experiences. For John Clifford, Patrick Dias, Robert Probst, and others, Bleich's argument implies the need to attend to the unique here-and-now students' classroom responses rather than the teacher's interpretive agenda. It implies slowing down the pace of the classroom to give students time to express their responses and to savor students' momentary, spontaneous responses. Contrary to expectations, students often have difficulty expressing their feelings about texts. When asked to cite reasons for their emotional response to a text, only one-fourth of 13-year-olds and two-fifths of 17-year-olds taking the 1980 NAEP assessment were able to do so (Education Commission of the States). One reason for this is that students, particularly males—as Bleich (*Double*) and Flynn ("Gender") have found—often adopt a detached, objective stance, thereby avoiding expressing their feelings. Another reason is that readers experience a sense of anxiety with focusing on subjective aspects of response. Drawing heavily on Bleich, Michael Steig, in *Stories of Reading*, attributes this anxiety to a need to ground interpretation in some system of ideas as opposed to one's own subjectivity. He cites the example of his own responses to *Treasure Island* while in his mid-forties. In his response, "driven by a need to come up with coherent and plausible interpretations for the purposes of teaching and 'doing criticism,'" (34), he developed a Freudian interpretation of the Oedipal relationships between Jim, a series of substitute fathers, and Long John Silver. At the same time, he sensed that this interpretation was limited, that something was missing:

> So I turned from approaching the text as objective meaning and sought for associations between my feelings about the text and my life. . . .
>     As Bill Bones, Doctor Livesey, Squire Trelawny, Captain Smollett, and Long John Silver provide Jim with important but ambiguous surrogate-father relationships, so I in childhood and adolescence had valued my five uncles as alternatives to my father. But as Trelawny, Livesey, and Smollett appear to give up on Jim after he leaves the Block House, and as Silver is alternately fatherly (or avuncular) and dangerous, so my relationships to those uncles alternated between close and distant, affectionate and antagonistic, and sometimes provoked jealousy and conflict between my parents and myself. (34)

Rather than being distinct from interpretation, Steig's subjectivity leads to an insightful understanding of the novel's meaning. Thus, contrary to distinction between the cognitive and the affective, the affective experience leads to cognitive understanding of texts. Moreover, Steig advocates relating personal, autobiographical experiences to texts. In his own teaching, he frequently shares examples of his own related experiences. In response to Clarissa Dalloway's difficulty in expressing what are threatening feelings in Virginia Woolf's *Mrs. Dalloway*, Steig shares with his students a description of his own repressed hostility toward his father ("Stories"). In reflecting on the question as to whether such an approach is simply a form of self-therapy, Steig argues that "any attempt to separate reading experience from life experience is arbitrary and repressive" ("Stories," 34). He cites the example of one of his student's commentaries about sharing personal response papers, a sharing that, according to the student,

> causes a vulnerability to be present in myself and also in my attitudes towards you, my other class members. I find I connect small bits of experience to all of you from one book to the next, or even one discussion to the next, and what is emerging is a cast of characters worthy of a novel on their own! ... [W]hat we are doing in this class is developing or further encouraging an involvement with literature as part of life, part of our life personally, and also visibly part of others' lives around us, all of you. ("Stories," 35–36)

Readers may also actively seek out the kinds of engagements afforded from reading as cognitively stimulating. In one of the more interesting, if not exhaustive, empirical studies of readers' engagement with texts, Victor Nell, in *Lost in a Book: The Psychology of Reading for Pleasure*, finds that avid readers read voraciously primarily for a sense of what Nell defines as entrancement associated with a sense of heightened consciousness in experiencing emotions and imagery. Rather than simply a form of escape, reading serves as a means of intensifying readers' cognitive and emotional experience, an intensity that is addictive.

## Experiencing the "Language of Emotions"

In their experience with literature, readers vicariously experience anger, sadness, pity, envy, intimacy, grief, fear, bewilderment, sympathy, love, vulnerability, shame, greed, etc. In the process, they are experiencing what Robert Solomon describes as the "language of the emotions," which he defines as a particular way of perceiving or judging reality. For example, having experienced the depths of despair and self-anguish of an Othello, grieving over the loss of his wife, readers may then acquire a new way of perceiving the vanity and jealousy that Iago played on. Having experienced the seething anger of Maya Angelou in coping with the adversities of poverty, segregation, and prejudice in her book *I Know Why the Caged Bird Sings*—highlighted by a scene in which a dentist refuses to treat her, saying, "I would rather put my hand in a dog's mouth"—readers gain a sense of the emotional trauma associated with racial prejudice. Or, having experienced Connie's sadness, anger, grief, and guilt associated with the death of his brother in Judith Guest's novel *Ordinary People,* readers acquire a perspective on the traumatic effects of misplaced guilt and suppressed anger. In my responses to "Mushrooms," I am experiencing a sense of the emotion of the precariousness of assuming power, particularly in terms of challenging the system.

By experiencing these emotions, Solomon argues, readers gain insight into the realities of being human—what it means to be vulnerable or anxious. For example, recent psychological research suggests that many adolescents experience an acute sense of shame, often due to having been shamed by parents or teachers (Karen). This research also indicates that adolescents are often so ashamed to express their shame that they can never overcome it. The traumatic, crippling effects of shame on one's self-concept is dramatized in the story "The Stone Boy" by Gina Berriault. In that story, a young boy accidentally shoots his brother, only to be confronted by parents who refuse to let him express his shame and guilt. In responding to this story, I feel the shame and guilt associated with having accidentally killed one's brother, as well as anger at his unsympathetic parents.

In order to learn how to recognize and express the "language of emotions," students could adopt a character's perspective and compose stories or poems as told through the eyes of that character. In this way, students would be perceiving experience in terms of what it would be like to be anxious, envious, jealous, angry, guilty, etc. Cox and Many cite the example of a student who writes a poem from the perspective of a young female character who runs away to her friend's house and contemplates the limitations of her life:

> I'm Marcia
> Everyone's ideal.
> Their precious darling.
> Their perfect angel . . .
> I am dead. Emotionally dead.
> I've died many times before my death . . . (30–31)

In responding to texts, readers adopt what D. W. Harding describes as the spectator's perspective. This allows them to *reflect* on the event, adopting what James Britton (*Language*) defines as the "poetic" discourse mode or the "language of reflection" of the text itself. For example, having read Fitzgerald's *The Great Gatsby,* they may adopt Nick the narrator's language or way of perceiving, in reflecting on their own experience. After leaving one of Gatsby's rowdy hotel parties, Nick walks out onto the dark street outside the hotel and looks back up at the window where the party continues, reflecting on the larger meaning of Gatsby's life. In adopting Nick's vantage point as the outsider, a reader, with Nick, reflects on experience in terms of larger ethical, philosophical, or religious meanings. In doing so, readers formulate their *own* perceptions of experience.

In order to reflect on their own responses, students need to learn to move between their hypotheses and perceptions of texts. As Garrison and Hynd find in their research, proficient readers learn to shuttle back and forth between "reader-based" engagement responses to a text and "text-based" perceptions of those aspects of the text associated with those reactions. For example, I respond to "Mushrooms" with a reader-based reaction: "I feel a sense of anxiety toward the end of the poem." I then note what it is in the poem that evokes that sense of anxiety by cycling back to a text-based response: "At the end of the poem, the mushrooms are tempting fate by challenging the whole system."

So that students can learn to shuttle back and forth between reader-based and text-based responses, they need to know *how* to extend their responses beyond their initial responses. Students may extend their response by formulating what Kathleen McCormick defines as a "response statement" about their own experience with a text, for example, " 'Mushrooms' creates the anxiety of knowing that one is doomed to fail," followed by some exploration of "text-based" reasons for their experience. In her college first-year instruction of Stephen Crane's story "The Blue Hotel," Patricia Buckler describes her own process of moving from a "reader-focused stage" to a "subject-focused stage," followed by a "text-focused stage" (141–46). The story involves a Swedish man who is so paranoid about his visit to a hotel in the "wild west" that he actually provokes his own death. In the reader-focused stage, the students talk about their own impressions of images associated with "wild west" and how those images are portrayed in the story. In responding to the Swedish man as outsider, they also talk about their own experiences as being misunderstood outsiders. In the subject-focused stage, the students talk about the portrayal of ideas of heroism, fate, intention, community, etc., in the story. Then, in the text-focused stage, students talk about the portrayal of characters relative to stereotypes of women, cowboys, and Native Americans, for example, the fact that Crane's techniques marginalize the portrayal of women. These stages are not necessarily sequential; students are recursively cycling back to previous stages.

Students could also use journal writing to explore their responses in a tentative, informal manner. In doing so, they are experiencing what Mariolina Salvatori describes as the "unfolding, rather than the concealing, of the drama of knowing—with all its uncertainties, obstacles, anxieties, resolutions, complications" (30). Journals can help students generate hypotheses, infer new insights, cope with difficulties of understanding, define analogies, and discover meaningful problems (VanDeWeghe). Teachers may also demonstrate a tentative stance by modeling their own ongoing, specific emotional reactions to a text. For example, Wendy Bishop hands out her written description of her responses. In responding to the lines from William Stafford's "Traveling through the Dark" ("Her side was warm; her fawn lay there waiting, alive, still, never to be born"), she writes:

> These lines overwhelm me with sensory and emotional detail. I, who have been dragging a stiff, dead deer, find, with a shock, that she is warm. As I register this information, I continue reading and learn that which I already half-guessed: "her fawn lay there." Then, a second shock occurs, equal to the first, in the alliterative emphasis given to the words "warm" and "waiting." The fawn is personified and vivified. . . ." (12)

By keeping a taped or written record of one's reactions, students could then stand back and reflect on the meaning of their experience. After her responses, Bishop notes: "I learned a great deal about timing. To read, I moved backwards and forwards through the lines in a manner I've never charted before. I also detected the in and out movement of reader identification with the narrator and reader distance from the narrator . . ." (13–14).

To encourage students to specify their engagement responses, Susan Lytle recommends the use of oral think-alouds. In think-alouds, one student expresses his or her thoughts to another student while reading specific lines of a text. The student-audience responds with reactions that encourage the student to continue doing the think-aloud. Over time, as students engage in think-alouds, Lytle finds that they gain an increasing sense of self-confidence in the legitimacy of their own subjective perceptions.

These open-ended modes of expressing response may also encourage students to explore some of the strange, unsettling, even perverse aspects of the literary experience that so delighted Roland Barthes. Unfortunately, prescribed methods for responding often serve to undermine these unsettling aspects of literature. Some feminist critics argue that this pedagogical concern for controlling the direction of response stems from a need to dominate or maintain control in order to avoid experiencing a sense of intimacy or involvement with a text

(Flynn). Patrocinio Schweickart notes that many response theories are "preoccupied with issues of control and partition—how to distinguish the contribution of the author/text from the contribution of the reader" (34). In contrast, some feminists are interested in "managing the contradictory implications of the desire for relationship (one must maintain a minimal distance from the other) and the desire for intimacy, up to and including a symbiotic merger with the other" (38). Rather than being bound to the "omnipotence of fiction" (55), as Poulet would have it, Schweickart argues for a dialectic interplay between student and text free from simply having to conform to a teacher's dictates. In their zeal to elicit engagement responses, teachers need to be careful not to dictate how to respond, thus undermining students' own motivation to explore their responses.

## Constructing an Imagined World

As part of their engagement with texts, students enter into an alternative, imagined world which they create, a process of envisionment (Langer, *Understanding Literature*). For Rosenblatt, the text consists of a set of instructions explaining how, in the transaction with the text, to construct an imagined text world. In this process, readers are creating their own conceptions of the text world, or what Judith Langer defines as "envisionments." Langer goes on to describe four basic processes involved in encountering, creating, and reflecting on these "envisionments" (7):

1. *"Being out and stepping into an envisionment,"* in which readers "make initial contacts with the genre, content, structure, and language of the text."

2. *"Being in and moving through an envisionment,"* in which readers are "immersed in their understandings, using their previously constructed envisionment, prior knowledge and the text itself to further their creation of meaning."

3. *"Stepping back and rethinking what one knows,"* in which readers "used their envisionments to reflect on their own previous knowledge or understanding."

4. *"Stepping out and objectifying the experience,"* in which readers "distanced themselves from their envisionments, reflecting on and reacting to the content, to the text, or to the reading experience itself."

Jill responds to "Mushrooms" primarily in terms of the first two phases, focusing on creating an envisionment. She displays little evidence of stepping back and reflecting on or objectifying her experience. In contrast, in critiquing my own middle-class stance inherent in my responses, I am stepping outside and objectifying my experience.

By comparing students' responses to literary texts and to informational textbook selections, Langer ("Reading") finds that the students employed these envisionments in quite different ways. In responding to the literary text, students' sense of the whole changed and evolved according to what Iser describes as a "horizon of possibilities." They kept expanding these possibilities by "projecting unspoken emotions and reactions beyond the ideas that were more directly expressed . . . their focus was always on the human situation, on the 'vicissitudes of life,' particular or general" (248). In contrast, students focused on a steady "point of reference" in responding to the informational texts. "As the envisionment unfolded, new details in the text clarified the nature of the whole, but they rarely changed it" (248).

In exploring different "horizons of possibilities," students are experiencing alternative ways of perceiving the world. In adopting the perspective of a Puritan in Hawthorne's "Young Goodman Brown," they experience the fear of "unGodly sin," the tension between perceived "good" and "evil," and a dedication to "hard work" as a means to achieving salvation. Once they are comfortable with that perspective, they may then experiment with "imaginative reconstruction" (Adams, 120) of the text world by adding other episodes, extending the story, creating an epilogue, imagining characters' thoughts or dreams, or rewriting the ending. They may then reflect on the disparity between the experience of being a Puritan and their own worldview.

In momentarily accepting their constructed text worlds as "real," readers experience a sense of estrangement from their "real-world" perceptions (Fredericks). Having experienced a totally different world of a fantasy or science fiction novel, they begin to perceive their own world through different eyes, and in some cases, this can be threatening. Thus rather than entertain optional perspectives, readers may rigidly cling to their existing perspectives, attitudes, and beliefs. This is evident when students impose their own attitudes and value assumptions onto texts, positing that characters should or should not have done something according to their own real-world assumption (Beach and Wendler).

## Identifying/Empathizing

In order that students recognize the limitations of their own real-world assumptions, they need to be able to identify or empathize with speakers', narrators', or characters' perspectives. The extent to which readers or viewers identify or empathize with characters often depends on whether they like a character or perceive him or her as similar to themselves (Hoffner and Cantor). Thus, in one study, children who wanted to be like a character were more likely to imagine themselves in that character's role than if they did not like the character (Noble). At the same time, readers or viewers may also empathize with characters they are concerned about. They also may develop long-term attachments to characters, to the extent that, in the case of familiar media characters, they confuse the character with the person playing that character. For example, Tim Piggot-Smith, who played the role of the despicable character, Ronald Merrick, in Masterpiece Theater's "Jewel in the Crown," noted in an interview that he had to wear a beard during his travels in America to avoid hostile encounters (Hoffner and Cantor).

These relationships with characters could be described as analogous to relationships with friends. In his book, *The Company We Keep*, Wayne Booth argues that readers could think of narrators or characters as extending invitations of "friendship offerings" (174) for "a richer and fuller life than I could imagine on my own" (177). For Booth, the quality of this friendship depends on readers' experience of intimacy, intensity, coherence, and the range of experiences offered, all of which entails a sense of responsibility on the reader's part to reciprocate "with the same kind of significant activity that they expect of us" (187). Booth's analogy suggests that, just as students describe their relationships with friends as "close," "distant," etc., so could they apply the same concepts to describing shifts in their relationships with characters. As with a friend, a student may have disliked a character, but then, over time, may develop a sense of trust in that character.

Such relationships with characters also serve as metaphors for readers to reflect on themselves and others in their own lives. The readers in Robert Coles's *The Call of Stories* frequently talk about themselves and their peers as characters in Dickens, Olsen, Percy, or Cheever. As Coles notes, the "story's character becoming embedded in their mental life" (138) as their experience with a text "works its way well into [their] thinking life" (214). In describing characters' difficulties, these readers literally come to terms with their own difficulties, adopting the text's language to recognize their own emotions. From these experiences, Coles argues, selecting texts for his courses "involves not so much matching students' interest with author's subject matter . . . as considering the degree of moral engagement a particular text seems able to make with any number of readers" (190).

*Visualizing*

Another important part of the literary experience is that of creating visual mental images in response to a text. These mental images of characters, places, actions are intimately related to readers' emotional experiences with texts and their understanding of texts (Nell; Sadoski and Quast; Sadoski, Goetz, and Kangiser). Central to Jill's response are her attempts to visually construct the growth of the mushrooms. She draws on her own knowledge of plant growth to describe the ways in which "mushrooms grow in the shadows of trees and bushes." Another reader envisioned this growth in terms of the explosion of the atom bomb (Purves and Silkey).

In moving through a text, readers are continually revising their images of characters, settings, and events. Bill Corcoran notes that images are more than "picture stills on a movie screen. After the *whole* movie has been run, what is more likely to claim our attention is a desire to share consideration of how the combined images affected us emotionally and intellectually" (46). Thus although readers may begin with a visual impression of a character based on their own preconceptions or attitudes, as they learn more about the character, they alter their impression to incorporate perceptions gleaned from other characters.

This does not necessarily mean that readers create specific "mug shot" portraits of characters. In some cases, characters are described as having no more than "a twitching hand" or a "gruff voice," inviting a reader to synecdochically create a larger image. William Gass argues that characters are simply blank slates, or "tabula rasas," who function as concepts within the larger conceptual meaning of the text. He therefore believes that envisioning a "mug shot" concrete image for a character may actually interfere with inferring these conceptual meanings.

Students may use visual images or icons to explore and extend their responses. In their useful book *Enhancing Aesthetic Reading and Response*, Anderson and Rubano suggest having students report the specific images they recall after reading a text, giving them the directions, "Think of your mind as some sort of box that contains the sights and sounds you have collected as you have read. Empty that box and write down its contents in the next few minutes" (46). Or, students list images that capture the ways in which a character is thinking about the world. They then ask the students to review their list to add some more images. The students then reflect on their pool of images, discussing the relationships between images, why certain images may be particularly important, and commonalities among the types of images recalled by the entire class. For example, in responding to "Mushrooms," students could pool their images associated with the mushrooms, leading to a description of an imagined video about the text.

Students could also construct paper icon cutouts or computer graphics that represent different aspects of texts. In their research, Robert Tierney and Pat Edminston ask younger children to describe their unfolding engagement responses as they are moving sets of paper cutout icons on a lighted white table. These icons represent different aspects of their experiences with texts—their feelings, the characters, events, or settings—or their own self as a reader. For example, if one icon represented "myself," as they moved it "closer to" or "further from" a character, they could talk about their identification with or distancing from that character. These icons therefore serve as visual prompts to encourage students to talk about their engagement responses.

Students could also express their responses with artistic visual renderings of their experience, using, for example, a montage of cutouts to represent their experience. In response to novels, e.g., Linda Reif's eighth-grade students, working in teams, created their own paintings containing images that represented their experience with these novels. As they worked on the paintings, they discussed their responses, often revising their perceptions through the process of having to visually convey their experience. The result was three large abstract paintings that were placed on a hallway wall of Reif's middle school. Students could also study artists' own responses to literature. As Gabrielle Rico illustrates, students may recognize a text as an experiential experience by comparing their responses to the artists' visual re-creation of text experience, a form of intertextual linking.

Students may also explore their engagement responses by completing semantic differential scales (Anderson and Rubano; Hansson; Maill). For example, students could rate their reactions to a character on seven-point scales such as "like 1 2 3 4 5 6 7 dislike." Or, they could rate their perceptions of characters on scales such as "strong 1 2 3 4 5 6 7 weak." These ratings may then, as Anderson and Rubano argue, "provoke responses that would not occur in free response settings. Unarticulated response does not mean unthinking response; it means that a mechanism is provided for the initial response prior to its articulation" (34).

*Connecting*

Another process of engagement is that of connecting past autobiographical experiences or previous reading to a current text. For example, in responding to "Mushrooms," I recall the experience of finding hundreds of mushrooms in my backyard. I then attempted to dig them up, only to find that the very next day, more had replaced them. Recalling this past experience gives me further insight into the tenacity of the mushrooms portrayed in the poem.

In recalling related autobiographical experiences, the more readers elaborate on those experiences, the more they can use those experiences to interpret stories (Beach; Petrosky). In elaborating on the details of actions or events in their experiences, they begin to explore their own attitudes about those experiences, often in terms of the character's perspective. They then use their recalled attitudes to reflect on the text. For example, in responding to the grocery store manager who fires Sammy in Updike's "A & P," a student recalls:

> I have worked under a manager who would play favorites with his female employees. I was miserable when he played favorites between us. I thought of quitting but instead I talked to him about the way we felt about his favoritism game. Although from that day I was never his "favorite" again, he never expected me to brown nose because he knew how I felt and why I felt that way. (Beach, 224)

She then reflects on this experience: "I'm glad I was honest. I maintained both a job and the respect I deserved by thinking before acting" (224). This leads her to distinguish between her own and Sammy's perspectives: "To quit was irrational and immature. I realize what he stands for as a character. Sammy is something that I am not—the heroic, romantic worker. He puts himself into his job and stands for what he believes" (224). Thus, by elaborating and reflecting on her own experience, she then gains further insight into the story.

What prompts readers to recall certain autobiographical experiences? For one, in responding to a text, experiencing a certain emotion—anger, envy, love—may evoke recollection of experiencing that emotion in the past. Michael Steig cites the example of a college student, Marian, who wrote about her first reading *Wuthering Heights* at age seventeen. She experienced "the intensity of the emotion between Catherine and Heathcliff, recalling it as a love quite apart from physical, sexual or natural love" (54). Marian also recalls a similar intimacy with her boyfriend Ted in eighth grade. Her intimacy then deteriorated as she rejected Ted and Ted changed as a person. In reading her past journal writing about her relationship with Ted, Marian associates her hurt feelings with her feelings about Heathcliff's relationship with Catherine. However, she is still confused, noting that "if Ted does play a Heathcliff role and I a Cathy role, why is it that I sympathize with Heathcliff? Perhaps our tales are closer than, even now, I care to admit" (57). Steig notes that this kind of writing helped Marian "understand [their relationship] as it seemed to be reflected in *Wuthering Heights*, first to an adolescent girl and then in a quite different way to the same person as a young woman" (61). Thus responses to texts afford insights into autobiographical recollections which then further illuminate the text.

Similarly, in making intertextual links, readers may go beyond simply the similarity in text or genre features (e.g., the fact that two stories are mystery stories) to base links on common subjective experiences. For example, the feeling of impending doom associated with "Mushrooms" evokes recollection of the sense of doom I associated with the main character's plight in novels such as Ellison's *Invisible Man*. By reflecting on the nature of the feelings that link texts, i.e., the feeling of doom, readers are able to clarify the meaning of those feelings.

### Judging the Quality of One's Experience with a Text

Readers may also assess or judge the quality of one's experience with a text. Readers bring certain expectations to what they hope to gain from their experience with a text. If they are seeking a mindless escape, they may not be critical of an escapist, bestseller novel. On the other hand, in reading a text presumed to be portraying complex human experiences, they may expect that these experiences will be treated with some degree of sensitivity. For example, in responding to sensationalized novels that trivialized the complexities of the Vietnam War, Phil Beidler argues that such trivialization "suggests that choices are not difficult [and that] increases the particular perniciousness of such illusion by making it somehow have an appeal by being close to common experience . . . 'that average people can relate to'" (74). Beidler cites the novelist Robert Stone, who criticizes a text that provides only the "easy gratifications of cliche . . . rather than more complex and painful effort of critical reflection" (74):

> The reassurance that it offers is superficial: in the end it makes life appear circumscribed. It makes reality appear limited and bound by convention, and as a result it increases each person's loneliness and isolation. When the content of fiction is limited to one definition of acceptability, people are abandoned to the beating of their own hearts, to imagine that things which wound them

> and inspire them may be a kind of aberration particular to
> themselves. (30–41)

Readers may also judge the quality of their experience according to aesthetic criteria. They may judge their experience as failing to satisfy expectations associated with what they expect from what they assume to be a "good" novel, poem, or movie. However, in contrast to their teachers, adolescents typically do not assess their experience according to aesthetic criteria (Carlsen). They are more likely to assess the degree to which a text approximates what they assume to be reality. Hence, the frequent complaint in the beginning of class: "This book is unreal." Because students, particularly early adolescents, select books primarily on the basis of content or topic portrayed—as opposed to aesthetic criteria—teachers need to publicize books in free-reading programs by using content summaries instead of citing aesthetic criteria.

### Reflecting on One's Responses to Texts

In reflecting on responses such as the aforementioned autobiographical recollections or intertextual links, readers may reflect on the larger social and moral dimensions of their responses. As John Dewey argued, learning to reflect fosters a sense of tentative open-mindedness associated with becoming a thoughtful person (see Neilsen for an application of Dewey's theory to literary response). Unfortunately, many adolescents have difficulty reflecting on their response experience. In his research with adolescents, Jack Thomson proposed a hierarchy of types of responses related to the levels of reflection: "unreflective interest in action," "empathizing," "analogizing," "reflecting on the significance of events and behavior," "reviewing the work as the author's creation," and "defining one's own and the author's ideology." Most of the adolescents were responding on the first three levels; unless prompted, few went beyond those levels to reflect about their responses. Similarly, as Judith Langer ("Process") found in her study, adolescents had difficulty "stepping back and rethinking what one knows" and "stepping out and objectifying the experience."

One reason that students have difficulty reflecting on their response is that they may impose a premature closure on exploring their response either in a discussion or in their writing. Many assume that once they have answered the question, they are done. They may be more likely to reflect on their experience if they engage in a series of oral and writing activities, each referring back to previous experience. For example, students may begin with an oral and written response, which leads to a small-group discussion about their oral/written response, followed by some writing about their oral/written response, all of which leads up to a small-group analysis of the types of response strategies employed (Durrant, Goodwin, and Watson).

It may also be useful to model the process of reflection. In their discussion of reflection process, Bond, Keogh, and Walker posit three phases of the process: returning to the experience, attending to feelings, and reevaluating the experience.

### Narrating about Their Experience

As Barton and Booth, Protherough, Steig, Fry, and others suggest, readers could return to their experience by telling stories about that experience, recounting how they responded to a text. Adopting the role of what Edgar Schon describes as the "master apprentice" who models ways of reflecting on their work, teachers could model this process by telling stories about their own or their colleagues' teaching experiences, noting how their narratives serve to organize their recollection of the experience in linear or spatial terms. Protherough cites the example of a sixteen-year-old's story about an initial reading of Joseph Heller's *Catch-22*:

> Very shocking—something completely new to me that sometimes I didn't know how to react to it, whether to laugh or get upset about it. I thought that there was an immense feeling of being trapped and of things being very repetitive. So many things made no sense. Somehow I would think that Youssarian was the only sane person but then when some madness happened it could be explained so that it almost made sense which was ridiculous— such as the things that Milo did for the syndicate! (78)

### Attending to Feelings about Their Experience

Once they have recounted their experience, readers may then attend to both positive and negative feelings about that experience, for example, their frustrations in trying to understand a text. Recognizing and acknowledging feelings about their experience can help readers more carefully assess and evaluate their experience.

### Assessing Their Experience

In assessing or reevaluating their experience, readers ask themselves: What did I learn from this experience? As Fish notes, a reader is "simultaneously a participant in the action and a critic of his own performance" (*Self-Consuming*, xiii). For example, in reviewing journal entries as part of a portfolio assessment, students may assess changes in how they responded from the beginning to the end of a course. Or, students may evaluate their use of particular strategies, noting, for example, that they had difficulty connecting their story response to previous reading experiences because they never explored their responses to the current text. Or, students may reflect on how their experience was shaped by their own attitudes and assumptions, a process which, as Rosenblatt notes, "can foster the process of self-definition in a variety of ways" (*The Reader*, 145). Or, at the end of a class discussion, students may do a five-minute free write reflecting on what they learned in that discussion. After some discussions of *Catch-22*, for instance, the same student quoted earlier talked about what he learned from his discussions, as Protherough notes, going beyond his more emotional initial reactions to adopt Britton's spectator stance of the language of reflection:

> I realize now that it is not simply an "anti-war" novel. I think Heller is a very caring man and this shows in the book. He cares about the people who are bullied and punished by those in power. He shows us that those in power are the ones with money. So you can't get anywhere in life without money—not just in war. This shows the injustices in life which we have to face. Therefore, I can "relate" to the characters in *Catch-22* as they are very real and could appear in everyday situations in the reader's life. Heller has been very clever as he has created all of these people in a wartime situation to show us how they appear in our lives and we recognize them. (78)

Through reflecting on what he learned from his discussions, this student has some understanding of his process of connecting to the characters. The student's response thus illustrates why experiential theorists are interested in more than simply the aesthetic response, why they are also interested in how one responds aesthetically to life experience using the language of reflection.

## The Limitations of Experiential Theories

One limitation of experiential theories is that theorists often generalize about the processes of responding based on their own or a few readers' experiences, assuming that all readers respond in the same manner as they or the few readers do (Purves). Having noted that readers infer connections in a particular manner, they then assume that all readers make connections in that manner. The danger in such generalizations is that teachers then assume that there is a particular way of responding that they then privilege as "the way." As attempts to impose "the composing process model" onto students have revealed, the assumption that all students respond according to the same model of response masks the range of different styles and modes of responding.

Another limitation stems from the idea that students should necessarily extend their initial engagement responses to more "mature" responses. Perceiving initial responses as "superficial" or as simply a preliminary step leading to more "sophisticated" responses devalues students' expression of responses, particularly students who lack the confidence to openly express their responses.

Experiential theories have also been criticized for perpetuating the myth of individual subjectivity. As I discuss in chapter 6, poststructuralist critics and critical theorists believe that readers are constructed by social and cultural forces. For example, Althusser argues that readers are "positioned" in a manner that makes them empathize naturally with the main character or speaker. In doing so, readers believe that they are achieving a privileged position entailing the same understanding as that of characters. For Althusser, this positioning serves to create an "illusion of independent thought" consistent with the myth of individuality. While experiential theories assume that readers are free to express their "own" unique response, poststructuralist theorists believe that responses represent their cultural socialization by various institutions and are therefore not "unique." As Pam Gilbert notes, "Readers are situated in culturally determined discursive traditions, and the effects of these traditions determine the nature of the reading a text will be given and the meaning assigned to it" (245). Thus rather than perceive the processes of engaging, connecting, envisioning, etc., as ideologically neutral, cultural theorists consider these processes to be shaped by institutional forces constituting the transaction. For example, the meaning of an adolescent female's vicarious identification with the heroine of an adolescent romance novel may represent her cultural socialization according to traditional gender roles. As John Willinsky notes in his critique of Rosenblatt's later work, focusing primarily on the unique, aesthetic response fails to account for the ways in which social and cultural forces constitute the meaning of response.

By privileging the reader as "a *subject of experience* rather than bearer of knowledge," experiential theories deny that status of experience as constituting knowledge (Easthope, 173). The cultural theorists discussed in chapter 6 prefer to describe experiences in terms of various discourse practices that constitute the individual reader's experiences. Experiences are therefore described as the effects of discourse practices rather than as caused by unique readers. "... The subject of cultural studies becomes divided against itself because it is positioned *both* in pleasurable consumption *and* in self-conscious critique of that pleasure, *both* in supposedly direct access to the text *and* in confrontation with constructions enabling such access" (Easthope, 174).

Despite their limitations, experiential theories remain a powerful reminder to teachers of the need to value individual students' responses as central to the drama of their transactions with texts.

# 4 Psychological Theories of Response

Psychological theories of response assume that readers' responses are shaped by their level of cognitive or intellectual development, cognitive abilities and processes, and subconscious forces. These theories are useful for teachers because they provide descriptive frameworks for explaining students' responses. Just as parents draw on child development theory to explain their child's temper tantrums as part of the "terrible twos," so applying a psychological theory helps teachers explain, for example, why early adolescents respond with more descriptive than interpretive responses. These theories also help teachers perceive students as individuals whose responses are shaped by a host of psychological dimensions.

Understanding responding as a psychological act draws on a range of quite disparate disciplines within psychology: developmental, cognitive, perception/cognitive complexity, personality, identity, psychoanalysis, and "cultural" psychology. (For book-length bibliographies on psychology and response, see Norman Holland, *Holland's Guide to Psychoanalytic Psychology and Literature and Psychology*; Norman Kiell, *Psychoanalysis, Psychology, and Literature: A Bibliography*; and Joseph Natoli and Frederick Rusch, *Psychocriticism: An Annotated Bibliography*.)

## Developmental Psychological Theories

In comparing my own responses to those of some sixth graders, I noticed that they were more likely to conceive of the mushrooms in Plath's poem as engaged in an adventuresome quest, whereas I was more likely to conceive of them in symbolic, existential terms. Developmental psychological theories can help teachers appreciate the profound differences between their own cognitive, social, and moral development level and that of their students. For example, a teacher may expect a sixth-grade student to respond in an interpretive mode, when in fact, the student at that grade level typically prefers to respond primarily with engagement or descriptive responses.

Response theorists draw on developmental psychology to chart the shifts in responses according to different developmental levels. For example, in *Becoming a Reader*, J. A. Appleyard argues that each developmental phase serves as a foundation for subsequent phases. He notes that "the young child's intermittent grasp of the boundary between fantasy and actuality . . . yields to the older child's sense of control and identity . . . (16). This is then "transcended by the adolescent's ability to see that romance is only one version of life's story . . . [which is] supplanted by the student's realization that stories are also texts . . . that require us to think about the conditions of their production, their effect on us, the issues they raise in the world of contemporary intellectual discourse, and the kinds of meaning they can plausibly claim to offer" (16).

In his model of development of responses, Appleyard defines five roles for the reader, each of which represents a different developmental phase:

### The Reader as Player

In the preschool and early elementary years, the reader, primarily as listener, engages in a fantasy world of images, fears, and desires. Research by Applebee, Cochran-Smith, Donaldson, Gardner, Pitcher and Prelinger, Sutton-Smith, and Winner on young children's responses and story production indicate that children actively create imagined fantasy worlds and characters (the "imaginary friend"). They focus on specific, concrete parts of stories rather than attempt any part/whole synthesis. According to Appleyard, a key theorist for understanding this phase is the late Bruno Bettelheim, whose book, *The Uses of Enchantment*, focuses on the child's emotional experience of desires and fears portrayed in fantasy and fairy tales. Drawing on Freud, Bettelheim argues that in experiencing the traditional fairy tale, children directly confront the difficulties and evil of life in such characters as the wicked witch or evil troll. Then, when good triumphs over evil, children acquire a sense of needed reassurance. By listening to, creating, and performing stories as "the envisagement of possibility" (Sutton-Smith, 316), children can begin to link the fantasy world with the realities of the pragmatic, social world.

### The Reader as Hero and Heroine

Elementary school/middle school students vicariously experience the romantic quest of adventure stories. In imagining themselves to be the hero or heroine, students experience a sense of independence and competence, which satisfies "the need to imagine oneself as the central figure who by competence and initiative can solve the problems of a disordered world" (Appleyard, 55). Students at this age respond positively to stories in which the main characters engage in quests and overcome obstacles—what Northrop Frye described as the Romance narrative pattern. They therefore enjoy serial adventure, fantasy, and detective novels in which the same heroes and/or heroines consistently overcome malevolent forces. Thus, as did the sixth graders previously referred to, they may conceive of Plath's mushrooms as engaged in an adventuresome quest.

Students of this age also typically identify with the idealized heroes and/or heroines who represent role models of adult competence and virtue. At the same time, they may also respond negatively to less mature characters who represent their prior childhood experience. As Appleyard notes, "The central characters in these stories may themselves *simultaneously* represent both what children want to be and what they once were" (77). And, in learning to adopt a character's or narrator's perspective, students begin to experience a sense of emotional self-consciousness, leading them to focus more on the character than simply the story's action. Thus intermediate students often respond primarily in terms of engagement with or description of their experience of constructing characters.

## The Reader as Thinker

In adolescence, students experience a newfound delight in what David Elkind calls "thinking in a new key" (62). They enjoy arguing, particularly when they discover contradictions, as reflected in questions such as, "If you say that Katy always does the right thing, then how come she violated her curfew the other night?" They also attempt to define their own sense of identity or subjective self, an inner being with unique feelings and thoughts (Erickson).

For Appleyard, the drive to define identity creates a number of tensions: Adolescents experiment with possibilities, yet face adult restrictions. They want to adopt new roles and try new things, yet they are highly self-conscious about their appearance and of being perceived as behaving inappropriately. And, while they trust peers and adults who help them entertain possibilities, they object when these same peers or adults attempt to impose limits. I typically find that, in responding to "Mushrooms," secondary students highlight the mushroom's rebellion against authority or "the system."

Given these developmental issues, adolescents may focus their attention on characters whom they perceive as experiencing similar tensions and complexities. As Appleyard notes, students are most likely to identify with characters who "match their readers' newfound sense of complexity, but do not exceed it" (106). For example, in *A Separate Peace* by John Knowles, Gene grapples with the tension between a trusting relationship with his role model, Phineas, and his own emerging awareness that he is distinct from Phineas. In responding to these characters, adolescents are vicariously exploring complexities associated with defining their own identity.

In contrast to elementary school students, adolescents are now willing to explore what they begin to realize are underlying meanings or motives associated with characters' actions. Their sense of multiple meanings is, according to Appleyard, related to their "newfound awareness that there is a disparity between the inside and the outside of experience" (112). At the same time, they are often cognitively limited by an absolutist intellectual stance that there must be one "right" interpretation, a stance that often leads to an "either-or" debate rather than a mutual exploration of multiple possibilities.

The "reader-as-thinker" phase of development is somewhat reflected in Jill's responses to "Mushrooms." As a fifteen-year-old, unlike a twelve-year-old, she is now able to entertain multiple meanings for the language in the poem, asking questions such as, "What did it mean by 'even the paving'? Are 'our hammers, our rams' supposed to be the tops of the mushrooms pushing?" In order to clarify the meaning of the mushrooms' behavior, she rereads the poem ten times. Jill also has some sense of the fact that the poet, as distinct from herself, is constructing certain meanings based on her own experiences in "watching mushrooms grow." At the same time, Jill does little or no interpreting of the symbolic meaning of the mushrooms. It is not until late high school and early college that students enter into Appleyard's next phase, the "reader as interpreter."

*The Reader as Interpreter*

During the late high school and early college years, students learn to perceive the text as problematic and as requiring interpretation. From learning to interpret texts, students move beyond the sense of the text mirroring a real world to perceiving the text as problematic and as inviting multiple, often contradictory meanings. My college students, for example, enjoy entertaining optional interpretations for what the "mushrooms" represent.

Learning to perceive the text as problematic also corresponds to a larger shift in intellectual development from absolutist "dualist" thinking to a recognition that there are optional, multiple perspectives of reality (Perry). As a result, students are more likely to interpret the characters' perspectives as representing a range of different attitudes and interpretative approaches—feminist, Freudian, archetypal, Marxist, etc.

## The Reader as Pragmatic User of Texts

In adulthood, pragmatic use of a text entails an ability for adults to voluntarily select texts and consciously respond according to their own adult needs and interests. Adults use fiction to escape, in some cases, achieving a sense of what Victor Nell describes as a positive entrancement. Or, they may respond to fiction as portraying "life's truths" that shape their own adult lives. Or, they may seek an image of a sense of completeness characteristic of the needs of mid- to late-life adults. Thus, while adolescents may respond to a novel in terms of the character's actions, adults may respond to the same novel in terms of its underlying philosophical perspective. I am using my own responses to "Mushrooms" in this book, as I might in the classroom, for a very pragmatic purpose—to demonstrate how my responses reflect the different perspectives described in this book. As teachers, we select and read the texts we teach with our students in mind—a pragmatic perspective. Thus, while adults are continually trying to track down texts that fulfill specific needs, younger readers are more likely to read simply whatever's available.

Each of these developmental shifts in Appleyard's model of readers' response orientations is based on a number of the following factors:

## Levels of Cognitive Development

Much of developmental theory of response in the 1970s was based on Piaget's stages of cognitive development. As students move from a concrete operational stage of late elementary school years to the early formal operational stages of junior high school years to the late formal operational stage of high school years, they are developing an increasing ability to abstract about or interpret experience (Elkind; see Pikulski for a review). In his application of cognitive-stage theory to responses of six-, nine-, thirteen-, and seventeen-year-olds in *The Child's Concept of Story,* Arthur Applebee found that six- and nine-year-olds prefer to respond with short summaries or evaluate according to categories. In contrast, the thirteen-year-olds are more likely to analyze or interpret and to evaluate according to specific characteristics of the texts. Similarly, Cullinan, Harwood, and Galda found that while fourth and sixth graders respond at a more literal level, eighth graders respond at a more interpretive level.

Take, for example, students' evaluations of texts. Students differ developmentally in the reasons they give for their evaluations. Applebee found that young children will evaluate simply on the basis of whether they liked a text. Nine-year-olds operating at the concrete operational stage begin to evaluate according to categories such as "action-packed or interesting." Thirteen-year-olds operating at the early formal operational stage begin to evaluate in terms of the techniques employed in the text. And seventeen-year-olds operating at the late formal operational stage evaluate the text according to its relationship to the world.

These differences in evaluation reflect a shift from more concrete to more abstract thinking. One reason for elementary students' literal-level responses is that, in thinking at the "concrete operations" stage, students apply set, defined categories or schema to texts. As story grammar research (Mandler; Stein and Glenn) indicates, if texts deviate from these set categories, students may have difficulty responding to those texts. Thus, they prefer to read texts based on familiar, predictable narrative structures.

As students enter the initial formal operations stage in late elementary and middle school years, they begin to make more abstract inferences. However, their inferences typically focus on surface, physical phenomena, as opposed to deep, underlying meanings (Petrosky), an orientation the British psychologist, Peel, termed a "describer" perspective. As I found in my own research (Beach and Wendler), eighth graders are more likely to conceive of characters' actions in terms of physical behaviors than are eleventh graders or college students. In contrast, college students are more likely than eighth or eleventh graders to conceive of characters' acts in terms of social or psychological motives or goals. Thus, when responding to character A saying hello to character B, an eighth grader may typically state that "A is saying hello to B," while an older student is more likely to state that A is trying to make a positive impression on B. Jill's responses to "Mushrooms" reflect a "describer" orientation. She focuses primarily on describing the mushrooms with little or no reference to social or psychological motives. In contrast, a college student familiar with psychological theory may infer that the mushrooms are "representative of the subconsciousness asserting itself against the super-ego." Hence secondary students will generally not infer social and psychological explanations characteristic of college students' responses, differences that have as much to do with exposure to social science theories as to cognitive development.

From ages nine to thirteen to seventeen, students are developing Britton's spectator stance by which they evaluate and reflect on their experience with a text. Drawing on D. W. Harding's and Britton's theories of the spectator stance and Applebee's developmental work on evaluation, Lee Galda hypothesized that students may be more likely to adopt a spectator stance in response to realistic fiction than to fantasy fiction. "One might recognize the similarities and differences between oneself and one's life and realistic characters and their lives more easily than with fantasy characters, those whose lives cannot be the same as ours because of the fantastic nature of the story being told" (263). When she compared sixth graders' evaluations of fantasy versus realistic novels, Galda found that these students evaluated the fantasy novel according to categories—"adventurous," "exciting," "interesting"—and evaluated the realistic novel according to reflection on the development of story and characters. Students may have been more likely to reflect on the realistic novels because they were more familiar with the content of those novels than they were with the fantasy novels.

There are, however, a number of limitations to cognitive-stage theories. Recently psychologists have questioned the validity of the cognitive-stage model, particularly when used to pigeonhole students as presumably thinking according to a certain stage. They argue that other factors—the nature of the task, the student's interest or motivation, and the social context—also influence responses. As Cai Svensson argues, cognitive-stage models fail to account for the influence of differences in readers' background experiences in reading. As noted in chapter 3, he found that the amount of previous reading had a stronger influence on the ability to interpret than did the level of cognitive development. Students who are read to at an early age and who read literature for pleasure were more likely to interpret than students who were not read to or who did not read literature for pleasure, regardless of grade-level differences. Thus, even within the same grade level, students may respond at quite different levels not only because of their level of cognitive development, but also because some students read more than others.

## Levels of Moral Reasoning and Response

Another model of development concerns levels of moral reasoning evident in response to moral dilemmas in a text. In his model of moral development, Lawrence Kohlberg defines three basic levels of development, with two specific stages within those levels:

1. *Preconventional:* Reasoning in terms of a behaviorist orientation; an "eye-for-an-eye, tooth-for-a-tooth" orientation.

   Stage 1—Chastisement: Characters attempt to avoid punishment based on concern for the physical consequences of their action.

   Stage 2—Tradeoffs: Characters decide in terms of return favors, as based on an "I'll scratch your back if you'll scratch mine" bartering.

2. *Conventional:* Reasoning in terms of conforming to group or community norms.

   Stage 3—Approval-seeking: Characters decide on the basis of approval from peers or adults in order to maintain goodwill.

   Stage 4—Rule Orientation: Characters decide on the basis of society's rules, norms, or conventions.

3. *Postconventional:* Reasoning in terms of beliefs, legal rights, or principles.

   Stage 5—Social Utility: Characters decide according to the legal system.

   Stage 6—Universal Principles: Characters decide according to the principles of justice, rights, or trust, even when such a decision violates a society's laws.

These different levels are evident in students' reactions to the reasons given by characters or in reasons they use to explain characters' actions (Bennett). Middle school/junior high students typically reason at stage 3 ("approval-seeking") or 4 ("rule orientation"), while high school students reason more at stages 4 and 5 ("social utility"). For example, sixth graders may argue that the mushrooms are doing the right thing in rebelling because if the mushrooms did not, they would be punished. Ninth graders may argue that the mushrooms are not doing the right thing because they are violating community rules. And twelfth graders may argue that the mushrooms are doing the right thing because it is their moral obligation to challenge a system that suppresses them. Again, however, none of these levels of response should be used to arbitrarily pigeonhole students. The same students often vary in the stages of their reasoning across and even within different texts. And aside from their level of reasoning, they may vary in the sensitivity to the moral issues portrayed; some students may readily react to moral issues that other students ignore.

Kohlberg and other moral developmentalists argue that adopting a neutral, "value-free" stance in discussions of moral issues simply reinforces a moral relativism. Consistent with developmentalist thinking, they believe that growth occurs through creating a sense of disequilibrium between one's current and subsequent, "higher" levels of thinking. Exposure to subsequent levels leads students to recognize the inadequacies of their current level.

By articulating or encouraging other students to articulate responses representing the next "highest" level of moral reasoning, teachers may create disequilibrium between the student's current level of reasoning and the next level. For example, if a student adopts an "eye-for-an-eye, tooth-for-a-tooth" preconventional level, teachers may adopt a conventional level, advocating the value of following the rules of the community.

In her critiques of Kohlberg, Carol Gilligan argues that his model privileges autonomy and independence based on the ideal of individual rights or justice. Thus women who reason about moral dilemmas according to a concern for relationships with others may be categorized as reasoning on a "conventional" level. Based on her research comparing male and female moral reasoning, she finds that females base their reasoning more on being considerate of others and on sustaining caring relationships than do males. In contrast, males base their reasoning more on maintaining individual rights than do females. As a result, in responding to a moral dilemma, females attend to how the other people in their lives would be affected by their decision, while males simply make the decision regardless of how it affects others. Gilligan, Lyons, and Hanmer cite the example of Anne. In an interview, they ask Anne to discuss an incident in which she rejects a request to buy cigarettes for someone. Anne initially notes that by buying the cigarettes, she would be contradicting her own belief in not smoking. She believes that she was morally right because her decision did not contradict her own beliefs. However, when she was asked to consider another perspective on the dilemma, she begins to discuss the problem of the self-centeredness of her friend, who fails to recognize the effects of her actions on others. She notes that her friend "does not always recognize that what she likes to hear is not what other people like to hear, but may hurt their feelings" (*xxv*).

From Gilligan, Lyons, and Hanmer's perspective, Anne moves from a "rights" orientation to a "caring" orientation. She initially conceives of the problem in terms of contradicting her own beliefs, a focus on her own autonomous sense of justice. However, in thinking about her self-centered friend, she argues that being self-centered may have detrimental effects on others. In making this shift, she is focusing on a consideration of others and how one's actions may affect others, an ethics of caring essential for establishing relationships. Anne's shift leads Gilligan and her associates to argue that in responding to moral dilemmas in text, females may be somewhat more likely than males to take into account contextual, interpersonal factors. However, given the propensity for male students to dominate classroom discussions, males and females need to openly share their responses to moral dilemmas so that each group is exposed to the other's ways of thinking.

## Levels of Intellectual Development

Another developmental perspective concerns students' levels of intellectual development. Students' willingness to express their ideas and opinions about texts reflects their level of intellectual development— their attitudes toward knowledge and truth. On the basis of his adult development research, William Perry defines what he calls "positions" of intellectual development:

- *"Dualist."* Students who think primarily at the first position, the "dualist" stage, believe that knowledge is defined in absolute, distinct, black-and-white categories: "good/bad," "right/wrong," "we/them." They are willing to take people's statements about truth at face value, without the need for supporting evidence. Because they assume that the teacher or textbook is the source of truth, "dualists" prefer "correct answer" tests and lectures in which the teacher dispenses the "truth." They are uncomfortable with texts portraying experiences or attitudes that conflict with their version of the truth or with discussions involving different or conflicting opinions. In responding to "Mushrooms," a student adopting a "dualist" stance may state that "the mushrooms must be women because the textbook says so."

- *"Multiplicity."* The next position, "multiplicity," involves an awareness of different or multiple perspectives. A "multiplist" recognizes that there are several different perspectives on the truth and that one needs to support contentions with evidence. "Multiplists" recognize, unlike "Dualists," that there are "no absolutes." However, they also believe that different truths are equally valid, and that it is difficult to determine one truth as more valid than another. As they may say to a teacher, "You have your opinion and I have mine, and we'll leave it at that."

- *"Relativist/committed relativist."* However, multiplist students still have difficulty with the academic assumption that they need to test out opinions with supporting evidence. As students are challenged to provide evidence supporting their opinions and beliefs, they acquire a more "relativist" position—the ability not only to consider a range of different perspectives on the truth, but also to test the validity of ideas against other ideas. It is often not until graduate school that some students reach the highest stage of commitment to their beliefs.

Perry's work was conducted primarily with groups of male Harvard students. In recent research with female students representing a wider range of different academic institutions and social classes, Belenky, Clinchy, Goldberger, and Tarule, in their report, *Women's Ways of Knowing*, found that women's intellectual development proceeds in a somewhat different manner. Based on extensive interviews with women, they modified Perry's categories to formulate five "perspectives on knowing":

1. *"silence"*—in which women believe that they have no say or worthwhile ideas—"as mindless and voiceless and subject to the whims of external authority"

2. *"received knowledge"*—in which women are capable of receiving knowledge from authorities believed to be all-knowing, but are incapable of creating their own knowledge

3. *"subjective knowledge"*—in which women begin to articulate their own knowledge or truth in terms of subjective, personal meaning

4. *"procedural knowledge"*—in which women apply more objective, academic procedures for defining knowledge

5. *"constructed knowledge"*—in which women conceive of knowledge as varying with contexts and of themselves as capable of creating their own knowledge (15)

In this continuum, defining one's own subjective voice based on personal experience plays a key role in women's development. Almost half of the 135 women in their study were thinking at the third stage of subjective knowledge. At that stage, women become more aware of their own inner, intuitive resources or voice, moving beyond a dependency on male authority figures. For example, the characters Celie in *The Color Purple* and Jamie in *Their Eyes Were Watching God* are initially operating at the stage of "silence." Students could describe their responses to these characters' movement out of the stage of "silence" to the stage of developing a "subjective voice," relating the characters' experiences to changes in their own development.

A large body of research indicates that most secondary students and many first- and second-year college students could be characterized as thinking at the "dualist" or "silence"/"received knowledge" positions (Davison, King, and Kitchener). It may be difficult therefore for these students to openly express their opinions about texts, particularly for those students who live in environments or cultures in which authority and absolutism prevail. Students are most likely to develop their "subjective voice" if they begin to trust the validity of their own response as worth articulating. That may occur only if others in the classroom, particularly the teacher, acknowledge the worth of their responses. Moreover, as Belenky and others argue, female students prefer to learn through connecting with others' personal lives. By sharing their own autobiographical responses to texts, teachers create a classroom environment that values connecting with others.

Each of these various models of development charts a path of development for how students learn to respond. Yet they are limited by the fact that they provide only a global, somewhat reductionistic explanation of why students respond as they do. For a discussion of more specific strategies of responding, I now turn to cognitive-processing models of response.

## Cognitive-Processing Models of Response

Another important psychological perspective is that of cognitive-processing models of readers' thinking about texts. Understanding readers' cognitive processes can help teachers develop activities or model ways of responding (see Marzano for a review of instruction in thinking processes related to reading/literature). By learning how to employ these strategies, students are acquiring what Deborah Brandt defines as "to do" plans for exploring and extending their responses. When students consider the question, "What do I do now?" they need to be able to "not merely [know] how to make a text make sense but how to make what they are doing make sense" (38). Students are able to extend their thinking about a text by knowing what it is that they are doing; they have a metacognitive awareness of what to do next. If they are puzzled about why a character is doing something, they know that they need to review their previous responses to recall possible reasons for the character's behavior.

The following are some of the "to do" cognitive processes that teachers could model for students, noting how and why they employ them and for what purpose.

## Hypothesis Making/Problem Finding

As part of constructing "envisionments" (Langer), readers are continually generating hypotheses to explain characters' actions. In doing so, they often discover that they do not understand a phenomenon. For example, in responding to "Mushrooms," Jill poses a number of questions:

- "What sort of person wrote this poem?"
- "What did it mean by 'even the paving'?"
- "Are 'our hammers, our rams' supposed to be the tops of the mushrooms pushing? Or is it the mushrooms imagining they have hammers and rams?"
- "They diet on water because plants don't eat good or do they?"

All of her questions serve to create problems to be solved. This is not a matter of her "misunderstanding" the text. Rather, it stems from her own need to more fully understand a text, so that, in essence, she creates her *own* "problems" of understanding. Having asked her questions, she then explores possible answers. Having asked, "Or is it the mushrooms imagining they have hammers and rams?" she then notes that "earless and eyeless tells us mushrooms have no ears and eyes." Thus posing questions serves to extend her thinking about the poem.

Students may be reluctant to engage in their own problem finding if they assume that they need to simply generate "correct answers." As Thomas Newkirk found, college students prematurely shut down their exploration of difficulties in understanding poems because they have no interest or incentive to further explore meanings. They assume that once they infer the main point, they are done with it. Or, they blame themselves for not understanding the poem, reflecting a lack of confidence in their own ability to explore meanings.

Various theorists have suggested that the problem-finding/problem-solving process involves the following steps (see Manlove, Leibman-Kleine for general discussions of the problem-solving process):

1. *Recognizing* that something in the text disturbs or bothers them, relying on their sense of "felt understanding" to infer the fact that they don't understand something (Baker and Brown)

2. *Defining* what it is that they don't understand—problem finding (Baker and Brown; Newkirk)

3. *Formulating hypotheses or schema* to help them understand what

they don't understand (Bruce and Rubin; Collins, Brown, and Larkin)

4. *Reviewing* the text to find information relevant to understanding what they don't understand (Newkirk)

5. *Testing out and revising their hypotheses* against prior information in order to settle on a possible solution or explanation.

To answer her question, "They diet on water because plants don't eat food or do they?" Jill hypothesizes that "a plant like a mushroom needs water to grow." This leads to posing a parallel explanation for why the mushrooms eat "crumbs of shadow" in that "mushrooms grow in the shadows of trees and bushes. They try to find any little bit of shadow they can grow in." She is therefore drawing on her real-world experiences to explain the mushrooms' behavior.

In modeling this process for students, I would describe the various problem-finding steps I go through in responding to a text, providing students with a heuristic for exploring their own responses.

### Defining Causal Links

Central to problem solving is the ability to define causal links between events. Take, for example, the following narrative:

> Mary enjoys running every day. The other day, late in the afternoon, she went out for her daily run in a nearby park. It was hot and humid. She had had a hard day at the office. She was tired. After a couple of miles, she felt a little dizzy. She sat down and rested, but still felt dizzy. So she took a long drink of water at a nearby water fountain. She then felt better and continued her run.

In responding to this narrative, a reader may want to explain Mary's dizziness. To do so, he or she makes backward inferences—explains her dizziness by connecting it to preceding events and/or prior knowledge (van den Broek). A reader may infer that Mary was dizzy because she was tired, according to information provided in the immediately preceding statement, "She had had a hard day at the office." Or, a reader may infer that Mary was dizzy because it was hot and humid. To determine which of these best explains the dizziness, a reader draws on her prior knowledge of running. On the basis of her knowledge of the relationship between heat, humidity, and running, she infers that Mary's dizziness may have been caused by the heat and humidity rather than by the fact that Mary was tired. And given what she knows about drinking water and running, she bolsters this explanation with the fact that after Mary drank some water, she felt better.

Readers need to draw on their prior knowledge to make these backward inferences. Younger readers are able to connect the act to be explained with prior statements. However, they are unable to causally connect the act with their prior knowledge. They therefore have difficulty understanding events so that they can readily move on in the text.

For Paul van den Broek, all of this suggests that simply encouraging students to apply their prior knowledge to texts or discussing related prior knowledge is insufficient. Students also need to learn *how* to apply their prior knowledge to making causal links. By engaging in think-aloud activities with each other, students can share and model the ways in which they draw on prior knowledge.

### Predicting

Consistent with Rabinowitz's "rules of contingencies" is another important strategy, predicting story outcomes. In making predictions, readers are constructing emerging text models that define the story development (Collins, Brown, and Larkin). When readers discover that their predictions are not valid—that their expectations conflict with what actually happens—they revise their predictions, creating an alternate model of the text. In order to predict what may happen to the "mushrooms" once they "inherit the earth," I draw on my knowledge of science fiction conventions, anticipating that the mushrooms will encounter a force with a counter-weapon that they will need to outwit. My prediction makes sense within the context of a science fiction text model.

In order to make predictions, readers review what they have already inferred about a text and match that up with their knowledge of prototypical story development. For example, knowing that a story is a comedy, they can predict that it will probably be resolved with a "happy ending."

In working with students, it is important not to imply that there are "correct predictions." Rather, students should feel free to create any predictions. What is more useful is to help students define the basis for their predictions in terms of reviewing the text or their emerging text models. And, teachers could model ways of revising predictions according to perceived disparities between the predictions and the text model.

## Inferring Act/Trait/Belief/Goal/Plan Relationships

Readers also learn to explain characters' acts according to their traits, beliefs, goals, and plans (Black and Seifert; Borwer and Morrow; Bruce; Viehoff), shifting between these "reader-based" constructs and "text-based" perceptions of characters' actions (Garrison and Hynds). To explain Willy Loman's actions in *Death of a Salesman,* a reader infers his traits—pride, stubbornness, blindness; his beliefs in the need to be the "successful salesman" and the value of "hard work"; his goals— be the successful salesman; and his plans—keep his job and socialize his sons to follow in his footsteps. To explain the mushrooms' actions, both Jill and I infer their traits, beliefs, and goals.

In making these inferences, readers draw on their knowledge of prototypical act/trait/belief/goal/plan relationships. For example, elementary grade students draw on their knowledge of the familiar pattern of the hero making three attempts prior to finally succeeding to explain the success of the hero's third attempt. To do this, they search their memory for knowledge of prototypical relationships between acts, traits, beliefs, goals, and plans acquired from previous reading. The more familiar the goals, the less difficult the search, suggesting the value of having students define characters' goals. For example, by defining the often competing goals for each of the family members in *Dinner at the Homesick Restaurant,* students could then use those goals to infer traits and beliefs consistent with those goals.

Readers also draw on their knowledge of interpersonal relationships to conceive of characters' acts in terms of specific traits—"brave," "outgoing," "lazy," "nervous"—or oppositions such as "weak/strong," "soft/hard," "masculine/feminine," "restraining/facilitating" (Miall). As Susan Hynds ("Interpersonal") has found, students' ability to infer multiple, competing traits for the same character depends on their level of cognitive complexity. A reader high in cognitive complexity is able to perceive a character as being both hateful and loving. Hence, he or she may perceive the mushrooms as both weak and strong. A reader low in cognitive complexity is more likely to conceive of characters in terms of stereotypical perceptions. As Hynds finds, while some students may perceive persons in their own lives in highly complex ways, they may not do so in responding to literature. Students who are heavy readers and who have an interest in the text are particularly more apt to apply their own personal constructs to characters than are light readers.

In her more recent work, Hynds ("Bringing," "Reading") has found that students may be more motivated to explore complexity in their own lives than respond to characters. As she notes:

> In real life, we are most interested in understanding people who affect us in some significant way, and who can teach us something about ourselves. Unfortunately, reading is often presented in a way that is neither personally significant nor enlightening to readers.
>
> In the words of one high school reader, "I see [my friends] every day, . . . I live my life with them . . . and a character in a book . . . it's not like they're sitting next to you, talking to you everyday, you know? ("Bringing," 50–51)

Evidently, there is a need to help students transfer their fascination with everyday social relationships and motives to responding to characters. By drawing parallels between the complexities of their own social lives and those of characters, students can then apply their social cognitive abilities to both.

Cognitive processes are also very much situated in or associated with specific social contexts. Brazilian street children who sell candy to live develop a remarkable mathematical ability to compute costs and prices despite their social situation. In her extensive research with students in kindergarten through fourth grade, Susan Lehr has found that the social context has a strong influence on their ability to make thematic inferences. Lehr's interest in students' ability to link two books with similar themes led to the following classroom exercise:

In order to create a comfortable setting for the students, Lehr and individual students sat on a couch or rug together, with the books to be matched spread out in front of them. Contrary to Applebee's findings, most of the kindergarten students were able to summarize the stories, a feat Lehr attributes to the social interview context in which she encouraged open-ended responses without concern for the "right" answer. Rather than strictly follow an interview schedule, she negotiated meaning with the students, allowing their social agendas to shape the flow of the talk. As I will argue in the next chapter, this process of social negotiation and interaction fosters levels of thinking that may not occur in the research psychologist's lab (Donaldson).

## Readers' Use of Schemata

In employing all of the aforementioned strategies, readers are applying their knowledge of schemata or, as are more commonly used by psychologists, schema. Schema are those cognitive organizers, scripts, or scenarios that help guide readers' attention to certain aspects or features of texts. To demonstrate this conception of schema as functioning in active ways, Asghar Iran-Nejad cites a story he has used in his research:

> The story, adopted from Thurmond, is about a nurse, named Marilyn, who leaves the hospital where she works to go home after a late-night shift. The hospital is presumably in the downtown of a large city. When on the freeway, she notices that she is running out of gas and becomes terrified. She remembers the recent surge in muggings, beatings, and so on in the area. Finally, she decides to go to Gabriel's gas station for gas. Gabriel has always seemed to her to be a pleasant person and she knows him by going to his station for gas.
>
> Gabriel fills the tank, returns the change, and, as she is ready to leave, he suddenly asks her to go inside the station office with him to see some birthday present he has recently received. Marilyn refuses, but Gabriel insists. She finally agrees. She parks the car out of the way at his request in front of the office window and follows him inside the office.
>
> Once inside, Gabriel quickly locks the door and pulls a gun out of the drawer. She becomes terrified and begins experiencing the symptoms of shock. She sees Gabriel walking toward her. His lips are moving but she cannot hear. She cannot defend herself and she yields to the pressure of Gabriel's hand on her shoulder forcing her to the floor. Gabriel is still looking out of the window with the gun clutched in his hand.
>
> Finally, she begins to hear what he is saying: "Sorry I had to scare you like that. I was scared myself when I saw that dude on the floor in the back of your car." (123–24)

As readers move through this text, they apply a range of different schema in order to understand what is happening. They may begin to apply a "mugging" or "rape" schema to Gabriel. However, once they discover that Gabriel is protecting Marilyn from someone else, they may then revise their schema to apply a "hero/savior" script.

As they apply different schema, readers attend to different aspects of the text. Readers who read a description of a home from the perspective of a home buyer focus on the positive features of the home, while those who read it from the perspective of a burglar focus on ways of breaking into the home (Pichert and Anderson). In applying a "revolution" schema or script to "Mushrooms," I attend to those details associated with the "mushrooms" overthrowing the system. I also use the schema, "revolution," to sequentially organize my perceptions of the mushrooms assuming power. Meanwhile, drawing on my knowledge of the French Revolution, I also envision the possibility of a backlash against the mushrooms.

How do readers acquire or learn these schema? According to Roger Schank's model of "dynamic memory," readers store schema in their memory as scripts or scenarios. Readers organize these script or scenario schemas according to a hierarchy of levels of abstraction. High-level scripts are often based on themes or long-range goals. For example, in responding to a narrative about a "first date," readers apply their global scripts for "dating" or "establishing a relationship." Their global scripts may include more specific scripts involving "introducing one-self" or "impressing another person."

Readers then search their memory for scripts that may be appropriate for understanding a text. By evoking a high-level script, readers can activate and try out lower-level scripts. My "revolution" script evokes a set of subscripts having to do with unrest, ferment, outbreak, and overthrow of the powers that be. When readers sense that their existing knowledge is inadequate—that there is a disequilibrium between their current knowledge and their experience with the text—they may then revise their scripts to incorporate novel, deviant, or more elaborate versions. From a schema perspective, learning to respond to literature could be defined as a process of continually redefining schema, resulting in an increasingly more elaborate knowledge network.

Readers' scripts have different meanings across different cultures, so that, for example, a script for "getting to know a member of the opposite sex" will have a totally different meaning in a Muslim culture than in an American culture. As a result, readers are better able to understand texts with culturally familiar content than texts with unfamiliar content. For example, in the Pacific Island of Palau, funerals involve the family's active participation to a much greater degree than they do in America. In responses to fictional letters describing a funeral, each rewritten according to differences in the Palauan versus American culture, groups of eleventh-grade Palauan and American students were each better able to understand the letter consistent with their own cultural schema (Pritchard). Their responses suggest that in working with students from different cultural backgrounds, particularly immi-grants to a new culture, teachers need to select texts with relatively familiar cultural content.

Another variation on schema theory is the idea of spatial "mental models." Readers use these "mental models" to create visual repre-sentations of scenes in texts (see McNamara, Miller, and Bransford for a review). In doing so, readers determine their own physical relationship with and stance toward the phenomena in the scene (Bower and Morrow). In imagining themselves looking across a room and through a window out onto a lawn, they may construct a visual model of an intruder lurking on the lawn. They may specify some phenomena, particularly the central unusual episodes, and leave other, less relevant phenomena as fuzzy.

Similarly, perceptual psychological theories of response are interested in how readers construct visual images when they read (Collins; Paivio). In responding to "Mushrooms," Jill and I construct a mental representation of the mushrooms in my mind's eye. In this process, meanings of images change over time. According to Christopher Collins, readers use six different cognitive modes to construct and revise their visual perceptions: (1) "retrospection" (recalling related past memories); (2) "perception" (taking in new information from the text); (3) "expectation" (anticipating future meanings); (4) "assertion" (applying beliefs to the images); (5) "introspection" (intuitively reflecting on the meaning of the images); and (6) "judgment" (assessing the personal consequences of events and actions portrayed). Readers thus move from past to future, drawing on knowledge and experience to enhance the meaning of the images; and their ability to recall aspects of texts has much to do with their recollection of these images, which serve as "pegs" or "hooks" on which other related memories are "hung" (Paivio). Thus, in responding to magazine articles, college students were better able to recall material perceived to have highly vivid imagery than material perceived to have little or no mental images (Sadoski and Quast).

Despite its seeming usefulness, as is the case with much reading comprehension research, most schema theorists remain tied to an assumption that the meaning is "in" the text and is distinct from the reader, who must learn to apply the appropriate schema. As Terry Beers charges, schema theory is a "theory of information processing based on a machine metaphor of human understanding . . . which unfortunately implies that the text and the personality of the reader can be separately analyzed" (92). Take, for example, studies such as Pichert and Anderson's home description experiment. Readers were assigned the schema "home buyer" and "burglar" as external perspectives prior to reading the description. Moreover, their responses were analyzed in terms of their efferent "correct recall" of those items in the description that they recalled, mitigating the potential for differences in readers' aesthetic experiences. And, in some cases, schema are defined as fixed, static "cookie cutter" constructs to which the text must conform. Rand Spiro asserts that because schema have often been defined as fixed and static, the theory cannot explain understanding of ill-structured phenomena in texts. He argues that readers need to apply multiple perspectives created by assembling a range of different schema. (For other critiques of schema theory, see Alexander, Schallert, and Hare; Sadoski, Paivio, and Goetz.)

### *Individual Differences in the Use of Cognitive Strategies*

In addition to applying different schema, readers also apply these various cognitive strategies according to certain defined styles or patterns. To illustrate these differences, I cite a study by Harry Broudy and Alan Purves of eight graduate students' oral responses to "Mushrooms." These students' responses represented three different styles reflected in their previous schooling and interests: "literalists," "associationalists," and "interpreters."

### Literalists

The one literalist student in the group perceived the poem as only about mushrooms, making few if any interpretations. Because he assumed that poems are primarily designed to impart information, he noted that it was no more than "a little tale of the growth of mushrooms. They do grow fast" (94). This student had little recollection of any poetry instruction.

### Associationists

Two students responded to the poem primarily by thinking of as many associations as possible, for example, a mushroom factory, *The Birds*, science fiction movies, and "a place back home called Santa's Village with mushrooms all around that you can sit on" (95). However, one of the students did not perceive the mushrooms as representative of people, noting that "there should be something more there, but I didn't see what it was." The other thought that the poem was indirectly about people, but "frankly, if mushrooms were not in the title, I probably wouldn't know what she was talking about, a human or a mushroom really." Neither of these students read or appreciated poetry.

### Construers

Another student perceived the poem primarily as a linguistic problem to be solved, assuming that he needed to work to create meanings out of the language. He therefore went through each stanza, deciphering each line. While he used the title to explore the idea of the mushrooms as "little people," he was primarily interested in what happened to the mushrooms, rather than any larger symbolic meanings. His prior literary education, taught by British teachers in Singapore, privileged the idea of "making sense" out of a poem.

Analogizers

Four of the students approached the poem with the assumption that the mushrooms represent people. These students drew heavily on their own prior instruction, knowledge of Sylvia Plath, and writing of poetry to interpret the symbolic meaning of the mushrooms. One student, drawing on his knowledge of Plath, perceived the poem as autobiographical: "It's a feeling of suffocation in a society where she can't make herself known; she just can't get along with society. She's already being crushed by society" (100). Another student, drawing on her experience in a poet's workshop, explored the personal meanings of the mushrooms as women:

> I also feel as she did—too consumed . . . too meek . . . too edible . . . too used . . . too voiceless . . . [I need to] feel the underlying layers of textures that underlie feelings and attitudes and the veneer of civilization, the necessity to keep on rooting in that . . . to delve, dwell in the unconscious, to explore it, to go below the surface, to live there. (106)

Another student initially applied a Freudian approach to define the mushrooms as sperm and then infants being born, and then moved on to adopt a religious interpretation. As was the case with the other "analogizers," he shared a common propensity for, as he noted, "reading it with the expectation of looking for interpretations, rather than just reading it for pleasure."

These individual differences in styles of responding suggest that students' use of various cognitive strategies reflects their stance—the extent to which they adopt an "information-driven," "story-driven," or "point-driven" orientation (Hunt and Vipond).

## Cognitive Linguistic Theory of Response

One of the most interesting recent developments in response theory is the work of "cognitive linguists" such as George Lakoff, Mark Johnson, and Mark Turner (for pedagogical applications of their theories, see Pugh, Hicks, Davis, and Venstra). These theorists refer to themselves as cognitive linguists because they locate the meaning of response in the metaphoric concepts readers bring to texts, concepts rooted in language. Readers draw on their knowledge of metaphoric relationships in order to understand the metaphors in texts or to apply their own conceptions to responding to texts. These theorists are particularly interested in the meanings of what they define to be conceptual metaphors. A conceptual metaphor consists of a *target,* the domain to be understood metaphorically; a *source*, the terms by which the target is to be understood; and a mapping between the target and source. For example, in saying, "I am searching for the meaning of my life," the target is "life," the source is the schema of journey, and the mapping is conceiving of life as a journey (Turner, 268).

Similarly, metaphors of madness are often used to describe love ("I'm crazy about you," "I'm going out of my mind over her," etc.), or metaphors of war are used to describe sports, particularly football ("He threw a bomb," "They ran a blitz," etc.). While cognitive linguists typically analyze metaphors in texts, more recently, as reflected in Mark Turner's book, *Reading Minds*, they have begun to focus some attention on the reader's own use of conceptual metaphors. For example, readers may draw on the conceptual metaphor of "life as a journey" to understand a character's utterance, "I'm getting nowhere," or their responses to an entire novel in which they conceive of the character's development in terms of a journey. When a reader describes a character as a "traveler seeking a destination," she is drawing on the conceptual metaphor of "life as a journey." In our responses to "Mushrooms," both Jill and I are drawing on the reverse of the "people as plants" metaphor to consider "plants as people." Such was also the case in my own response to a contemporary novel, *Love Is Rich*, by Josephine Humphries, in which eighteen-year-old Lucille attempts to cope with deteriorating love relationships in her family. I was struck by the number of references to her acts of seeing or watching other characters. Lucille would often focus on the other characters' faces or eyes to understand their motives or personalities. These references to seeing or watching suggested an underlying, familiar conceptual metaphor that understanding others entails seeing. With that conceptual metaphor in mind, I adopted Lucille's perspective, focusing with her on others' blank looks, neutral gazes, or shifting eyes as telltale markers of their character.

Cognitive linguists also discuss the ways in which the meanings of conceptual metaphors are associated with direction and symmetry: up/down and right/left movements. "Up" is typically associated with power, while "down" is associated with lack of power. In describing the movements of the mushrooms, Jill and I are assigning meaning to the mushrooms in terms of pushing up through the soil, associating "up" with assuming power. And, in conceiving of the mushrooms as the "downtrodden," I am associating being "down" with having less power. Similarly, in entertaining the possibility of a "backlash," I am invoking the idea of a symmetry that has been or will be violated. As all of this suggests, teachers could ask students to reflect on how their conceptual metaphors or categories shape the meaning of their experience. While the meanings of the conceptual metaphors readers apply to texts are derived from cultural and psychological sources, I can only hope that future work in this area will draw on the work of cultural theorists (see the last chapter) and psychoanalytical theorists, who posit that the meanings of language derive from subconscious forces.

## Psychoanalytical Theories of Response

Psychoanalytical theories of response consider the ways in which readers' subconscious fantasy themes shape the meaning of their experience. For Norman Holland, the leading advocate of a psychoanalytic perspective on response, the earlier application of psychoanalytic theory to analysis of subconscious elements in characters' actions shifted to analysis of subconscious elements in readers. For Holland (*The Critical I*), this shift occurred in three phases. In the first phase, critics focused on instances of latent, unconscious content inherent in characters' dreams, jokes, or Freudian slips. In the second phase, beginning in the 1920s with Freud's notion of the tensions between the superego, ego, and id, critics focused on the writers' or characters' language as transforming through a series of defenses the fantasy elements of the id into a conscious form. However, Holland notes, theorists assume that these defenses were "in" the text. In the third phase, through case-study research, theorists began to recognize that the defenses were not simply in the text but in the reader. A reader transforms experience into a conscious level that expresses, through identification with the fictional character, the reader's repressed, subconscious experience. Holland ("Unity") summarizes this process by the acronym, DEFT: "defense," "expectation," "fantasy," and "transformation" (814). A reader applies certain defenses to the evoked fantasy elements—denial, repression, or intellectualization. Responding to texts encourages readers to break through defenses to project their subconscious fantasies onto the text and, by transforming them on a conscious level, to understand their meaning. For example, a woman responding to a Gothic novel recalls childlike fantasies of a female confronting dangers and sexual threats from a domineering male and a dark castle, a suppressed fantasy related to exploration of the body. In responding to the text, she reformulates this often-repressed fantasy experience into a conscious understanding of her sexuality. As David Willbern notes, "Freudian theory . . . is about the representation of self, body, others, emotions, and relationships in the enactments of behavior and discourse—the ways we transfer and translate work and event into meaning and utterance" (168–69). For example, Peter Brooks, drawing on Freud, argues that in responding to narrative, readers enjoy the pleasure of arousal and expectations for ultimate fulfillment. Thus the sexual experience transfers to the literary. However, as Susan Winnett points out, these Freudian models of arousal and fulfillment derive primarily from a male perspective, failing to account for possible connections between the quite different female sexual experience and response to narrative.

According to Holland (as well as Alcorn and Bracher), in reformulating their subconscious experience into a conscious understanding of fantasy themes, readers are applying their own unique personality or "identity style." A reader's identity style represents his or her unique, consistent way of coping with experience. For example, a reader who is a perfectionist may attend to every detail in a text. To demonstrate the influence of identity style on response, Holland has published numerous case studies of individual readers' responses: *Poems in Persons, 5 Readers Reading,* and, with Eugene Kintgen, "Carlos Reads a Poem." In the latter, Kintgen and Holland devised the "I-Test," which determines students' personality orientations. This test, based on George Kelly's interpersonal construct theory, asks students to define analogies and to answer some open-ended questions about themselves—preferred activities, an animal they might want to be, etc. On the basis of their analysis of students' answers, Kintgen and Holland inferred certain consistent personality orientations. They noted in Carlos, for instance, a consistent propensity to want to be in control, to dominate, and to achieve success. In an oral think-aloud response to a poem, Carlos consistently tried to unify disparate images. He linked the poem to various historical and religious traditions such as Christianity, considering which would dominate. He sought progressions in the poem, treating it as actively doing things; his responses reflected his controlling, authoritative identity style.

In responding to "Mushrooms," I am playing out a tension inherent in my own identity style, a tension between assertion of power—both political and sexual, as reflected in the metaphor of the physical upheaval of the mushrooms—and an awareness of the dangers inherent in the assertion of power. I trace this tension to recollection of my own socialization as a male child to assert myself in a competitive manner and my later recognition, as an adult, of the debilitating effects of a competitive outlook. I am also aware of the need to distance myself from coping with this tension by adopting a safe, analytical, middle-class stance.

In a more recent version of his model, as delineated in *The Brain of Robert Frost,* Holland meshes his psychoanalytic theory with a cognitive-processing, problem-solving model. He argues that readers create their own self-regulating "feedback" consistent with their own identity style or needs. Noting that behavior controls perception rather than vice versa, he posits that readers create expectations and then test them out as part of a "feedback loop." He illustrates the idea of feedback with an analogy to driving a car. A driver turns the steering wheel to determine how the car responds to the road conditions, and then adjusts the steering accordingly. In doing so, a driver is setting standards according to the degree to which he or she is emotionally satisfied with his or her own driving under certain conditions. Similarly, by noting the consequences of creating expectations, readers compare their perceptions with their standards for what is satisfying, standards related to their own subjective identity needs. Holland summarizes this feedback loop in terms of how Robert Frost may have responded to texts:

> In the most abstract terms, he—his identity—has a certain aim or desire which becomes a personal standard. To achieve that aim the identity puts out behavior, which amounts to a test of the environment. The environment gives a return, thereby closing the loop. The identity compares the return with what was tried out and the standard. If they match, then the identity feels satisfied, the loop closes, and the system called Robert Frost settles down. If they do not match, if the desire continues, and the identity feels dissatisfied, the Robert Frost system continues to try behavior on the environment until it achieves a match. (90)

Readers draw on their identity style to assess the validity of their hypotheses according to what feels satisfying. As with learning to drive, readers learn to balance perceptions and the resulting feedback according to their own identity style.

Holland's theories of identity have been criticized as assuming a unified theory of self. Rather than seek unity in a text, he seeks unity in the reader's self, a unity that may not exist. As Elizabeth Freund argues, this leads to his "inability to decide whether the 'self' is the provisional product of interpretation or an 'unchanging essence'" (126). Given the ways in which the self is shaped by social and cultural discourses, Jonathan Culler (*Pursuit*) notes that Holland's case-study students' free-association responses reflect their own cultural attitudes and socialization rather than their own unique identity. And, in his criticism of Holland's case-study methodology, Bleich ("Identity") charges that Holland consistently fails to consider the influence of the social context and the presence of the interviewer/researcher—Holland—on his students' responses. Bleich also notes that in analyzing his students' responses according to his theory of identity style, Holland often imposes his own preconceptions on his analysis so that, in essence, he finds what he is looking for.

Bleich's more recent work, contained in *The Double Perspective*, meshes his earlier psychoanalytic work dealing with the subjectivity of the unique reader with the social constructivist theories of Vygotsky and Bakhtin. For Bleich, readers' perceptions of and attitudes toward the social context reflect certain psychological or personality orientations. For example, in his case studies focusing on gender differences, a male's personality propensity to assert status or dominate the situation shapes the way he shares his responses in a group. As I will discuss in the next chapter, on social perspectives on responses, Bleich's theory, unlike Holland's, admits to a social constructivist model of the self—that the self is constituted not as a unique, autonomous identity, but through social interactions with others.

Holland's critics also charge that the unique self is constituted by both the language of the text and the language constituting the reader's self. Theorists turn to Jacques Lacan's psychoanalytic theories for justification that the linguistic system shapes response. For Lacan, the child's rejection of the mother is precipitated by language development dictated by the subconscious cultural structures already in place. In developing his or her own ego in the "mirror phase," the child begins to develop an image of his or her own body. The child creates a self-image as an imaginary "ideal ego" that does not coincide with his or her body. The same process occurs in relating to and communicating with others. The person creates an imaginary sense of the other by harking back to an image of the "ideal ego." This ideal ego represents a stable consciousness that does not always represent the unstable, shifting unconscious. Thus the "I" of the conscious self does not necessarily reflect the "I" of the unconscious.

Drawing on Lacan's psychoanalytic theory of language, Marshall Alcorn and Michael Brancher posit that the self is anchored in specifics of language. Particular words in a material sense have a biological control over the body, leading to hysteria, hallucination, or paralysis. The reader's projections are therefore modified or "filtered" by the text's signifiers, which unconsciously shape the meaning. As Alcorn notes, "when we respond fully to the material signifiers of the text, we use the text to embody in signifiers our partly conscious and partly unconscious values" (146). When readers apply their ideals of the self to the text, these signifiers "defile" these ideals. "The reader responds actively to the objective and material signifiers of the text, seeking to rework the content of his or her projection" (151). Rather than treating the text as simply an inkblot that evokes subconscious meanings, a reader's experience with the language of the text triggers subconscious associations. Thus the language of the unconscious serves to position readers, sharing their experience with the text.

These subconscious forces play a particularly strong role in response to the dreamlike experience of film. In her application of psychoanalytic theory to response to film, particularly the work of Christian Metz, Sandy Flitterman-Lewis notes that the "viewer is positioned, by means of a series of 'lures,' as the *desiring producer* of the cinematic fiction . . . when we watch film we are somehow dreaming it as well" (180). Viewers may also believe that what they are watching is true, requiring them to acknowledge that what they are watching is false or fictional. For Flitterman-Lewis, this tension between belief in the dream and knowledge of reality mirrors Lacan's split between the unconscious and the conscious: "The spectator is, in a sense, a double-spectator, whose division of the self is uncannily like that . . . between the conscious and the unconscious" (181). Experiencing the image of "ideal ego" in the mirror parallels the fascination with the screen. In the process of constructing the ego through the dreamlike experience, the ego is strengthened. Simultaneously, there is a loss of the ego, which identifies with the "other" on the screen. Thus, "the film viewer both loses him/herself, and finds him/herself—over and over—by continually reenacting the first fictive moment of identification and establishment of identity" (184).

In contrast to being enveloped by the movie screen, viewers' responses to the smaller television screen differ from their responses to film (Flitterman-Lewis). While the dreamlike experience of film involves "a sustained gaze," the experience of television is a momentary "glance" (187). Television also projects an image of the here-and-now present, an immediacy that differs from a sense of distance in time in the film experience. Television viewers are also often attending to or are distracted by other people and events in the room, undermining the sense of loss of self-consciousness in the film experience.

Viewers also experience differences in the organization and editing of television versus film. In television, the viewer leaps from one momentary narrative segment to the next, including the interruptions of commercials, undermining the unity inherent in a sustained film experience. And, in the film experience, the seamless editing creates an illusionary sense of a world in space and time. This is accomplished through the use of reverse-angle and point-of-view shots that create a " 'suturing' system of looks, a structured relay of glances" between the camera position and the filmed object or between the characters on the screen (Flitterman-Lewis, 194). In experiencing these different perspectives, a viewer has a sense of his or her own perspective as someone "offscreen" who is related to the action "onscreen." This creates the perspective of the onlooking voyeur that evokes "certain unconscious fantasy structures such as the primal scene (an early 'scenario of vision' in which the unseen child observes the parents' lovemaking)" (194). While a viewer may assume that he or she is constructing a coherent text-world, the fragmentation of the television experience undermines this sense of coherent involvement.

Thus psychoanalytic theory portrays the dramatic tensions between a reader/viewer who is seeking unity and order inherent in the ego but is also experiencing the disunity of the unconscious. Not only does this serve to explain readers' entrancement with particular texts, but, as Victor Nell argues, it also explains the appeal of the hypnotic, trance-like experience of reading itself. Readers and viewers actively seek out reading (or viewing) as alternative states of consciousness linked to the experience of subconscious forces.

There is some question as to whether psychoanalytical theory bears any relevance to the classroom. It would be difficult, if not impossible, for teachers to deliberately attend to or accommodate differences in students' "identity style." However, the idea that larger subconscious forces shape our lives is a healthy antidote to students' assumptions that they are self-directed "individuals." Mark Paris encourages his college freshmen to explore their own experience with repression of subconscious forces shaping characters' actions as well as their own responses. For example, in responding to *The Yellow Wallpaper,* students experience the repression of the female protagonist confined to her bedroom by her husband's diagnosis of her "hysterical tendency." They then note the ways in which social forces serve to repress female sexuality, drawing parallels to social repressions in their own lives. From all of this, students may recognize that their experience with texts is constituted by larger psychological forces.

## The Limitations of Psychological Theories

One major limitation of cognitive psychological perspectives is that they conceive of responses in terms of an "interactionalist," information-processing model as opposed to a transactional model. The problem with this information-processing approach is that it fails to account for the variations in social or cultural contexts that shape meaning. (The controlled, "scientific," reading-comprehension research used to study cognitive processes often attempts to "control" for the "contaminating effects" of these contextual features.) This assumes that the reader is a rational, autonomous, accessible, consistent self who is described as an entity separate from social and cultural forces. The belief in the reader as a rational, autonomous, consistent self reflects, for Kenneth Gergen, a modernist, scientific conception of the world as "composed of fixed and knowable entities" (38). From a modernist perspective, the self experiences characters who themselves are perceived to discover their "true selves." Gergen portrays this ideal of the modernist self that permeates much of psychological research and educational philosophy:

> The modernist self . . . is knowable, present in the here and now, just slightly below the surface of his actions. . . . his reasons guide his actions and his voice is clear and honest. . . . Everyone is created equal, and it is up to us as parents and good citizens to mold the young. With proper molding, and the help of science, we create the future of our dreams. (47)

For Gergen, this modernist vision of the coherent, unified self, for better or worse, has been eclipsed by a postmodern world, creating what he defines as a "saturated self." In contrast to the intimate "face-to-face" communities of the past, the various "technologies of social saturation"—advances in transportation, communications, and the media—have "propelled us toward a new self-consciousness, the postmodern" (49). Overwhelmed by this social saturation, the self becomes fractured into partial identities and multiple selves. This shift from a modernist to a postmodernist conception of self calls into question many of the assumptions underlying the psychological theories reviewed in this chapter.

The failure to account for the effects of specific social and cultural forces leads Jerome Bruner to argue for a new psychological orientation, which he describes as "cultural psychology" (19). Dismayed by the failure of experimental and cognitive psychology to examine how the self defines meaning, Bruner argues that psychologists need to consider how the self is shaped by social and cultural forces as reflected in how persons relate their experiences through autobiographical narratives. For example, in his research on adult members of a family of seven who all still live in Brooklyn, Bruner (122–36) finds that each member conceives of self and his or her experiences in terms of life inside and outside the family circle. The home as inside is contrasted with the real world outside the home (132–35). The home is perceived to be the site of intimacy and trust, while the real world is perceived to be a threatening, dangerous place requiring street smarts. Bruner argues that these conceptions represent a withdrawal from a belief in social commitment to the well-being of the community. These beliefs about the dangers of the outside world therefore shape the meaning of their responses.

In contrast to the cognitive or psychoanalytic perspectives, Bruner therefore locates meaning-making in the "folk psychology" that sustains everyday social and cultural life. The self learns the practices of interpreting acts, experiences, and contexts—both real and in texts—according to learned cultural norms or values. As I will discuss in the next two chapters, on social and cultural theories of response, focusing on the individual's own psychological orientation needs to be complemented by a recognition that the meaning of readers' transactions are constituted by their participation in social and cultural contexts.

# 5 Social Theories of Response

The other day, I asked my seventeen-year-old son, Ben, to talk with me about the poem, "Mushrooms." I asked him to first read the poem a couple of times and to jot down some of his thoughts. Then, in discussing the poem, we both shared our perceptions of the meaning of the mushrooms. He shared some of the ideas he had jotted down—that the mushrooms represent a "human innocence" and that they were naive about the consequences of their actions. He perceived them as engaged in a political revolution to overthrow the system, drawing links to the French Revolution that he was studying in school. I shared some of my own responses—that the mushrooms represented the downtrodden, exploited masses, including women. Ben was also intrigued by how Plath uses figurative language and sounds to invite these meanings. His overall approach reflected a thematic analysis that he learned in school, an approach that seems to focus on extracting thematic meanings. On some points our perceptions converged, so that we would then begin to collaboratively construct some composite perceptions of the poem. Having talked about the fact that the poem reminds me of the movie *Invasion of the Body Snatchers*, Ben begins, picking up on his interest in the human side of the mushrooms, which launched him into analogies to the French Revolution.

In reviewing the taped transcript of our forty-minute discussion, I was struck by how the meaning of our exchange was constituted by our social roles and relationship. Each of us responded according to the social roles of "student," "son," "teacher," "parent," and "researcher." Given the idea of responding to a poem, Ben seemed to adopt a student role associated with the thematic analysis strategies employed in his classroom. In the beginning, I assumed a teacher role, asking questions such as, "Do you see the mushrooms as being anything else?" By assuming the teacher role, I reified the idea that he was (or should have been) responding according to a student role.

At the same time, I shifted out of my teacher role to share my own responses as peer or father. And, in my researcher role, as I told him toward the end of our talk, I was interested in determining how our social roles or the contexts shaped our response. Adopting these different roles, each with different agendas, created some tensions. As teacher, I wanted to help him express and elaborate on his responses. Hence the follow-up questions. As father, I was looking forward to some intimate sharing of my thoughts and feelings with my son, particularly since I had not seen much of him recently. And, as researcher, I wanted to determine how our social roles and interaction shaped the meaning of our exchange. So, having asked that we "both talk about the poem together" (as father/son), in the very next breath, I slip into a teacher role, asking him to "tell me some of your feelings about the poem," a request driven by my researcher role of wanting to see if he could respond with some initial emotional reactions.

These tensions were also evident in Ben's responses. While he seemed to be adopting a student role associated with learned classroom strategies, he was also responding as a son in a one-to-one exchange. When I asked Ben to compare how he responded in our discussion to how he might respond in a classroom, he noted that "I would probably have worded it a lot quicker... I would not have gone into much depth, not expand so much on my thoughts because I wouldn't have wanted to occupy so much time in the classroom." Asked how he would have responded to the poem had he been sharing it with his friends, he noted that there would have been "more humor, more criticism of the poem ... we may have been more apt to find things that were funny because we weren't discussing it for any real reason." He therefore associates different ways of responding with different social roles and contexts, which suggests that responding is a learned social process. As James Paul Gee notes, "One always and only learns to interpret texts of a certain type in certain ways through having access to, and ample experience in, social settings where texts ... are read in those ways" (209). The reader defines self in social contexts as a social being through his or her use of various response or social strategies. The self, as Raymond Williams notes, is therefore "the active construction, within distinct physical beings, of the social capacity which is the means of realization of any individual life. Consciousness, in this precise sense, is social being" (41–42).

While I did not have access to the social context shaping Jill's responses, it certainly was the case that Patrick Dias's own initial modeling of the rereading and free-association writing influenced her responses. In considering the effects of social contexts on responses, it is important to recognize that, as a social context, the classroom is infused with pedagogical intent, that teachers deliberately create contexts to foster certain kinds of learning.

In this chapter, I discuss those response theorists who are particularly interested in how readers' social roles, motives, needs, and conventions, operating in particular contexts, constitute the meanings of their response, theory relevant to creating a positive social environment in the classroom.

## Social Constructivist Theory

Basic to social theories of response is social constructivist theory of knowledge, which challenges the idea of knowledge as a set of external, scientifically verifiable truths. In questioning the idea of "scientific objectivity," Thomas Kuhn proposed that ways of knowing and testing reality are relative to different paradigms—the legal, religious, economic, psychological, as well as the empirical/scientific. No one of these paradigms can claim to have a corner on the truth.

The same assumptions about knowledge apply to specific social contexts. As the speech-act theorists argue, the meaning of language depends on how language is used in specific contexts. The meaning of my statement, "The door is open"—whether it is a description of an open door, a request to close the door, or a command—depends on participants' perceptions of others' roles, status, motives, needs, and "definitions of the situation." Learning how language means therefore involves learning to "read" these various social dimensions in specific contexts. As Lev Vygotsky argues, learning evolves from social interactions and collaboration, which are then internalized as inner dialogue: "Every function in cultural development appears twice: first, on the social level, and later on the individual level; first between people, and then inside . . . all the higher functions originate as actual relationships between individuals" (46).

The incentive to formulate one's responses is often driven by the social need to share those responses with others. I wanted to share my interpretation of the mushrooms as downtrodden victims with Ben, now going through a "political period," to see how he would react to my interpretation. I am also often using my responses to create social relationships. In sharing my responses to a movie with a friend, the fact that I agree with his judgment of the movie as "just plain awful" serves to bolster our friendship. At the same time, readers may even use their responses to socially exclude others. For example, in observing classroom discussions, David Bloome ("Social Construction") examined various kinds of intertextual links students made to and for each other. He found that in some cases, students made intertextual references to texts or experiences familiar only to peers they wanted to favor, thereby excluding unfavored peers. Thus, for Bloome, understanding the meaning of intertextual links requires a social perspective.

Similarly, in a more recent version of the conception of "point-driven" reading, Vipond, Hunt, Jewett, and Reither adopt a social perspective to explain how readers define the "point" of a story. They argue that in everyday conversation, participants mutually attempt to stick to the point or deviate by getting off the point. Just as the point of conversations is socially constructed, the point of a transaction between reader and text is also socially constructed. Thus the meaning of an interpretation or "the point" evolves out of social exchange of responses.

### The "Interpretive Community"

Stanley Fish's notion of the "interpretive community" embodies this social perspective. For Fish, the meaning of any reader/text transaction is a function of the interpretive strategies and conventions adopted by readers as members of a particular interpretive community. In responding as members of an interpretive community, readers share certain strategies and conventions valued by the group. Thus, in responding to "Mushrooms," members of a group may, for example, subscribe to a feminist, Marxist, or deconstructionist approach to their response.

Fish questions Iser's assumption that something—the text—is an objective, determinate given. He argues that the meaning of a text is a product of one's reading strategies operating in specific social contexts. For example, in beginning to teach a class on religious poetry, he found a list of linguists on the blackboard from the previous class. He then asked the students to treat the list as a poem. In their responses, students began attributing religious meanings to the linguists' names. Fish attributes this to the students' membership in an interpretive community accustomed to responding to symbolic meanings of poems (332). These strategies, Fish argues, "are finally not our own but have their source in a publicly available system of intelligibility. Insofar as the system (in this case a literary system) constrains us, it also fashions us, furnishing us with categories of understanding, with which we in turn fashion the entities to which we can point" (332). Thus the meaning of the transactions is due to neither the reader nor the text but to the "interpretive communities that are responsible for the shape of the reader's activities and for the texts those activities produce" (322). The meaning of Milton's sonnets are not constituted by the text but by the particular kinds of strategies applied to the sonnets.

Fish's notion of the interpretive community has been widely criticized as too nebulous to provide a workable explanation for variations in meaning (Culler [*Pursuit*], Dasenbrock, De Beaugrande, Eagleton, Freund, Mailloux [*Rhetorical*], Ray). Critics charge that if the meaning of a transaction is totally constituted by a set of institutional strategies, then the reader and the text disappear, along with reader-response theory as a viable perspective (Freund). Other critics charge that Fish endows the "community" with considerable, possibly coercive, power to shape the responses of individual readers. De Beaugrande cites the example of a student who gave him two opposing readings of an e.e. cummings poem. The student interpreted the poem as both about death and about the end of a love relationship. De Beaugrande notes that "Fish would either have to say that the student's interpretive community allows both readings equally—but then it cannot be true that the 'text is always set' as long as 'a particular way of reading is in force' (629)—or Fish would have to say that the student was moving between two communities—but then we have the explosion of communities that makes the whole notion pointless" (551–52). It may therefore be difficult for readers to clearly distinguish between allegiances to different interpretive communities. In responding to a text in a classroom, a student may be not only a member of the classroom community, but may also import perspectives as a member of a family, social club, a neighborhood, etc.

Fish also assumes the readers readily accept the belief systems inscribed in the community's strategies, acceptance that may curtail the possibility for doubt or self-scrutiny, leading to acceptance of the status quo. For William Ray, "Fish's reader knows no anguish, can provoke no change in himself . . . He can never outflank the beliefs of the institutions that define him; he can trigger no revolutions: the discipline will always have already understood, assimilated, indeed produced, any arguments for its realignment he might generate" (169).

As Reed Way Dasenbrock argues, the idea that the meanings of texts are relative to the interpretive communities may simply serve to reinforce the parochial cultural perspectives of its members. Dasenbrock argues that readers adjust and alter their theories to fit particular social situations, applying what Donald Davidson describes as a "passing theory," a momentary modification of set beliefs or theories. In continually adjusting and revising their theories to meet new, anomalous challenges, readers learn that others do not always share their beliefs. Rather than assume that texts are understood "only on our own terms," Dasenbrock argues for "a genuine hermeneutics of difference, particularly cultural difference" (17). Teachers and students therefore need to recognize that they are responding as a member of a specific class, family, neighborhood community, school staff, political party, or professional organization. Moreover, as members of these competing groups, readers may momentarily entertain "passing theories" that reflect the belief systems of these different groups.

Regardless of the validity of Fish's concept of "interpretive community," it is often the case that certain ways of responding are privileged in certain classrooms, schools, or even countries. For example, in an international study of eight countries, Alan Purves asked students, ages 14 and 18, and educators to select those response types they most preferred from a list of twenty different types. Analysis of these preferences indicated that students and educators in different countries differed considerably in their preferences according to two continuums: an emphasis on the personal versus impersonal, and an emphasis on form versus content. For example, while students and educators in Belgium and Italy emphasize impersonal and formal responses, those in Chile, England, and Iran emphasize the personal and content-oriented responses, and those in the United States emphasize impersonal and content responses (characterized by the formal, literary critical essay). The most telling finding of this study was the fact that between ages 14 and 18, the preferences become more definite and consistent with teachers' own preferences. This leads Purves to argue that students are socialized to adopt the response modes privileged by educators in a certain country.

## Social Roles

As my exchange with my son Ben illustrates, certain ways of responding may be associated with certain social roles. Readers adopt certain social roles in a group—leader, facilitator, devil's advocate, outsider, etc.— that entail certain ways of responding. The "leader" may respond in ways that guide the direction of the discussion, while the "devil's advocate" continues to raise questions that challenge the majority opinion. These roles entail different purposes for responding to texts. For example, viewers' responses to television vary according to the social roles they adopt during viewing of television. If they are engaged in social conversation and trying to "be friendly," they may ignore the television. When Dorothy Hobson watched a popular British soap opera, *Crossroads*, with viewers in their homes, she found that the viewing situation itself varies considerably:

> To watch a program at meal time with the mother of young
> children is an entirely different experience from watching with a

seventy-two-year-old widow whose day is largely structured around television programs. Family situations change both the ability to view with any form of concentration and also the perspectives which the audience have on a program. (111)

In a classroom setting, the social roles of teacher and student, as well as a host of other roles—class clown, teacher-pleaser, burnout, school politician, etc.—influence their responses. And, the role a teacher adopts—entertainer, authoritarian, provocateur, facilitator, etc.—often invites students to adopt reciprocal roles. If students perceive the teacher to be the "critical authority," they may attempt to mimic that role in their own responses or they may resist that role by not listening attentively or by challenging the teacher. As David Bartholomae has argued, college students are often expected to imitate the role of authority on a literary text, even though they have little knowledge of that role and of the expectations of an academic audience. In their essays, students therefore mimic the formal voice and mannerisms of formal academic analysis, relying on "institutional authorities" to make their argument (Mortensen).

To define their roles in school settings, students learn to adopt or resist role expectations associated with certain groups. By doing well in school, participating in athletics and extracurricular activities, or wearing certain clothes, some students align themselves to a pro-school "jock" group. In contrast, as Penelope Eckert's study of a Detroit high school indicated, by resisting academic norms and expectations and by behaving or dressing in "deviant" ways, other students align themselves to "burnout" groups. A student assumes certain stances toward the many groups in a school by adopting or resisting role expectations associated with these groups. By doing well in school, she may define herself as a "good student." Or, by resisting academic norms, she may define herself as a "burnout."

When the student enters the classroom, these social negotiations are often limited by the need to perform or resist the role of the "good student" (Brooke). Being a good student means that one performs according to the teacher's dictates and criteria. By responding in the "right way," a student identifies herself to her peers as a "good student." In order to define and evaluate what it means to perform as a good student in a particular classroom, a teacher assumes the role of evaluator.

As every teacher knows, students resist having to adopt these classroom roles. By deliberately not responding, a student publicly conveys to his peers in the class that he does not care about being the good student, perhaps to ally himself with a burnout group.

Students express their resistance through what Brooke describes as "underlife" behaviors. In his analysis of writing in freshman composition classes, he notes instances of students passing notes to each other, mimicking and parodying the instructor, or defying formal conventions of classroom behavior. By displaying these underlife behaviors, the students are expressing their own sense of individuality—the fact that they are more complex and unique than their classroom roles as "students."

Given the limitations associated with the student role in the writing classroom, Brooke argues that teachers need to create social contexts that encourage students to adopt the role of writers as opposed to students. In Brooke's own writing workshop class, students assume a range of different writers' roles through actively exchanging and responding to each other's writing. In reading published writers' reflections on writing, they discuss their own concerns as writers.

Similarly, students also learn to adopt roles of "responders" by experimenting with new and alternative ways of responding without fear of responding "the right way." To provide such mentoring, teachers need to shift their role from "evaluator" to "coach" (Geisler, 22–26). As a coach, a teacher encourages students to take risks by reading and responding in new ways to their peers, rather than simply to or for the teacher. As a coach, a teacher downplays his or her evaluative role by providing descriptive, nonjudgmental feedback to students. And, as a coach, a teacher models the process of adopting alternative roles, talking about how they read as an adult, parent, writer, critic, political being, mystery buff, and teacher.

Concern with the social aspects of response to texts is also related to issues of censorship. Advocates of censorship argue that reading certain texts results in certain deviant social behaviors or the development of deviant attitudes. Their argument assumes a cause-and-effect relationship between reading texts and behavior and/or attitudes. In some cases, censors dramatize their charges by arguing, for example, that rock music lyrics regarding death cause adolescent suicides.

Arguing that a cause-and-effect relationship occurs between a text and a reader/viewer assumes that readers or viewers will all respond in a similar manner. However, as social theories of response suggest, reader/viewer responses are shaped by social roles and attitudes defined by family, school, and community. Thus the claim that a particular book will have a particular effect on a group of students— that it will *cause* them to behave in deviant ways or to change their attitudes—underestimates the strength of their socially constituted roles and attitudes (Beach, "Issues"). The very fact that adults object to certain books in a particular community often reflects the effects of their own well-defined roles and attitudes constituted by the values of that community. As a result of his interviews with Kanawha County, West Virginia, parents, James Moffett vividly documents the social reasons behind their attempt in 1974 to censor a textbook series, as well as their sense of powerlessness in dealing with the schools.

Thus, in focusing on meaning as constructed in specific social contexts such as the classroom, social constructivist theories suggest the need to attend to those social conventions and roles constituting responses in these contexts.

## Dialogical Theory

Another social perspective is that of dialogics or dialogic criticism (Bakhtin, Bialostosky, Bleich, Clark, Holquist). Central to dialogic theory is the idea that the meaning of any utterance depends on the situation in which it is used. For the most prominent dialogic theorist, Mikhail Bakhtin, the meaning of an utterance involves two levels of dialogue. At an *internal* level, a person constructs an intrapersonal dialogue that takes into account the potential *external* dialogue. The meaning of this internal dialogue is intimately related to the social and ideological meanings of the external social context.

For Bakhtin, dialogue is central to existence. When persons make an utterance or respond to a text, they are "answerable" for what they are saying. Because they are accountable for the potential social implications and effects of their utterances, they must consider the meanings that are constituted by their social interaction. To truly understand the social meaning of my exchange with Ben, I needed to reflect on my own internal dialogue that reflected tensions between my roles as teacher, father, and researcher. As Gregory Clark notes, "Such understanding is constructed in a second internal, intrapersonal dialogue, this one within the person to whom an utterance is addressed, a dialogue conducted in response to the utterance of another" (12).

Bakhtin points to the centrality of articulating response in achieving understanding: "Understanding comes to fruition only in the response. Understanding and response are dialectically merged and mutually condition each other; one is impossible without the other" (282). In responding to writers' utterances, readers create their own internal dialogue by incorporating the writers' utterances with their own. These internal dialogues then surface in the reader's own external social interaction as "a text that embodies that reader's experience as organized by the writer's language and one that will be expressed . . . in an external dialogue that reader will join" (Clark, 14).

An important distinction in dialogics theory is the difference between a "monologic" and a "dialogic" perspective. A monologic perspective imposes a single, unified, fixed perspective on experience. In contrast, adopting a "dialogic" perspective, persons entertain multiple layers of conflicting, competing meanings, or what Bakhtin describes as "heteroglossia." In adopting a dialogic perspective, persons are exploring "relations among voices and a practice of actualizing multiple relations among internally divergent voices" (Bialostosky, 224). Members of a dialogic community resist monologic orientations in order to "keep talking to themselves and to one another, discovering their affinities without resting in them and clarifying their differences without resolving them" (224). One goal of education is to help students move from simplistic, monologic perspectives to entertain the complexities of dialogic perspectives through the responding to and writing of literary texts (Bizzell).

In responding to literature, some students may be more willing to entertain a dialogic than a monologic perspective, differences due to their own social role in the school. In a recent study (Beach, "Complexities"), I examined five tenth graders' explorations of complexities or tensions in literary responses to two stories and their story writing. I also interviewed the students regarding their perceptions of family members, their leisure-time activities, what they value in life, their attitudes toward school and gender, their moral reasoning, and their perceptions of their stories.

These students varied in their responses along a continuum from monologic to dialogic. The two students who were more likely to adopt a monologic orientation, Kerry and Mike (pseudonyms)—both relatively good students—wrote stories and responses that were consistently judged as involving little or no examination of tensions or contradictions. Analysis of the language of their interview transcripts, freewritings, and story/response writings indicates that both adopted a relatively traditional gender attitude. Neither student questioned his family's or school's values. Kerry consistently focused on the dualism of "good versus evil," without exploring the complexities inherent in that dualism. Mike consistently focused on the theme of achieving individual autonomy through physical actions, particularly sports. In the classroom, these students generally played it safe, avoiding expressions of deviant ideas.

In contrast, the three students I perceived to be adopting a more dialogic perspective were not necessarily good students. All three of these students consistently examined tensions and contradictions in both their story writing and responses. They frequently challenged institutional norms, entertaining optional explanations or interpretations. Both Adell and John questioned their families' patriarchal values, and Dee questioned the teacher-centered mode of instruction that predominates in her classes, proposing alternative teaching methods. In his highly autobiographical story, John portrayed the tensions of coping with his parents' traditional attitudes. The latter group was more likely to be experimenting with alternative social roles and attitudes beyond that of simply being the "good student." These students would therefore apply their experience of coping with the tensions in their own lives to their responses to texts.

Thus dialogic theories point to the value of exploring the conflicting perspectives and tensions associated with the heteroglossia inherent in the transaction with texts.

A number of feminist theorists, drawing on Bakhtin and others, have examined the ways responses are shaped by the quality of social interaction in the classroom. Catherine Lamb notes that classroom response is often driven by models of argumentation associated with a masculine gender orientation. Students are typically asked to formulate a hypothesis and then defend that hypothesis with "evidence from the text." The student's job is to "win over" their audience—usually the teacher—with persuasive evidence. For Lamb, the metaphor of "winning over" implies an adversarial power relationship. These ways of responding are also encouraged in writing critical essays. In an analysis of literary critical essays published in *PMLA* from 1975 to 1988, Olivia Frey found that all but two adopted what she perceived to be the "adversarial method" (509).

This adversarial relationship reflects Bakhtin's monologic stance. To adopt a more dialogic or dialectical orientation, Lamb advocates the use of mediation and negotiation. Rather than attempt to win over an audience, students attempt to construct insights or knowledge that both they and their peers judge to be mutually acceptable. In contrast to a monologic orientation that often suppresses conflicts or tensions, negotiation and mediation serve to acknowledge and define conflicts. Rather than lining up according to competing *positions*, Lamb recommends focusing on differing *interests* or *issues* represented in the different perspectives, leading to a consideration of reasons for these differing perspectives.

In contrast to responding in a detached, impersonal mode, the aforementioned theorists also recommend the idea of "connected knowing" (Belenky, et al) through social connections or relationships with teachers, peers, or authors whose materials they are reading. Patrocinio Schweichart cites the example of Adrienne Rich's essay on Emily Dickinson. In order to connect with Dickinson as a historical figure and person, Rich visits Dickinson's home in Amherst to imagine the ways in which Dickinson's own context influenced her writing. And, in describing her own experience with Dickinson's poetry, Rich focuses on her own interpretive context "shaped by her experience and interests as a feminist poet living in the twentieth-century United States" (37): "She reaches out to Dickinson not by identifying with her, but by establishing their affinity. Both are American, both are women poets in a patriarchal culture. By playing this affinity against the differences, she produces a context that incorporates both reader and writer" (38).

It may be the case that gender differences shape the purpose for responding in a classroom. In her analysis of male and female uses of conversation, Deborah Tannen finds that women use conversation primarily to create and sustain relationships, while males use conversation primarily to complete tasks. In a classroom discussion, females may therefore prefer to share responses as a way of creating social relationships, while males may prefer to focus on completing what they perceive to be classroom tasks, for example, analyzing the text in an objective, detached manner (Bleich, Flynn).

The idea of women valuing sharing response in social groups, particularly in book clubs, may stem from historical experiences. In her study of the women members of the upper-middle-class Hamilton family of the 1880s and 1890s, Barbara Sicherman finds that reading and discussing literature served as more than idle escapism. Reading served as a means of "removing [women] from their usual activities, permitted the formulation of future plans, or more generally, encouraged vital engagement with the world" (215). Moreover, these women's social exchanges served to help them experiment with alternative social roles and sources of fulfillment beyond the traditional expectations of marriage. Sicherman notes that in the cultural world of late-Victorian American life, "reading was more likely to be liberating than confining" because it provided "the occasion for perceiving one's inmost needs and wants—desires that could be later acted upon" (217).

## Speech-Act and Sociological Theories

Another relevant social perspective is that of speech-act and sociological theories, particularly those posited by "social interactionalists" such as Erving Goffman. These theories are interested in how language means within the social contexts of everyday conversation. For example, when I was a kid, I would walk into a hot dog restaurant in downtown Durham, North Carolina, and simply state the words, "All the way." The meaning of my utterance was understood within that specific social context to mean that I was performing an act of ordering a hot dog and that I wanted mustard, ketchup, onions, and chili on the hot dog. The meaning of my utterance depended on how I used those words in that context for a specific pragmatic purpose.

Context is relevant to response theory because readers draw on their knowledge of social uses of language in making inferences about characters' own language use (Beach and Brown). For example, I make inferences about the mushrooms as characters by applying my knowledge of what it means to make assertions, particularly rather bald assertions such as, "We shall, by morning/ Inherit the earth." And, these theories help explain the meaning of responses as social acts in specific social contexts.

## Knowledge of Speech-Act Conventions

Speech-act theory, as originally formulated by J. L. Austin and later by John Searle and H. Paul Grice, posits that the meaning of language is constituted by how it is used in specific contexts. Speakers use language to perform speech acts of requesting, ordering, inviting, asserting, etc., by meeting certain conditions constituting the use of certain acts. In Searle's model, speakers must conform to sets of codified conditions in order that an act such as a request succeeds. For example, in order that the words "the door is open" be taken as a request to close the door, a speaker needs to have the status or power to make such a request, believe that his or her audience is able to fulfill the request, and be sincere about making the request. Other speech-act and pragmatics theorists, who are less bound to formal conditions, focus more on the underlying social assumptions that constitute speakers' interactions. (For general discussions of these theories, see Adams; Bakhtin; Beale; Brown and Levinson; Cohen; Davis; Green; Grice; Leech; Levinson; Wardhaugh; for specific applications to responses to texts, see Harris; Felman; Hancher; Petrey; Pratt; Sperber and Wilson; Straus.) For example, in Grice's theory of the Cooperative Principle, speakers and audiences seek to cooperate with each other by following certain maxims—saying no more than is necessary, being truthful, being sincere, and citing valid evidence. While speech-act theory has typically been used to analyze characters' or narrators' speech acts, more recently it has provided some insight into how readers may make inferences about speakers' or characters' speech acts. Take, for example, Grice's maxim of sufficiency: say no more than is necessary. If, upon saying the words, "All the way," to the clerk in the hot dog stand, I had also said, "And would you please also add the usual toppings," I might have received a strange look from the clerk, signaling to me that I had violated the maxim of sufficiency. From that and thousands of other social experiences, I learn what it means to violate that maxim. Then, in responding to a narrator or character who violates this maxim by blathering on needlessly, I can, drawing on my tacit social knowledge, infer that something is wrong with the character. In other cases, I may deliberately flaunt this maxim by being laconic. For example, if someone asks me to describe the hot dogs in the stand, I might state, "The water's good." I am cooperating by answering the question, but I am also deliberately saying no more than necessary to imply a meaning—that the hot dogs weren't very good. Similarly, in responding to a character, Mary, whose assessment of Bill is a simple "He's OK," I know that Mary is deliberately flaunting the maxim to imply that Bill has some problems.

I am also able to draw on my knowledge of Grice's maxim, "Be sincere," to sense instances in which characters or narrators are being insincere or unreliable (Pratt; see Smith for activities on responding to unreliable narrators).

Readers also mesh their knowledge of speech-act conventions with knowledge of textual/genre conventions to make inferences about dialogue embedded in texts (Beach, "Discourse"; Beach and Brown, "Discourse"). In applying rules of notice to anticipate the unusual or extraordinary, a reader is particularly attentive to instances in which characters' dialogue violates speech-act or conversational conventions. For example, in *Pride and Prejudice,* Mrs. Bennett talks incessantly about her difficulties, much to the consternation of those around her, particularly Mr. Bennett, who retreats to his library. In responding to the novel, readers mesh their knowledge of Grice's sufficiency maxim with knowledge of comic, nineteenth-century British novels to infer that Mrs. Bennett's blathering constitutes a violation of norms, violations that are also mitigated by the comic norms of the novel. Readers are thus drawing on their knowledge of both social and text conventions to make inferences about characters' traits, beliefs, motives, and goals. As one reader notes in describing Mr. Bennett's often deliberate misunderstanding of Mrs. Bennett:

It's possible that he really doesn't understand but I think just the tone that was set in the beginning of a kind of humorous irony leads you to conclude that he does understand, that he is simply being humorous, and in fact, as it goes on, one of the things that gives you a clue is that the kind of questions are really so dense, that they's too dumb to be true. For example, when she says, "I'm thinking of him [D'Arcy] marrying one of our girls," and he says, "Is that his design in settling here?" Well, nobody would really be that dumb; and in fact, it's his wife that doesn't get it, because she takes him seriously in this obviously leading or stupid question, so that the impression you get is that she's the one who's misunderstanding and he really understands it very well and is just playing a game. (Beach, "Discourse," 117–18)

Readers also draw on their knowledge of what theorists such as Erving Goffman define as the process of strategic social interaction accomplished through face-saving or avoidance rituals. In applying Goffman's theories of strategic interaction to a theory of response, Mary Rogers describes the strategic moves that both author and reader make to constitute a social relationship. An implied author or narrator attempts to gain a reader's trust by such moves described in Goffman's theory as revealing certain details, making asides, citing reservations, directly addressing the reader as "friend," or disqualifying their status to mislead the reader. Readers also make various moves, which Goffman describes as "naive moves" involved in accepting the speaker: "the assessment an observer makes of a subject when the observer believes that the subject can be taken as he appears" (Goffman, 15). Or, readers go beyond naive moves to make "uncovering moves" to go beneath the surface appearances. On the basis of their experiences in everyday social interaction, readers learn to sense when to apply naive and uncovering moves. When, for example, they sense some incongruity between what a character says and does, they are more likely to apply uncovering moves.

All of this suggests the value of relating students' own social experiences with language use to their responding to characters' or narrators' language. A teacher can model that process by making explicit his or her own thought processes. For example, in responding to the mushrooms assertions, I talk about my experience with speakers who make unqualified assertions in order to convey a sense of power.

## The Classroom as a Social Community

Applied to the classroom, these theoretical perspectives posit that the meaning of texts is constructed through readers' and writers' social interaction (Bruffee). Knowledge is perceived not as a fixed, external entity to be imparted from teacher to student; rather, it is mutually constructed and verified through social interaction (Nystrand). And, within the context of the classroom as an "interpretive community," students learn to share certain common assumptions and strategies specific to the classroom as a social community.

In the past decade, these theories have had a profound effect on writing instruction (Brandt, Brooke, Cooper and Holzman, Dyson, Phelps). In shifting toward writing as a social exchange within the classroom, teachers create a context which endows students with a sense of purpose and responsibility associated with producing texts to communicate with and influence others. In contrast, a recent survey of secondary school literature instruction indicates that much of secondary and college literature instruction continues to focus primarily on teacher presentations and teacher-led, large-group recitations/ discussions (Applebee). Thus, while students become social activists in the writing classroom, they often adopt a more passive role in the literature classroom, operating according to the familiar ritual of answering teacher questions. In the process, they lose their sense of purpose and motivation associated with membership in a writing community.

The ritual-like nature of literature discussions stems from assumptions about the social roles of teacher and students. One reason that much of the talk in the classroom fulfills a "presentational" function has to do with fulfilling the teacher's agenda as "evaluator" (Barnes, Britton, and Torbe). In presenting the right answers to the teacher's questions, students are using language to satisfy the teacher. As Barnes, Britton, and Torbe note, "It is abbreviated, it serves the purpose of educational control and it brings pupils' statements in line with the teacher's frame of reference" (73). Presentational talk focuses on reproducing, in a relatively definitive manner, what they already know. In contrast, "exploratory" talk "occurs when peers collaborate in a talk, when they wish to talk it over in a tentative manner, considering and rearranging their ideas" (50). As is the case in any thoughtful, engrossing conversation, the quality of students' response—their willingness to explore and extend their responses—depends heavily on teachers' own willingness to themselves engage in thoughtful, engrossing conversation. On the basis of his observations of schools throughout the country, Rexford Brown notes:

> In poor schools, there's no vibrant conversation, there's no sense of a tradition of inquiry or argument. You find in them a preponderance of the kind of bureaucratic instrumental rationality which

focuses on skills and processes and control. You do not see the kinds of conversation that lead to thoughtfulness, except rarely. Where we did see thoughtful schools and thoughtful districts, there was a huge and vibrant and exciting conversation with a capital "C" going on in the community and in the school, among the adults. (35)

On the basis of their observational studies, Goodlad, Sizer, and Powell, Farrar, and Cohen charge that many classrooms are "overly-structured" in that students often cannot dictate the direction of the activities. For example, an analysis of discussions in fifty-eight eighth-grade classrooms (Nystrand and Gamoran) indicated that little time is actually devoted to class discussion. Only 12 percent of the teachers' questions were "authentic" (i.e., they were genuinely seeking answers) and only 11 percent of the questions were follow-up probes to students' answers.

Similarly, in his analysis of high school students' discussion in high-ability English classes, James Marshall found that teachers generally dominated the discussions. After a teacher's question was answered, the focus or floor returned to the teacher. The teachers' turns, which were two to five times longer than the students' turns, were used to inform, question, and respond to students, while the students used their turns primarily to inform.

In addition to dominating the discussions, the teachers asked questions in a manner that served to establish their own framework for keeping the students "on track." For example, 73 percent of the teachers' questions focused on the text. The teachers typically described the text, applying their own background knowledge, followed by an interpretive question. The students then responded with the appropriate interpretive answer. Marshall cites the example of the following sequence in a discussion of *The Grapes of Wrath:*

> *Teacher:* "Who's the first one who sees (Casey). Through whose eyes do we meet him?"
> *Student:* "(inaudible) Tom Joad."
> *Teacher:* "Through Tom Joad, the main character. So through Tom we meet the preacher. And they talk. What do you know about the preacher? Maybe I shouldn't call him that. Why not? Why shouldn't I call him the preacher?"
> *Student:* "He has strange ideas."
> *Teacher:* "He has strange ideas, a little strange" (20).

In this exchange, the teacher is using his own perceptions of the novel to frame the direction of the discussion. As Marshall notes, "the students' statements, while few, are woven into that context, becoming a part of the summary that [the teacher] himself is providing" (36). By framing responses according to his or her own interpretive agenda, the teacher forecloses the possibility of the students defining their own agenda for exploring their own opinions or ideas.

Similarly, in teacher-controlled recitations, as Susan Hynds notes, "there is no openness to multiple responses. . . . Turn-taking proceeds from teacher to student, and back again, with only a very small proportion of the classroom talk emanating from the students" (27). In this context, students in classrooms often respond in a presentational mode, giving the preferred response as defined by the teacher's questions (Rogers, Green, and Nussbaum). If students fail to give the preferred response, then teachers may rephrase their questions or ask another question in order to put the student on track. Or, given a number of optional responses, a teacher may imply that one of those responses is to be preferred. Eventually, students learn that certain ways of responding are to be preferred over other ways (Rogers). In employing presentational talk, students are learning what David Bloome ("Reading") defines as "procedural display," responding according to the expected script or scenario. They passively respond to the teacher's questions with "correct answers," with little or no exploration of their own personal opinions or ideas. As a result, they are less likely to explore differences of opinions or ideas.

In contrast to these teacher-controlled, large-group discussions are the small-group discussions in which the members shape the direction of the discussion, creating an environment characteristic of the book club. In a study comparing classroom discussions with those conducted by members of informal adult book clubs, Michael Smith and James Marshall found that in contrast to classroom discussions, the book club discussions featured more fluid movement between episodes initiated by all members and relatively longer, more cooperative turns in which members worked together to formulate ideas. Group members also were continually citing intertextual links to other texts, links that served to bolster their social interaction. Members of the book club were also more likely than students in classrooms to use exploratory talk to tentatively experiment with optional responses. While members of a book club, unlike students in a class, attend voluntarily, attempts have been made to create small-group, book club discussions in the classroom. A three-year study of book clubs in fourth- and fifth-grade classrooms (Raphael et al.) found that the students used their book clubs to fulfill a range of purposes: to share reading log responses, clarify points of confusion, discuss ideas, relate to other texts, discuss their own response process, and relate their personal experiences and prior knowledge to the text. In addition, asking students to establish classroom book clubs around topics, issues, or genres of particular interest fosters a sense of social accountability to the success of that club (Short and Pierce).

In order to duplicate a book club environment in the classroom, small groups need some autonomy so that they can shape the direction of the response and support each other in exploring responses (Eeds and Wells; Hickman; Roser and Martinez). The quality of discussions is also bolstered by writing completed prior to or during discussions. This may take the form of freewriting prior to discussions or exchanges of dialogue-journal entries. Given the fact that many students lack the confidence to easily and openly express their responses in front of others, writing prior to discussion helps these students privately formulate responses which they can then share publicly. In one study (Smith and White) of discussions without any prior writing, about half of students' responses consisted of surface descriptions. In discussions with prior writing, only 28 percent of the discussion consisted of descriptions; 72 percent, consisted of abstractions about the stories.

Students may also exchange dialogue-journal entries to mutually explore responses through social collaboration. For example, as Nancie Atwell has demonstrated, sharing letters about texts motivates students to extend their responses. In an oral conversation, speakers respond immediately to the other person. In written conversation, because there may be a gap of several days before a partner reacts, students need to use their entries to create a social relationship. In our own research on peer dialogue journals (Beach and Anson), during the more effective exchanges, students initially established a social relationship or bond, often through self-disclosure of their own experiences, feelings, or attitudes, or, as Schatzburg-Smith found, by sharing their complaints and concerns about a course.

The quality of small-group discussions may also depend on whether, having brought up a certain topic, issue, or question, students can mutually work through it. In his analysis of discussions of poetry, Keith Hurst notes that students engage in what he calls "cycles of utterances." One student begins the cycle by throwing out a question or something that he or she finds puzzling. Then, other students chime in with possible alternative answers or hypotheses that may then be tested out against alternative hypotheses. Hurst notes that the cycle is completed when the group members tentatively accept one or more hypotheses and then move on to another question. Thus students were willing to pursue a particular topic, issue, or question in a sustained manner.

Various forms of drama can bolster the social quality of classroom responses (Heathcote; O'Neill and Lambert; Porter). In some cases, students' social roles in the classroom may become ossified to the point that these roles may limit the degree to which students may express their responses. In drama activities, students break out of their classroom roles to experiment with alternative ways of behaving and speaking. A quiet student who says little or nothing in class may, in the role of a character, suddenly come alive now that it is safe to deviate from his or her usual role. As in the book clubs, it is equally important that students engage in drama activities in which they have the authority to construct the situations, apply their own knowledge, and create their own interpretations. As Heathcote notes, students "become involved at a caring and urgently involved level if they are placed in quite a specific relationship with the action, because this brings with it the responsibility and more particularly the viewpoint which gets them into effective involvement" (168). In traditional role play or play production, students often have less involvement in and responsibility for constructing social situations and roles. In responding to texts, students could assume the frames or perspectives of teachers who had to teach the text, historians, media representatives, psychologists, relatives of central characters, or witnesses to key events, and conduct interviews with characters or each other (Edminston). As one study found (Edminston), in adopting the role and responsibility associated with being the teacher, for example, students are more likely to ask questions, express their own feelings, and converse as if they were outside the classroom.

The teacher's own social role also influences the quality of classroom talk. In adopting the teacher role, teachers may experience a sense of two-sidedness—a tension between their own felt-identity and their official role as defined by the school (Fox). The teacher is often caught between allegiance to the socially constituted classroom community and allegiance to external dictates associated with mandated textbooks, assessment tests, or school policies that serve to undermine the unique social fabric of that community. Thus, while teachers and students may mutually develop an interest in a particular topic, they may suddenly need to drop that topic in order to prepare for tests such as the New York State Regents Exam (Perl and Wilson).

Teachers may also be concerned with meeting institutional expectations as to whether one is, for example, "covering" the appropriate content or "maintaining standards." Concerns with these expectations may blind one to the here-and-now social and emotional realities and climate of the classroom. In reflecting on how her own expectations shaped her teaching, Jane Tompkins notes that her concern with not being "good enough" created "anxiety and self-doubt" and prevented her from developing the confidence to attend to the here and now. As she notes:

> If only I had known how important it was to open up intercourse with the class, to be there with them in a human way, take the temperature of their feelings, find out what was really on their minds, give them an opportunity to take control of the material for themselves, let them run with it and see how it felt. If only I had let them get access to one another, allowed the class to become a community instead of a collection of people. . . . If I had known about these things and realized that I had the freedom to do them, life would have been a lot easier for me and more rewarding, and I think the students would have had a better time. (604)

Creating this sense of community includes reacting to students' responses in a descriptive, reader-based manner. In reacting in writing or on tape to students' written essay or journal responses, *how* one reacts shapes the quality of the exchange. As Nancie Atwell found from responding in dialogue journals, "when I bombarded kids with teacher questions, I turned the dialogue journal into a test" (276). Or, as I (Beach, "Evaluating") found out from interviewing students about my reactions to their journals, the students preferred comments in which I shared my own perceptions and experiences rather than comments that were "pro forma" or evaluative. All of this suggests that creating a classroom as a social community fosters students' expression and exploration of responses.

## Limitations of Social Theories

Social theories of response attend to the ways that the meanings of responses are constituted by specific social "literacy events" (Bloome and Bailey). The quality of an event depends on how participants perceive the degree of social involvement or responsibility in an event; how participants interpret an event constitutes the meaning of an event. Understanding the meanings, as ethnographies of the classroom illustrate, requires attention to what could be defined as the *local*, the particular, or, as in Tompkins's case, the here and now. While it is difficult to dispute the value of this orientation, in some cases, this perspective may not capture the larger, more global cultural and ideological forces that, in invisible ways, shape the meaning of the event. For example, take what could be defined as "controlled literary events" evident in current televised sports events or rock concerts. Driven by the need to build excitement, the producers of these events continually prompt participants at the scene to applaud at certain moments, or they interject commercials at every opportune moment. A social analysis of such events would reveal the ways in which these events seek not only to control but also to create certain behaviors. However, what may be missing from such an analysis is the application of a cultural critique of how the entertainment business creates what Jean Baudrillard calls "hyperreality" (7) which blurs the distinction between fiction and reality (see also Eco's *Travels in Hyperreality*). Similarly, in considering the classroom as a social community, what may be missing is a consideration of how responses in that classroom also reflect larger cultural attitudes and values. While teachers may strive to create communities in which all students are actively participating, the *meaning* of their responses is still constituted by the fact that they are engaged in a host of cultural practices associated with defining identity according to gender or class. It is to these matters that I now turn.

# 6 Cultural Theories of Response

In my responses to "Mushrooms," I perceived the mushrooms to be downtrodden members of an unfortunate underclass who ultimately assert themselves against a system that suppresses them. I believe that the mushrooms know that the only way to gain power is to join forces with others so that their numbers "count" in attempting to face overwhelming odds.

In responding to "Mushrooms," I am also responding to a "culturally-activated text as a culturally-constituted reader" (Bennett, 216) according to my white, middle-class, male, "liberal" attitudes acquired during the 1960s. In conceiving of the "mushrooms" as "downtrodden" or "underclass," I am putting them in safe, academic categories, thus distancing myself from the messy political complexities they evoke. At the same time, the fact that I create a narrative in which they challenge "the system" reflects a political response to the poem.

Theorists interested in how readers' attitudes and values shape their response draw on a range of different disciplinary perspectives: post-structuralist, feminist, anthropological, historical, and Marxist. These perspectives generally assume that readers respond according to "subject positions" acquired from socialization by cultural institutions. As part of that socialization, readers acquire various cultural practices—expressing cultural identity or resisting social and economic domination (Giroux and Simon). As Teresa Ebert notes, "texts do not so much duplicate social practices as produce the representations through which we live those practices and make them intelligible" (54).

According to Edgar Schein, such cultural practices include, among others, the following (6–12):

- sharing a common language and conceptual categories
- defining norms and boundaries for appropriate interpersonal behavior
- recruiting, selecting, socializing, and training members
- allocating authority, power, status, and resources

- dispensing rewards and punishments
- coping with unpredictable, stressful events.

Schein notes that these cultural practices are evident at three levels: artifacts, values, and assumptions/paradigms. Artifacts are visible behaviors that reflect a cultural climate or style. He cites the example of a workplace in which the doors to offices are always open and in which there are a lot of discussions and arguments, behaviors that reflect an "open" culture. In a culture, members cite certain values to justify their behavior. The head of the workplace will order the doors to be open because communication is highly valued. Less visible are the underlying assumptions or paradigms that members take for granted, for example, the assumption that members need to test out their ideas with others in the group.

Similarly, readers' cultural practices of identifying with a character reflect their cultural attitudes and values of certain groups. Understanding how students respond as members of a certain gender or class—the focus of this chapter—may serve to explain their responses.

## Poststructuralist Theories

Many of the textual theories reviewed in chapter 2 were based on structuralist theory. As I noted, central to that theory is Saussure's semiotic distinction between the signifier and the signified. The signifier, a word such as "joint," may represent a range of different concepts, i.e., what is signified. "Joint" may be used to refer to a brace, a building, or marijuana. While structuralists assume that the relationships between signifier and signified are relatively well defined, as I also noted, poststructuralists such as Barthes perceive the relationship as relatively unstable. The fact that meanings of signifier continually change—the fact that joint as signifier for marijuana did not exist fifty years ago—suggests that the sense of permanence and stability of language is problematic. Poststructuralists examine the ways in which schools, businesses, organized religions, or governments limit the signifieds of the signifier to meanings consistent with their own institutional ideology. They focus on how these institutions socialize readers to respond according to certain "subject positions" consistent with these ideological stances. They argue that a reader's subjective, vicarious experience with the narrator's or main character's subjective experiences gives the reader the false impression that he or she is deriving these insights independently. "The reader is thus placed in a privileged position, one of *dominant specularity* [which] . . . provides the illusion of independent thought and reinforces the myths of individuality. . . . "(Webster, 83). As Barnes and Barnes found in their analysis of literature instruction in British schools, students are typically encouraged to conceive of characters' difficulties in terms of their own personal difficulties independent of or even in opposition to institutional forces. As evident in units or textbook sections on the individual *versus* society, the individual protagonist is often valued for resisting the need to conform to institutions instead of perceived as being shaped by institutional forces.

Understanding the meaning of response therefore requires an understanding of the ideological stances inherent in these cultural and historical forces. In his analysis of James Joyce's development as a young reader and writer, Robert Scholes describes this as a process of "reading" the culture "as a mediating factor, a structure of possibilities that presented Joyce and others of his generation with pathways that were already organized in the form of axiological or binary structures of value and choice" (28).

The forces of this process are described by French sociologist and critical theorist Michel Foucault as "discourses" or discursive practices shared by institutions such as medicine, law, religion, or education. These discourses constitute relationships among persons according to the power, status, and rights inherent in institutions. Contrary to the idea that persons define their experiences in terms of their own words or signifiers, "discursive formations" or "practices" exist prior to individuals' own experiences. Discourses also serve to limit the definitions of language to ways legitimate only for that speech community. Speech communities attempt to persuade other speech communities of the legitimacy of their discourse, competing with each other "to be statutorily recognized as the legitimate authority for defining some phenomenon-word relation" (Mosenthall and Kamil, 1022). For example, the discourse of science when applied to discussions of "the audience" often masks the complexities of actual audience responses. Ien Ang documents the ways in which, in making decisions about television programming, producers rely on ratings based on behavioristic, often pseudo-scientific research. These ratings assume that it is possible to generalize about the larger viewing audiences' responses from determining whether or not a sampling of viewers did or did not watch a program. Simply determining whether a viewer watched a program says little about the ways in which that viewer responded to that program. Moreover, given the increasing number of choices of channels available through cable television, viewers have more autonomy over what they watch, making it more difficult to predict their responses.

Literary criticism is itself a discourse practice often distinct from the writing or production of texts. New Criticism may have distinguished itself from production of literature by tying itself to philology or to more "scientific" or "positivistic" attempts to "purify" the problematic nature of language associated with literature itself (Schuster). As a result, "English as a discursive practice has allocated status, money, and power to literary scholars and critics, at the expense both of people who actually create literature and of people who think it important to help everyone to write with as much skill and confidence as possible" (Schuster, 798).

Education is also constituted by a discourse that serves to reify the authority of educators. For example, in an exchange of letters between a group of teachers and their students—when the teachers attempted to alter their roles to "be like students"—they had difficulty divesting themselves of their authority roles granted by the institution (Brodkey). Thus, in responding to the students' dramatic personal narratives, the teachers were reluctant to acknowledge class concerns—that their students were experiencing difficulties that were institutionally different from their own lives as professionals. The educational discourse therefore creates a "discursive hegemony of teachers over students [that] is usually posed and justified in developmental terms—as cognitive deficits, emotional or intellectual immaturity, ignorance, and most recently, cultural literacy" (139). Even given the diversity of cultural differences represented in students, schools continue to assume the role of socializing students to acquire academic norms reflecting the values of the academic institution. As Marjorie Godlin Roemer notes, "differences in race, gender, class, and the traditions that 'place' us all are ostensibly left at the parking lot while we on campus take the 'objective' stance of scholars" (915).

Discourse practices are embedded in a continually changing, fluid set of relationships that continually challenge what Foucault described as the "will to truth" that is "reliant upon institutional support and distribution," which "tends to exercise a set of pressures, a power of constraint on other forms of discourse . . ." (219).

From this poststructuralist perspective, truth and knowledge are located in shifting, unstable discourses. As James Porter argues, readers and writers are participants in a process of continually negotiating knowledge and truth as "probable, local, and temporary" (116). For Porter, readers and writers negotiate knowledge within the context of a "forum, . . . a trace of a discourse community, a defined place of assembly or means of publication for discourse communities." Forums may include journals, conferences, classrooms, dinner tables, clubs, organizations, etc. Members are socialized to understand the shared ethos or attitudes of a forum, often through intertextual references to previous texts or literacy events.

## Acquiring Reading Formations

As part of this socialization, readers acquire certain "reading formations" or "subject positions" (Bennett and Woollacott; see, also, Morgan). Reading formations are those acquired ideological stances that constitute certain subject positions or desired ways of responding. On the basis of his analysis of viewers' responses to a British soap opera, "EastEnders," David Buckingham found that "viewers are not merely 'positioned' by television: They are also positioned in society and history, and will therefore bring different kinds of prior knowledge to the text. . . ." (115).

Readers acquire reading formations through what Bennett and Woollacott describe as "textual shifters" (16) or ideologically similar intertextual links and experiences. For example, during the 1950s and 1960s, readers' responses to Ian Fleming's James Bond novels were shaped by a host of different kinds of texts: films; film reviews; interviews with, and publicity about, Sean Connery and Roger Moore; fan magazines; etc. These intertextual links cut across different media: responses to the Bond films shaped responses to the Bond novels. In acquiring this reading formation within the context of the Cold War, readers learned to perceive Bond as a representative of Western, anti-Communist, masculine values. While the women in the Bond novels and films were sexually liberated, they were liberated in terms of male control. Thus, the book covers, films, and male magazines consistently placed women as the objects of the "male look" or "male gaze." A reader or viewer was therefore invited to perceive the "Bond girl" through a patriarchal, sexist perspective, a perspective or reading formation consistent with the appeal of Bond novels and films to males of that generation.

Discourses may thus serve to mask tensions and contradictions by creating an "illusion of regularity" (Spellmeyer, 719), creating a "monologic" reading formation. For example, in responding to a text, students often infer the theme as a moral platitude—"hard work pays off in the end"—without reflecting on the tensions or contradictions inherent in such thematic inferences. In contrast, by exploring what Barthes described as "obtuse" meanings (*Image*, 64–65), students use the experience with the text, according to Patricia Donahue, to "challenge the universality of the symbolic meaning and to question common sense as seamless, inviolate truth" (75). For example, Donahue's students typically infer a symbolic meaning for Poe's "The Fall of the House of Usher" as meaning "madness leads to destruction and death; therefore, madness must be avoided at all costs" (74). In order to infer the obtuse meanings of the story, students note the ways in which the character Roderick influences the narrator in perverse ways, serving to undermine the thematic meaning that madness can be controlled. In entertaining obtuse meanings associated with a more dialogic stance, students explore the problematic aspects of monologic thematic inferences.

## Institutional Socialization of Response

Readers are therefore socialized by various institutions to adopt certain reading formations. To understand this process, theorists observe readers' responding within the context of cultural institutions.

For example, John Fiske studied adolescents' responses to Madonna by "listening to them, reading the letters they write to fanzines, or observing their behavior at home or in public. The fans' words or behavior are . . . texts that need 'reading' theoretically in just the same way as the 'texts of Madonna' do" (97). In reading these various "texts of Madonna"—the music videos, movies, magazine articles, posters, etc.—Fiske goes beyond what I have described as a textual approach to recognize "that the signifieds exist not in the text itself, but extratextually, in the myths, countermyths, and ideology of their culture" (97). This allows him to determine "the way the dominant ideology is structured into the text and into the reading subject, and those textual features that enable negotiated, resisting, or oppositional readings to be made" (98). He cites the example of 14-year-old Lucy's response to a Madonna poster:

> She's tarty and seductive . . . but it looks alright when she does it, you know, what I mean, if anyone else did it it would look right tarty, a right tart you know, but with her its OK, it's acceptable . . . with anyone else it would be absolutely outrageous, it sounds silly, but it's OK with her, you know what I mean. (November 1985, 98)

For Fiske, this response represents Lucy's grappling with the cultural oppositions of patriarchal versus feminist perspectives on sexuality:

> Lucy can only find patriarchal words to describe Madonna's sexuality—"tarty" and "seductive"—but she struggles against the

patriarchy inscribed in them. At the same time, she struggles against the patriarchy inscribed in her own subjectivity. The opposition between "acceptable" and "absolutely outrageous" not only refers to representations of female sexuality, but is an externalization of the tension felt by adolescent girls when trying to come to terms with the contradictions between a positive feminine view of their sexuality and the alien patriarchal one that appears to be the only one offered by the available linguistic and symbolic systems. (98)

Through her grappling with the conflicting codes of the poster, Lucy is not only defining her gender identity within the context of competing patriarchal and feminist values, she is also making intertextual links according to learned cultural categories. Fiske cites the example of the cultural category of "the blonde":

Madonna's music video "Material Girl" provides us with a case in point: it is a parody of Marilyn Monroe's song and dance number "Diamonds Are a Girl's Best Friend" in the movie *Gentlemen Prefer Blondes:* such an allusion to a specific text is an example of intertextuality, for its effectiveness depends upon specific, not generalized, textual knowledge—a knowledge that, incidentally, many of Madonna's young girl fans in 1985 were unlikely to possess. The video's intertextuality refers rather to our culture's image bank of the sexy blonde star and how she plays with men's desire for her and turns it to her advantage. (108)

Readers therefore associate certain cultural meanings with categories such as "the blonde"—sexiness, power, vulnerability, youth, celebrity, etc., meanings—in this case, associated with the cultural practice of defining gender roles. Through a range of different "textual shifters," such as record labels, movies, music videos, celebrity magazines, etc., Madonna evokes the contradictory images of "innocent virgin" and "worldly whore." For many adolescent females, during her popularity, Madonna represents an assertiveness against a patriarchal system— an attitude that "I can do what I want," an autonomy not always associated with a 1950s image of "the blonde" as dependent on patriarchy.

Lucy's response to Madonna also represents another cultural practice: defining her membership in a particular group at a particular time— Madonna fans in the mid-1980s. Through her response, she aligns herself with attitudes and values of a cultural community. To take another example, Per-Anders Forstrop observed and interviewed the members of a "fundamentalist" Swedish church community. He found that their socialization in that community shaped their responses to the Bible. The church members learn to "read" the Bible as the absolute and infallible "word of God." In the process, members learn to conceive of "reading" the Bible as "walking" or "living" "the word"—the will of God—a stance that leaves little room for critical analysis or individual differences in interpretations of the Bible.

This community's way of responding is a learned cultural practice. Through their responses, members establish their allegiance to these community values. Group sessions in the church consist of testimonials of how the "truths" of the Bible affect their daily lives. Old members socialize new members into this reading formation because old members believe that they are responsible for "bringing the word" to new members: "spiritual children" who need the "food" or "nutrition" of the Bible and testimonials of its application to life. Through this socialization, members acquire what could be characterized as a fundamentalist reading formation.

At the same time, readers are not simply cultural dupes who passively acquire reading formations. As members of cultures constituted by inner contradictions, they ultimately acquire the cultural practice of resisting norms. From experiencing gender or class perspectives, readers learn to resist traditional beliefs through exploring new and alternative sensibilities. In the act of breaking in new ways of experiencing texts, current feminist critics are therefore interested in exploring the idea of multiple or competing sensibilities associated with responses to texts (Ebert). As Tania Modleski notes, reader-response critics often assume that

> an *already-existent* meaning resides *somewhere*, and that the critic's job is to locate it (in the text, in the reader, in the interpretive community, or in the relations between the three). On the contrary, a fully politicized feminist criticism has seldom been content to ascertain old meanings and (in the manner of the ethnographers) take the measure of already-constituted subjectivities; it has aimed, rather, at bringing into being new meanings and new subjectivities, seeking to articulate not only what is but "what has never been." (58)

Drawing on speech-act theory, Modleski celebrates the very performance of responding as an act or practice of resisting and redefining traditional models. She cites the example of Virginia Woolf's position in *A Room of One's Own* as challenging historical reality to construct alternative sensibilities.

### Responding and Group Membership

David Bleich argues that readers' responses reflect their *membership* in these competing cultural communities. He reflects autobiographically on his own memberships in competing cultural and ethnic communities:

> At age fourteen I asked, why don't I understand or like Shake-
> speare, while other Jewish boys in my school seemed to know
> and understand many of his plays? At twenty-one I wondered,
> why don't I like Ezra Pound and T.S. Eliot, while the Jewish
> professor in graduate school taught them as if they represented
> an eternal standard of literary achievement? Why do I think Kafka
> is funny, while the Jewish professor who taught him wanted me
> to "deduce the narrator" from a given text? . . . Members of my
> own culture and ethnic group accept what they "received" in high
> school, college, and graduate school . . . it is the membership
> of . . . students in various communities that is more pertinent to
> their studies of language and literature. (21)

To further explain this phenomenon, within a high school setting, students' responses reflect and display their negotiated membership in a number of different social groups. In her ethnographic study of a large suburban high school, Penelope Eckert found two predominant "cultural categories" shaping students' perceptions of school: "jocks"— students who were middle class, pro-school, involved in athletics and extra-curricular activities—and "burnouts"—students who were representative of working-class backgrounds and less involved in school and more involved in work and neighborhood activities. The jocks learned to use the social networks in the school to gain the information necessary for success in the school; they associated school with certain forms of "preppy" dress, "pro-social" behaviors, and athletics. In contrast, the burnouts, who were more accustomed to functioning in small, coherent neighborhood or workplace groups, had more difficulty coping with the large, bureaucratic structure of the school; they associated dress, behaviors, and allegiance to neighborhood groups and workplace with cultural rejection of the jocks' world. Moreover, because of their symbolic display of what were perceived to be "deviant" attitudes, burnouts were often excluded from academic courses and social networks of the school's organizations. Thus each group defined itself in opposition to the other. As Eckert notes, "clothing, territory, substance use, language, demeanor, academic be-havior, and activities all ultimately serve as conscious markers of category affiliation . . . that strengthens the hegemony of the category system in adolescent life and increasingly restricts individual perceptions and choice" (69).

Readers act out these cultural practices through their responses in ways that define their cultural identity. In his essay, "The Life and Times of Joe Bob Brigges, So Far," Calvin Trillin cites the example of a reporter for the *Dallas Times Herald*, John Bloome, who began to write a regular, weekly movie review column, "Joe Bob Goes to the

Drive-In," in the paper's entertainment section. In his column, he adopted the totally different role of "Joe Bob," writing as a redneck reacting to films by adopting a highly sexist, racist stance: "So this flick starts off with a bimbo getting chained up and killed by a bunch of Meskins dressed up like Roman soldiers in their bathrobes" (44). His column became so popular that it was syndicated in fifty papers. While the column was eventually terminated due to complaints, Bloome continued to assume the role of "Joe Bob," writing books and appearing on talk shows. Through his responses, he was resisting the norms of mainstream, "liberal" newspaper writing, a cultural practice associated with conservative, white, racist values.

Similarly, adolescents derive immense pleasure from resisting school norms by "maintaining a sense of subcultural difference, a social identity that is not constructed by and for the interests of the dominant" (Fiske, 118). Thus burnouts may thumb their noses at requests to "express their responses" as a political statement of opposition to "good student" cultural practices. For example, in a study of 125 tenth graders who were members of three "regular" and two "honors" classes, I found that membership in these two groups influenced their responses. In this study, students responded to the story "I Go Along" by Richard Peck. In this story, Gene, a member of a regular English section, decides to accompany the honors students on a field trip to a poetry reading at a neighboring college. On the bus, Gene is befriended by a popular female student, Sharon. When Gene tells Sharon that he could write poetry as well as the poet, she tells him at the end of the story that if he worked harder, he might qualify for the honors section. Many of the regular students, particularly the males, were critical of Gene for going to the poetry reading. They perceived the poetry reading as an esoteric affair which was removed from their own lives. Many of the honors students, reflecting a pro-school reading formation, did not understand Gene's lack of motivation. They argued that if he applied himself and worked harder, then he would be promoted to the honors class.

Some of the students also explored multiple sensibilities associated with memberships in competing groups outside the school. For example, one student, Adell, responded to the stories in terms of a growing awareness of the tension between what she perceives as the patriarchal attitudes of her father and the more feminist attitudes of some of her relatives. She describes her family as

> very traditional. It's me and my mom doing the dishes after supper which me and my mom fixed. Dad will come home and

> expects that supper will be ready and that the table will be set. That's just how it is. My mom grew up in a farm family. It's something she grew up with.

Adell perceives her father as holding to outmoded gender attitudes: "I went out with someone last night. The first three questions my Dad asked me was, 'Does he hunt, does he fish, and will he walk you to the door and open it when you get there.' And, oh . . . jeez."

Adell distinguishes herself from her mother's attitudes. As she says, "I see the way my mom does things and I say that I'm not going to be like that. I want to be equal." Adell believes strongly in "respect and equality. I don't like anybody being put down because they are less equal." She also attributes her interest in gender equality to her aunts, whom she describes as feminists. She describes one of them as "wild, she's crazy, yet she's very down to earth. She's very successful, yet she has her family. She works hard, yet she goes out and does fun things." Adell also sees herself as distinct from "the system: it's so built into everybody I've seen that I don't know if I have much chance of getting out of it." In her response to "I Go Along," just as she is able to stand back and perceive herself as being socialized by her family, she locates Gene within an institutional context. Echoing her critical concern with "the system," Adell describes him as "locked into a system where he can't get out. If he is bright enough to be in their advanced class his chances of being moved up are slim." She also recognizes the potential arrogance inherent in Sharon's attempt to help Gene, noting that Sharon could be perceived as having "too 'high and mighty' a reputation for her actual personality." Adell identifies with Sharon's efforts, as someone "who will look even at others when their friend is looking down or up." In response to another story, "Fairy Tale," Adell describes the students as "very obvious— you immediately like Cynthia and Sam, and dislike Sherri and Ruth. It is also inevitable that Cynthia will become interested in Sam. It's so typical it's almost unlikable." At the same time, she adopts the perspective of the main character, Cynthia, exploring optional explanations of her motives: "I don't know if she did like Sam or didn't want to betray him, (in a sense) by accepting 'The One's' offer."

In reading students' written responses, teachers typically read in terms of whether those responses measure up to an ideal answer or form—whether or not the students have cited evidence from the text to support their claims. By reading students' responses for instances in which they are exploring the tensions associated with characters, teachers can foster reflection of cultural complexities.

## "Reading Formations" in Historical Contexts

Drawing on the work of reception theorists such as Jauss (reviewed earlier), theorists have also examined reading formations evident in readers' diaries, letters, or reviews written during a particular historical period (Baym, Freedberg, Greenberg, Machor, Montgomery, Railton, Reynolds, Tompkins). For example, understanding how Shakespeare's audiences responded to his plays requires some historical spadework to examine those audiences' cultural attitudes and beliefs regarding child-rearing practices, political beliefs, the law, or religion (Greenblatt): While today's students are often socialized in schools to privilege interpretation as the reader's ultimate goal (Purves), Shakespeare's audiences were more interested in responding according to the effects of texts (Tompkins).

Students may better understand the ways in which their own reading formations shape their responses in contemporary forums or cultures by examining the historical reading formations operating for the particular text they are studying. In doing so, students need to examine more than simply the historical or social facts about a particular period; they need to understand the prevailing cultural worldviews and narratives constituting the reading formations of that period (Schilb). They may also examine the author/audience relationship as a dynamic one in which the audience was not only responding to the author's text, but in which the author was also responding to the prevailing, assumed reading formations. For example, in creating parodies of characters' political positions in *Huckleberry Finn*, Twain makes certain assumptions about his audience's reading formations operating in the 1880s (Mailloux). During that period, adolescents were perceived to be highly impressionable. Adults therefore believed that they needed to protect adolescents from the potential influence of the increasingly popular dime novel and the "bad-boy" novel, fears only inflamed by testimony from members of the Jesse James gang, who claimed that reading dime novels led to a life of crime. The bad-boy character in these novels was perceived to be representative of deviant, delinquent behavior that could corrupt adolescents. These fears served as justification for the Concord Free Library to ban *Huckleberry Finn* in 1885 as representative of the bad-boy genre. Mailloux argues that by assuming that his audience condoned this highly moralistic stance, Twain then parodied these beliefs in the novel.

Within particular cultural groups, the meaning of certain texts evolves over time as the vestiges of past readers' experience influence the responses of current readers. For example, two texts, *Piers Plowman* and *The Pilgrim's Progress*, become important texts for members of the Protestant faith largely because of the ways in which readers' response to these texts, as well as to printed illustrations, served to define their religious and economic importance.

Readers' responses are also influenced by their perceptions of the literary reputation of texts, which, in turn, are shaped by the critics' prevailing attitudes during certain periods. By the 1850s in America, there were nearly 700 periodical publications which contained reviews that shaped reading formations during that period. During the 1840s and 1850s, the largely male critical establishment privileged the reputation of certain writers such as Hawthorne as part of the canon over less well-known women writers such as Susan Ashton-Warner (Tompkins). Because Hawthorne, unlike Ashton-Warner, was perceived to be associated with the same cultural elites as those of the educated critics, he received more positive recognition. Nina Baym, who studied the reviews of women's literature written during the first half of the nineteenth century, found that these reviews frequently devalued women's literature. Underlying many of these reviewers' comments was a suspicion of the seductive, corrupting power of novels. Reviewers often assumed that readers who read novels were more susceptible than those who read history or philosophy. Reviewers also evaluated novels according to their effectiveness in conveying moral lessons. However, overly didactic techniques in novels were equally suspect in that, as James Machor notes, they "prevented fiction from doing the work reviewers ascribed as proper to it: 'to elevate the moral sentiments and to strengthen the virtuous impulses of . . . readers' so as to maintain social stability and traditional cultural values (*Godey's* November 1858: 469)" (56).

Machor argues that reviewers of the period also modeled certain response strategies consistent with the moralistic reading formation. In order to socialize their readers to read in a thematic mode, they included extensive plot summaries, bracketed by inferences about the themes of the text. These thematic reading strategies were equated with a "commonsense" ideological reading formation associated with middle-class values.

Throughout the nineteenth and early twentieth centuries, this didactic orientation prevailed in the teaching of reading in the schools (Greenfield, Morgan). Much of the reading instruction at the turn of the century focused on "reading for character," through which students were socialized to respond by adopting the character's point of view as a moral guideline for appropriate behavior. Teachers often provided various response strategies that served to encourage positive response to "good" literature and discouraged involvement with texts viewed as corrupting. Morgan cites one Toronto teacher, who, in 1886, observed:

> If any pupil of ours should in future years lay down some spicy sensational novel, or leave the sheets of some violently illustrated periodical uncut, because of some dim remembrance of a warning note, sounded in old school days, the knowledge should make us more satisfied with our work than had he obtained all the honours that the Universities could bestow (1886)." (333)

Reading formations also shape responses to visual images. In the previously mentioned analysis of documented responses to art images, during the medieval and Renaissance periods, Robert Greenberg finds that prevailing religious beliefs and superstitions shaped people's perceptions of the meaning of images. In some cases, people were so outraged or angered by images they perceived to be blasphemous that they slashed or damaged paintings in museums. They were also reluctant to put pictures of relatives in their bedrooms for fear that they would be possessed by those relatives.

The meaning of images can also vary according to the prevailing cultural attitudes of particular historical periods. As John Berger, Judith Williamson, and others demonstrate, advertising images convey ideals of culturally appropriate appearance and behavior. In charting shifts in the images of women in advertising during this century, Stuart Ewen found that ads contained images of increasingly slimmer body weight, reflecting a shift in cultural attitudes regarding body weight. Ewen also found that ads in the first part of this century appealed to the products' utilitarian value—the fact that clothes kept one warm. In subsequent decades, ads appealed more to the lifestyle image associated with using a particular brand name—the fact that wearing Levi's jeans defined one as young and sexy. Given the cultural practice of defining identity through projecting the "right image" as an expression of "lifestyle," persons responding to ads may adopt the reading formation of admiring voyeurs who vicariously imagine themselves in terms of the images contained in the ads. When Ewen asked his students to describe those experiences that contribute to their own sense of "style," they consistently described style in terms of physical appearance or "images" associated with particular brand names that "make statements" about themselves to their peers. Just as the viewers of medieval and Renaissance periods were socialized to endow religious meanings to images, so contemporary adolescents are socialized to respond according to consumeristic cultural values.

These anthropological and historical studies reveal the reading formations operating for certain communities and historical periods. I now turn to theories of how these "reading formations" serve to define reader roles in terms of gender or class.

## Gender Roles and Attitudes

Readers' gender roles and attitudes—their culturally acquired propensity to adopt "masculine" versus "feminist" orientations or reading formations—also influence responses. In reflecting on my responses to "Mushrooms," I notice that I am responding in a relatively detached, objective manner to what the mushrooms could "stand for" without empathizing with what their move to power means emotionally. I attribute some of this to the way I have been socialized to respond according to a masculine reading formation.

While there is no single feminist theoretical position on response, feminist critics share a basic concern with the very limitations of responding to what is largely a male canon and what they characterize as a male reading formation. In her review of feminist theories of response, Patricinio Schweickart argues that "reader-response criticism needs feminist criticism" in that much of reader-response theory ignores "the issues of race, class, and sex, and give no hint of the conflicts, sufferings, and passions that attend these realities" (21). Moreover, rather than advocating the idea of adopting a singular feminist perspective, feminists, adopting a poststructuralist perspective, are exploring the idea of recognizing multiple, competing, subjective sensibilities inherent in the act of responding (Ebert).

Rather than grappling with competing perspectives, it may be the case that, given the high school canon, many secondary students are adopting a relatively one-dimensional reading formation associated with gender. A recent survey of the most frequently required literature texts indicated that of the top twenty texts (Applebee), only one was written by a woman: *To Kill a Mockingbird* by Harper Lee. To some degree, reading texts representative of traditional patriarchal values serves to socialize students in a masculine reading formation associated with the practices of "doing gender." In traditional cultural contexts, males are socialized to define their identity through physical actions or performance in competition with others. As previously noted, in contrast, females are socialized to be considerate of the consequences of their actions on their interpersonal relationships (Gilligan; Gilligan, Lyons, and Hanmer). Thus, when British adolescents were asked to write narratives (Moss), males typically wrote action-adventure stories in which they dramatically defeated their opponents in feats of physical prowess. In contrast, females wrote stories focusing on their development of interpersonal relationships. Rather than perceive these stories as simply playing out traditional sex-role stereotypes, Moss argues that these stories represent adolescents' need to define and explore the complications of defining gender roles. She found that many of the stories contained some of the underlying tensions and ambiguities associated with defining these roles. For example, the female students' romance stories frequently grappled with the issue of male power. As Moss notes:

> The writer's attention is focused by the genre . . . on boys' reading of that sexuality and on the space for female sexual desire in a world named by men. The male view of women, the female view of men, are seen as being in conflict. The women's view of the man includes the knowledge that the man's view of her is wrong, and that if she succumbs without a struggle to his initial view of her, fails powerfully to contest it, she will be the loser. [They are] depicting the tensions between alternative ways of reading masculinity (the thriller) or masculinity and femininity (the romance). (114–15)

In her analysis of avid female readers' responses to romance novels, *Reading the Romance*, Janice Radway finds a similar set of tensions associated with responding to romance novels. On the one hand, for these women, the very fact of reading romance novels as a pleasurable activity in the home served as a means of asserting their independence in patriarchal contexts. On the other hand, they responded positively to the nurturing female heroine who typically transforms the passive, cold, aloof male into a more nurturing partner. For Radway, these responses serve to reify their cultural role as nurturer in the home within a patriarchal value system. However, Radway's methods have been criticized for relying primarily on interviewing, which precluded observations of women's own lives, particularly negative aspects of their lives, and how those lives may have influenced their responses (McRobbie). Moreover, in explaining the women's responses in terms of a relatively singular fantasy narrative of achieving satisfaction through love, Radway does not explore the contradictions between conscious and unconscious fantasies and between competing discourses that shape both her own and the women readers' responses (Modleski).

These competing perspectives occur even in adolescent females' lives. In Christian-Smith's study of "low ability" adolescent female responses to romances, the females often admired the heroines for their assertiveness, a trait they found lacking in their own relationship with the school and teachers. In responding to the novels, they also employed an expertise not often tapped in usual school activities. At the same time, they identified positively with what Christian-Smith describes as the portrayed "codes of beautification" associated with femininity and positive relationships with males. Thus the assertiveness is constrained by the larger fear of being " 'too pushy' because this could result in alienating boys and destroying any romantic prospects" (113). These two studies suggest that a female reading formation involves a continuing tension between multiple sensibilities associated with asserting independence and accepting patriarchal values. Consistent with poststructuralists' critiques of the "unified self," it may be more useful to think of a reader "as a divided subject whose identity and even gender are constructed through her participation in such signifying practices of culture as texts" (Ebert, 58).

The expression of the internal contradictions between assertiveness and compliance/dependency in these studies reflects a willingness to reveal emotional tensions. In contrast, feminist theorists charge that texts like Hemingway's stories and novels invite readers to adopt a stance of patriarchy. The speaker in those texts employs a sparse, unemotional, objective register associated with a stance of distancing oneself from emotional matters and preferring instead to prove oneself through solitary actions. As described by Peter Schwenger, this stance of masculinity avoids self-reflection:

> One of the most powerful archetypes of manhood is the idea that the real man is the one who acts, rather than the one who contemplates. The real man thinks of practical matters rather than abstract ones and certainly does not brood upon himself or the nature of his sexuality. To think about himself would be to split and turn inward the confident wholeness which is the badge of masculinity. (110)

This masculine orientation or reading formation perceives experience primarily in terms of competition, power, and hierarchy. In his case-study analysis of his adult students' responses, Thomas Fox cites the example of Mr. H., who describes his role in the classroom: " 'In my sub-group I am the leader. I begin every discussion by stating my opinions as facts. The other two members of my sub-group tend to sit back and agree with me . . . I need people to agree with me' " (61). Thus Mr. H's language reflects his need for power. He also describes himself as " 'an intensely competitive person,' " for whom playing basketball at West Point " 'was a dream come true' " (62). His sense of competition is manifested in his responses to a scene in Zora Neale

Hurston's *Their Eyes Were Watching God,* in which the male protagonist, Tea Cake, overhears a conversation between Janie and Mrs. Turner, a black woman who " 'can't stand black niggers' " (210). He relates his own experience with competition at West Point to Tea Cake's hatred of Mrs. Turner:

> I was being degraded and stripped of my pride by people who once were in my same shoes and who belonged in my same race. This race: we were all West Point cadets. Just as Mrs. Turner was a black woman who thought she was better and superior to darker negroes; older cadets thought that they were better and superior to me. . . . I was actually hated by some people because I was just starting my career at West Point. (63)

Mr. H's language portrays a world driven by competition and hierarchy which disadvantages him. Moreover, in the context of the classroom, given his need to compete with the other students in the class, he directed his responses primarily at the teacher, Tom Fox. As Fox notes, "Mr. H's tough and independent self needed to be constructed in order to compete and survive in the world of unjust hierarchies" (70). In contrast, students adopting a feminist stance may be more likely to be engaged with interpersonal perspectives (Bleich, Flynn, Kolodny) through engaging with the voices of an author or other students (Schweickart, 31), a form of connected knowing (Belenky et al.). These students may feel less comfortable in classrooms that privilege competition, rules of evidence, and the need to get it right, characteristics that reflect a more traditional male perspective (Frey). As noted in the previous chapter, current feminist criticism often reflects a more dialogic, personal, self-reflexive, exploratory orientation involving exploration of a range of interpersonal perspectives (Messer-Davidow). As Jane Tompkins explores in "Me and My Shadow," the distinction between public and private discourse that equates the private with the personal devalues females' ways of learning and thinking.

Adopting a patriarchic reading formation also invites stereotypical perceptions of females. For example, in my own research on adolescents' responses to ads featuring women in teenage magazines (Beach and Freedman), the prevailing reading formation was that of the admiring voyeur of the ad person's perceived power, success, or status. Many of the males in the study responded to the females in the ads from the stance of the "male gaze" (Mulvey, "Visual Pleasure," 9) that, as Erving Goffman argued, reflects a "ritualization of subordination" (23). In response to the Coty Musk ad, one male responded: "The sexy, good-looking girl is the first thing that catches your eye."

And, for females, as McRobbie notes, these magazines and their advertising function to

> anchor femininity while at the same time unsettling and under-mining it. If there is always another better look to be achieved or improvement to be made, then there is no better way of doing this than by introducing an element of uncertainty and dissatis-faction [associated with] getting behind or of getting lost in the style stake, which embraces not just clothing but the whole field of personal appearance. (176)

Students acquire this reading formation from their experience with television and teenage magazines that emphasize consumption asso-ciated with a $65 billion "youth market." In articulating their response, advertising agencies frequently employ the ad talk of merchandising discourse: "awesome," "sexy," "cool," "hot," "exciting," "attractive," "glamorous," "beautiful," and "handsome." Through the very act of responding through such language, young consumers create an ideal-ized, glamorized world. For example, an eleventh-grade male responded to a Zum-Zum gown ad portraying a female dressed in a gown dancing with a navy officer: "A very nice romantic evening. Roses on the floor, smiles on their faces as if they are in love. Peaceful, serene, placid. I would love to be the man or the woman." Similarly, an eleventh-grade female responded: "The girl looks like a prom queen. She looks very popular—every guy's dream girl. He looks like the lucky soldier—an all-American clean-cut boy. The perfect couple." Having created this world by using this ad talk discourse, both of these students become participants in these worlds—"I would love to be the man or the woman"; and "I wouldn't mind being the prom queen. She looks so happy with no worries."

In contrast, many students disliked responding to stories which they perceived as portraying unpleasant realities. As one student noted about the characters: "The confusion and hurt feelings that each of them feel are things that I can easily live without." And another: "I don't care for more misunderstanding, confusion, and mix ups, es-pecially with relationships." Given their experiences with the positive, feel-good stance associated with much of the mass media, students may react negatively to texts perceived to be challenging that stance.

In the study, some females resisted the male-gaze stance. Their resistance reflects the larger problem of female students' difficulty in identifying with traditional patriarchal perspectives. Women's acts of responding in nine nineteenth-century British and French novels was portrayed in largely negative terms as acts of challenging domesticity (Peterson). As Adrienne Rich notes, females cannot identify with the idea that "becoming a man means leaving someone or something . . . moving on, lighting out of the territory: a practice that also constructs the female as what is left behind, what is stability, what needs to be abandoned for the male to become himself" (quoted in Scholes, 114). And, in resisting the stance of the male gaze, they reject the idea of having to be looked after (Mulvey). For example, in responding to the stereotyped character, Caddy, in Faulkner's *The Sound and the Fury*, Karen Kaivola notes:

> Knowing what it is to be the screen of masculine projection and representation, women cannot respond to Caddy solely from a masculine position. While the text positions her as a blank screen upon which we can project our desires, and thus puts us in the masculine position, she is at the same time a discursive representation of ourselves. For women, simple appropriation of the masculine position as it is constructed in *The Sound and the Fury* is impossible, given our personal and social experience—which has already engendered us as women, and encouraged us to model ourselves as the object of masculine desire, to be the blank screen, to occupy object as well as subject positions. (30)

Readers may also resist the sexist oppositions inherent in the text's language. In responding to Thoreau's *Walden*, Irene Goldman notes that in the oppositions of man/Nature, Thoreau equates the dark side of nature with feminist sensuality that, for Thoreau, needs to be suppressed. In his portrayal of this opposition between the masculine versus the feminine dark side of nature, Goldman finds that a female reader "has no place to locate herself" (129). Or, as is the case with literature written for adolescent females, much of it is so unappealing that females read fiction for boys (Reynolds). It is only recently that young adult novels with female main characters have achieved a level of quality that males may cross over and read about female characters.

Gender differences in response are related to differences in purposes for reading. In her comparison of males' and females' responses to supermarket tabloids, S. Elizabeth Bird found that males often read tabloids to find information that helps them understand the world or that is consistent with their own interests while females react more personally, often for the purposes of identifying with or sharing gossip about celebrities.

Defining these gender differences in response serves, as does Deborah Tannen's work on gender differences in conversation, to demonstrate that readers' and viewers' responses are constituted by cultural socialization associated with "doing gender."

## Class

As my own middle-class conceptions of the mushrooms as the underclass or downtrodden suggest, readers' class ideologies also influence response. Critics such as Fredric Jameson, Terry Eagleton, Catherine Belsey, Raymond Williams, Tony Bennett, and Richard Ohmann examine the ways in which readers acquire ideological stances associated with their class membership (see Goldstein's review). These critics typically perceive much of reader-response theory as failing to grapple with readers' instabilities created by capitalist economic forces. Eagleton parodies the idea of a middle-class, liberal Reader's Liberation Movement to obtain consumer rights in reading through an "all-out *putsch* to topple the text altogether and install the victorious reading class in its place [by setting up] creative enclaves, equivalent in some sense to workers' co-operatives within capitalism" (184).

For these critics, reading formations are shaped by acquired class ideologies. In his analysis of critics' response to *Catcher in the Rye* over a twenty-year period of the 1950s and 1960s, Ohmann found that most critics during that period conceived of Holden Caulfield's problem in terms of "conformity" to various institutions. For Ohmann, these responses, reflecting the capitalistic ideological orientation of that period, blame the victim's problems on himself rather than on the class institutions—the prep school, his family, or the economic system. Ohmann ("History") also argues that readers in the late nineteenth century were socialized to believe in ideological superiority of the upwardly mobile professional middle class that was emerging in the 1890s. He cites the example of a story portraying the successful rise to economic success of a young, middle-class businessman. In the story, a young woman rejects the hand of a wealthy suitor in favor of an enterprising businessman. Through their hard work and technical expertise, the young couple then succeeds in setting up a new business, success associated with the values of the capitalistic ideology of that period.

For Ohmann, a reading formation associated with middle-class values avoids dealing with value perspectives that challenge middle-class values. Readers or viewers identify positively with reading formations that make readers "feel broadly content with their place in the world, so that the flow of their anxiety may be channeled into smaller concerns like the need for a healthy breakfast or for a laundry soap that won't shrink clothes. . . ." (121). For example, Elizabeth Long found that members of a suburban, middle-class women's book club typically focused their attention on identifying with the personality traits of the characters, measuring them against the morally significant idea of a unified character. They made little reference to historical, cultural, or political forces shaping characters, an orientation that for Long reflected their sense of security with their middle-class lifestyle. Avoiding the problematic aspects of their privileged economic status served to reify their own social status.

In another study, Radway examined the ways in which the editors of the Book-of-the-Month Club evaluated books under consideration for distribution to club members. Concerned with selecting books for what they perceived to be largely middle-brow readers, the editors selected books according to their own middle-class ideological assumptions, tending to be wary of books that challenged those assumptions. They preferred books that centered on "the coherent, unified personality" who was a "recognizable, interesting individual" (272). In addition, they preferred books that provided moral and ethical judgments regarding appropriate social behavior. As Radway argues, institutions such as the Book-of-the-Month Club succeed by reifying the middle class values of their members.

Similarly, response to television serves to reassure viewers in their class membership by celebrating middle-class consumeristic values as the prevailing social reality (Scholes). In a comparison of middle-class versus working-class women's responses to television, Andrea Press found that the middle-class women—those who were college-educated professionals—were more likely to identify with the characters and subscribe to the image of the glamorous, sexy female than were the "working-class" women—those who were blue-collar or pink-collar workers. On the other hand, the working-class women were more likely to perceive television as realistic than were the middle-class women. Press notes that these women were therefore more vulnerable to the assumption that television's portrayal of middle-class life constitutes a social reality, despite the fact that 69 percent of all female-headed households earn less than nine thousand dollars a year. Likewise, Benjamin DeMott charges that films such as *Working Girl, Pretty Woman,* and *Dirty Dancing* avoid the realities for class differences. In these films, the lower-class characters are suddenly transformed into members of the middle class. A secretary in *Working Girl* becomes a powerful executive; a prostitute in *Pretty Woman* becomes a well-heeled girlfriend. Demott notes that "treating class differences as totally inconsequential strengthens the national delusion that class power and position are insignificant" (22). The fact that characters from different classes easily shift in their status serves to reinforce a middle-class myth that "all citizens enjoy the same freedom of movement that they [the middle class] enjoy" (22).

In their study of working-class adults, Nicholas Coles and Susan Wall found that adults often respond to essays about work as practical, informative guides. Rather than respond critically, these adults adopt a utilitarian orientation that assumes that information is "in" the text and not shaped by writers' or readers' political acts. Because they are reluctant to critically conceive of institutions as constituted by political actions, they tend to personalize their own problems, blaming themselves rather than institutions for their social status. "As students, they embrace an individualist ideology that holds them alone responsible for their failures . . . that they imagine will result if they don't effectively turn the information education affords into a guide for success" (303). In contrast, those students who are able to generalize about parallels between, for example, Richard Wright's experience with racism, are able to turn their identifications with text into critical awareness. Thus students' beliefs in the validity of their own responses may reflect their own self-efficacy, which, in turn, reflects class differences.

At the same time, teachers need to recognize that students bring background experiences to texts which, from a teacher's middle-class perspective, are what Glynda Hull and Mike Rose characterize as "unconventional responses." Hull and Rose compare the responses of a student, Robert, from a working-class Caribbean family, and Rose's responses to a poem. The poem describes a woman living in a poor desert area, washing her clothes near some trees next to some shacks. While Rose perceives the "small cluster of wooden shacks" or the woman washing clothes in the poem as representative of a system of poverty, Robert responds quite differently. Robert recognizes that the woman hung her clothes by the shacks because the trees near the shacks prevented the dust from tractors from getting on the wash. Given his middle-class background, Rose has difficulty understanding Robert's perspective:

> The conventional reader could point out that such a windbreak would be necessary as well to protect residents, but given Robert's other interpretations, it makes sense, is coherent, to see the shacks—sheds of some kind perhaps or abandoned housing—as part of this eucalyptus-protected place where women hang the wash. What's important to note here is that Robert was able to visualize the scene—animate it, actually—in a way that Rose was not, for Rose was focusing on the dramatic significance of the shacks. Robert's reading may be unconventional and inappropriately jurisprudential, but it is coherent, and it allows us—in

these lines—to animate the full landscape in a way that enhances
our reading of the poem. (296)

Robert's response suggests that teachers need to be sensitive to the
ways of responding that are seemingly unconventional from a middle-
class perspective, but which actually represent rich background experiences in a range of cultural contexts.

## Teachers' Reading Formations

Teachers' reading formations reflect their own cultural attitudes, which
may or may not be consistent with the cultural attitudes of their
students, colleagues, or of the community. Responding to literature
ultimately brings out differences in cultural attitudes because, as Mary
Louise Pratt notes, there is "always doubt, conflict, disagreement,
because interpretations are always there in multiplicity denying each
other the illusion of self-containment and truth" (228). By making
explicit the value assumptions associated with these oppositions, teachers can demonstrate the very process of self-reflexive analysis of
responses as a cultural activity they seek to foster in students (Graff).
Thus teachers need to help students reflect on the process of responding
itself, as driven by cultural reading formations. In this way, students'
"idiosyncrasies, their particular cultural circumstances, are the subject
of investigation . . . [the] teacher problematizes responses in order to
build a more culturally and politically aware conception of reality
(Roemer, 919–20).

## Responding as Ethnographic Exploration of Cultural Worlds

Students can reflect on their own reading formations by thinking of
responding as analogous to conducting ethnographic research. In
responding as ethnographic exploration of either a text or an actual
cultural phenomenon, a student and an ethnographer are both constructing cultural worlds. In observing people's behaviors in various
cultural contexts—the peer group, family, classroom, school, workplace,
or organization—the ethnographer defines the cultural norms, attitudes,
and categories constituting behavior in these contexts. In conducting
these studies, ethnographers discover tensions and conflicts within a
cultural world. For example, on the basis of her observations of high
school students' behaviors in the *Jocks and Burnouts* study previously
mentioned, Eckert extracted the categories of "jocks" and "burnouts"
as two competing social groups. Researchers also recognize that they,

too, share the same internal cultural tensions of the people they are studying. During her study on women's responses to romance novels, Radway experienced both revulsion with these women's patriarchal attitudes and sympathy for their need to escape their constricted home lives. In reflecting on their own internal tensions, researchers and students ultimately learn to reflect on their own reading formations.

To understand the methods of ethnographical exploration, students may view a documentary film such as *Roger and Me*, which portrays the decline of Flint, Michigan, after the closing of a GM plant, the city's major employer. The producer of the film, Michael Moore, serves as a narrator/guide to the world of Flint, introducing the viewer to various groups in the town—local GM officials, former employees, chamber of commerce spokespersons, law-enforcement officers, and townspeople who were not affected financially by the shutdown. Moore also portrays another world outside of Flint—that of GM executives in Detroit responsible for closing the plant. Throughout the movie, Moore is engaged in a quest to track down and confront Roger Smith, the CEO of GM, in order to garner an explanation for the plant's closing. Moore documents various attempts by town officials to combat the high unemployment rate and rising crime rate by investing in a new hotel and theme park called AutoWorld, both of which closed within a year.

In responding to the documentary, students define several different, competing worlds, each with its own version of reality. On the one hand, the local GM officials and chamber of commerce spokespersons attempt to portray the town as having a positive future, even without the GM plant. Moore includes a public relations ad developed by the chamber that shows a young couple on a vacation visit to Flint talking with a friendly gas station attendant who tells them about all of the tourist sites in the town. In contrast, the laid-off workers and townspeople describe the difficulties of eking out a living on unemployment checks and low-paying jobs. Students compare these different groups' discourses—the often abstract, vacant booster's "salestalk" or the officials' legalistic jargon—with the townspeople's graphic descriptions of their own misfortunes. They also examine Moore's own selection and organization of material to construct his version of Flint. Drawing on Moore's techniques, students discuss how they could construct a similar documentary of their own town or city.

Students then conduct their own small-scale ethnographic studies of a particular cultural event or institution—a sports event, religious ceremony, fair, club meeting, amusement park, shopping mall, school, festival, family gathering, etc. In conducting their research, students take field notes and interview people (see Glesne and Peshkin for an introduction). In recording their observations, instead of vague, evaluative comments such as "friendly," "outgoing," "nice," "wonderful," "pleasant," etc., or abstract summaries, students should provide concrete descriptions of behaviors and events, followed by written reflections on the cultural meaning of these behaviors and events.

As they are conducting their research, students apply the same strategies to responding to written texts, treating their act of responding as ethnographic exploration or research. They also compare their research with real-world phenomena and their response to a text. They compare the organizational structure of the real world and the text world—the fact, for example, that both their school or workplace and the male peer group in *Lord of the Flies* are organized according to competing subgroups in a hierarchical power structure. They describe how as outsiders they use guides or narrators to gain an insider's perspective, raising questions about their guide's or narrator's veracity. And, they continually pose the question, "What's missing?" For example, in responding to Jane Austen's *Emma*, students in Richard Ohmann's class noted that rural populations were rarely portrayed. This led them to examine "whose values, whose interests, whose project of idealization, whose project of social order" (Ohmann, 182) are being served—that Austen's portrait of early nineteenth-century England may have reflected her own ideological conception of class differences. From all of this, students reflect on their alignment with these worlds—how their own attitudes and values are congruent with or distinct from the attitudes and values constituting these worlds.

## Limitations of Cultural Perspectives

There are a number of limitations to the cultural perspectives surveyed in this chapter. One limitation is that many of the theorists make questionable claims about the ways in which *groups* of readers or viewers are socialized to accept the ideological reading formations of texts. They do so because, with Foucault, they perceive the idea of "the individual" as a myth. Such sweeping generalizations are often insensitive to the variation of individual responses suggested by the other four theories of reader response presented in this book. Moreover, as John Hartley has argued, these cultural theorists' conceptions of audience, for example, as "the Valley High romance reader," are often fictions, created by critics, editors, and media producers to serve their own ends. As Turner notes, "We do not live our lives as members of audiences . . . we are many other things besides: workers, commuters, readers, parents, and so on" (162). This suggests that readers do not always apply the same reading formations presumably acquired from the culture or society. Given differences in their purposes, needs, expectations, or social context, the same reader may apply quite different formations. While readers may be cued by textual shifters to perceive Fleming's James Bond novels, movies, magazine stories, etc., as all representing a singular set of masculine, anticommunist attitudes, readers may actually respond quite differently to different Bond texts. As with Fish's "interpretive community," the idea of a reading formation may be insensitive to the particulars of a reader's experience.

Another limitation is a nagging ambiguity regarding the role of the readers'/viewers' subjective pleasure and its relationship to ideology. Viewers, particularly women, return again and again to enjoy movies such as *Working Girl, Pretty Woman,* and *Dirty Dancing,* which reify patriarchal values. The question that arises is whether the pleasure afforded serves to reify or challenge their gender and class attitudes. Barthes and other poststructuralists distinguish pleasure associated with the popular mass media from ideology, a distinction that does not sit well with Marxist critics. In his review of current media response theory, Graeme Turner argues that cultural theorists need to more carefully examine the relationship between pleasure and ideological socialization:

> One does not ask for a return to the analyses of a decade ago, which took an elitist view of popular pleasures in order to see them as the uncomplicated bearers of dominant ideologies. However, one might argue that it is important to acknowledge that the pleasure of popular culture cannot lie outside hegemonic ideological formations . . . we simply do not know how pleasure aligns us with or supports us against dominant views of the world. (221–22)

And, finally, the emerging body of "radical" or "confrontational" pedagogy based on these theories (see Davis, Gabriel and Smithson, Giroux and Simon, Kecht, Marshall, Merod, Morton and Zavarzaheh) tend to presuppose that students will be open to questioning social and cultural norms outside the school. However, if students, given the forces of poverty, broken families, drug and alcohol use, unemployment, a widening gap between the rich and the poor, a consumeristic culture, etc., lack the capacity or ability to question these very forces, teachers are then caught in a vicious circle. Given the power of these social and cultural forces outside of school, teachers may be limited to acknowledging to students that they are determined by forces outside schools while trying, at the same time, to help them transcend these delimiting forces.

All of this points to a major limitation of cultural theories—their deterministic stance. In conceiving of readers as adopting subject *positions,* these theories raise the possibility that the theories themselves imply a subject position—the subject position of cultural critical theory, with its own limiting hegemony. As Anthony Easthope argues, this can lead students to assume a position of presumptuous mastery, as if, as cultural critics, they hold the final word. Moreover, assuming a deterministic stance may preclude the possibilities that readers are open to change, that they are not locked into set subject positions. If readers are perceived as responding only as members of a certain gender or class group, such perceptions can limit the possibilities that readers can and do entertain optional subject positions.

Regardless of these limitations, cultural theories of response contain the seeds of dramatic new approaches to teaching literature, approaches that broaden the scope of literature study to include a range of disciplinary perspectives.

# 7 Applying Theory to Practice: Making Decisions about Eliciting Response

Given these five different theories of response, teachers apply these theories to plan activities for eliciting responses in the classroom. Planning response activities involves an ongoing series of decisions that takes into account a range of factors (Beach and Marshall):

- student attributes (needs, interests, abilities, attitudes, knowledge, and stances)
- the teachers' own attributes
- instructional goals and related evaluation criteria
- relevant response strategies and activities
- the social/cultural context
- long-term planning

For example, in planning response activities for "Mushrooms," teachers may categorize and ask themselves the following questions:

*Student Attributes*

Will my students enjoy or understand this poem?

What do they know about the world that is relevant to responding to this poem?

Given their everyday and/or reading interests, what in the poem may intrigue them?

What stances does the poem invite them to adopt?

*Teacher Attributes*

How do my knowledge, interests, attitudes, beliefs, and stance shape my response to the poem?

How may my responses differ from my students' responses?

*Instructional Goals and Related Evaluation Criteria*

What do I want students to learn from responding to the poem?

How will I know if they have achieved these goals?

*Response Strategies and Related Activities*

What kinds of response strategies (engaging, conceiving, explaining, connecting, etc.) could they employ?

What activities would help them employ these strategies?

How will I show or tell them how to do these activities?

How will students assess their own responses?

*Social/Cultural Context*

How does/will social climates/roles in the classroom influence students' willingness to articulate and share their responses?

How are students using their responses to negotiate and signal social membership in a range of different worlds/groups—peer, school, home, community, gender, class?

What activities can I employ to foster an articulation/sharing of responses in the classroom?

How will I accommodate those differences in my students' social/cultural backgrounds?

*Long-term Planning and Assessment*

How do I sequence, organize, and contrast texts and/or response activities to foster development of responses in a unit or course?

How can I help students inductively infer underlying intertextual relationships between texts and/or response activities?

How can I determine ways in which students have changed over time?

## Applying the Five Theoretical Perspectives to Planning Response Activities

These questions are all interrelated in that the answers to one affect the answers to others. Thinking about students' ability is related to long-term planning. At the same time, teachers do focus momentarily on considering answers to particular questions. It is at that point that each of the five theoretical perspectives reviewed in this book becomes useful. Each of the perspectives serves to address certain questions. Take, for example, questions about student attributes. While the textual perspective illuminates questions about students' knowledge of text conventions, the cultural perspective illuminates their cultural attitudes. Moreover, each perspective implies possible links between these questions. In adopting, for example, a psychological perspective, a teacher links his or her perceptions of students' cognitive abilities with plans for possible response strategies and related activities. Thus each perspective may, as illustrated here, entail a particular approach to eliciting students' responses. And, given differences in these perspectives, these approaches entail quite different assumptions about what is valued in responding. For example, privileging students' own unique subjective experience may detract from their exploring their responses as reflecting larger cultural roles. Hence, teachers need to examine the inherent tensions between the perspectives, tensions endemic to any thoughtful reflection on teaching.

## Textual

In adopting a textual perspective, teachers are particularly concerned about students' knowledge of text or genre conventions and the kinds of literary know-how they will need in responding to a text. To anticipate that knowledge of conventions, I reflect on or unpack my own responses to "Mushrooms." I notice that I need to know how to infer the symbolic function of the title, apply knowledge of narrative conventions to infer a pattern of increasing power for the mushrooms, and perceive the role of figurative language and sounds in creating meaning. I then consider whether or not my students possess this literary know-how. Assuming that they lack this knowledge, I then define my goals—to help students recognize that they have the know-how entailed in, for example, inferring the function of the title or perceiving a narrative pattern.

I then plan some classroom activities based on those response strategies I want my students to learn. In this case, I want them to learn to perceive consistent patterns in a text and to interpret the meaning of these patterns. Next, I select activities that entail use of that strategy. In thinking about the specific processes involved in perceiving and interpreting patterns, I select an activity—listing the mushrooms' behaviors in a chronological sequence. I therefore ask the students to list the mushrooms' behavior. Following that, I ask them to review their list and infer the meaning of any perceived patterns; for example, the fact that the mushrooms grow more assertive implies a narrative pattern of emerging power associated with the horror genre. I also know that by recalling some other related texts, students may inductively be able to infer this pattern.

At this point, in adopting a social perspective, I sense a potential tension between a textual and a social perspective. In thinking about my own social role in the classroom, I am wary of adopting a "he-who-knows" role based on my presumed superior knowledge of literary conventions. I therefore try to have the students work collaboratively so that they draw on each other's own prior experience with and knowledge of literature. Knowing that some students bring more prior knowledge of literature than others, I hope that by working in small groups, these students may model their know-how for the less knowledgeable students. I am also wary about students' propensity, in adopting a textual perspective, to assume that there are certain responses that are more valid than others. I therefore solicit a wide range of different responses without privileging any one response over the other, thus implying the equal validity of different responses. I also know that students, given their cultural backgrounds, will lack knowledge of literary conventions to the point of not being engaged in or even resisting these activities. I thus give students the option of parodying or performing the poems in ways that exploit their own cultural perspectives (Dyson).

In my long-term planning, I reiterate, extend, or transfer what is learned from the "Mushrooms" activities to subsequent responding and writing activities. I find another Plath poem, for example, "The Arrival of the Bee Box," and have the students compare their responses to the two poems. And, I ask students to recall other related poems, and talk about reasons for similarities in terms of language and style. I would also include some postmodern, experimental poems that challenge their expectations as to poetic forms. From this, they may inductively recognize how their emerging knowledge of a language and style shapes their responses. I then have them write their own poetry. By having them reflect on their poetry writing, they may recognize how their knowledge of conventions shapes their construction of poems.

### Experiential

In applying an experiential perspective, I think about the various strategies involved in responding to the poem—engaging, constructing an imagined world, identifying/empathizing, envisioning, and connecting. Recognizing differences in their learning styles, I give them optional activities: a visual activity—constructing their own drawings or storyboards based on a music video about the poem; a writing activity—a freewrite after each of many rereadings; or an oral activity, such as a think-aloud with a partner. I then have them reflect on how their processes of entering into and reflecting on their envisionments (Langer, "Process") changed across different rereadings.

In selecting strategies for planning activities relative to students' attributes, I am concerned about the students' ability to use these strategies or employ the activities. I am therefore continually asking whether or not students are capable of employing a strategy or doing an activity, for example, whether they would be able to adopt the role of the mushrooms by describing the world through the eyes of the mushrooms. If I anticipate that students may have difficulty, I then back up and consider the need for prerequisite activities that may best prepare them for doing an activity. Knowing that they may have difficulty adopting the mushrooms' role without some preparation, I decide to first have the students describe their classroom in writing from their own perspective. I then have them discuss in pairs how the mushrooms may perceive the world, prior to having them describe their classroom in writing from the mushrooms' perspective.

In all of this, I attempt to assess the effects of participating in such activities on students' responses and attitudes along the lines of a study by Marian Price. In that study, she examined the effects of participating in a college freshman course on writing about literature that was based on response activities on students' essay responses and their attitudes toward writing. She found that when compared to students in two traditionally taught classes, the students in the response-centered groups did equally well on their essay responses. More important, they developed a more positive attitude toward writing than students in the other groups. As did Price, I would interview individual students to ascertain reasons for changes in their learning. Price found that the students attributed their change in attitude to the ongoing experience of writing in their journals, which bolstered their confidence in articulating their own responses. In contrast, the students in the other groups never developed a sense of confidence because they were consistently concerned about making "correct" interpretations.

## Psychological

In adopting a psychological perspective, I consider the influence of my students' developmental level on their responses. For example, if

I were teaching "Mushrooms" to a group of eighth graders, drawing on Appleyard's notion of the early adolescent's romantic quest to test the limits of experience, I would anticipate that they might conceive of the mushrooms in terms of a quest or search for identity. I would therefore have them recall and compare experiences with other texts involving a quest or journey.

From a cognitive problem-solving perspective, I plan to have students openly discuss their difficulties in understanding the poem, difficulties precipitated by questions they might ask. As students share their difficulty, others will hopefully suggest ways for coping with those difficulties, thereby modeling problem-solving strategies.

Meanwhile, I am continually monitoring students' growth in thinking or cognitive strategies, noting, for example, students' willingness to grapple with complexity or dissonance (Odell). I also consider how certain tasks invite such complexity—the fact that when students are actively engaged in a role-play or rap-lyric performance of the poem, they are more likely to entertain complexity than if they are simply discussing the poem (Griffin and Cole; Means and Knapp).

## Social

In adopting a social perspective, I anticipate the ways in which my students' social roles will influence their discussion responses to the poem. I know that those students who feel alienated by the group or are disinterested in the poem will say nothing. And, conversely, I know that other, "good" students will dominate the discussion, stifling participation by others. Because some of these social behaviors are endemic to performance in large groups, I move to smaller groups, placing responsibility on the groups to collaboratively define how they want to respond to the poem. I rely on role-play, too, as a way of helping students experiment with alternatives to their classroom school roles.

I also attempt to build a sense of a classroom community in which students are mutually dependent on each other for sharing their responses. To shift their perceptions of me as their primary audience/ evaluator to their peers as audience, I have them share their journal entries and their essay writing with each other. And when I do assume the role of audience/evaluator, I model ways of providing descriptive, "reader-based" conversational reactions or questions (Elbow) designed to encourage students to continue thinking about a text, reactions such as: "I felt the same way about the marriage in *The Color Purple*; I wonder why it went on as it did?" By modeling these reactions, students will hopefully react to each other in a way that facilitates sharing of responses.

I also consider ways in which the students' social relationships with each other serve as a metaphor for their social relationships with characters. I therefore have them compare their experiences in real-world social relationships and their relationships with characters, asking questions such as Booth's: "Would I be friends with this character?" I also have them draw parallels between their own social experiences and the experiences depicted in texts. From all of this, students will hopefully recognize that meaning is socially constituted.

### Cultural

In adopting a cultural perspective, I recognize that many students have difficulty empathizing with cultural perspectives different from their own. I therefore plan activities designed to foster an awareness of cultural differences—how one person's or character's cultural outlook differs from that of others.

In their program, designed to foster multicultural awareness amongst the largely white student population in a Long Island school district, Adams, Pardo, and Schneidwind describe three steps they take to foster cultural consciousness. They begin with helping students gain an awareness of the normative nature of culture—that there are ways of doing things other than their own. They then move to an awareness of how the dominant culture fosters a version of reality that perpetuates the status quo. For example, in looking at the use of sports teams' names derived from Native Americans (the Atlanta Braves, the Washington Redskins, etc.), students may realize how these names reflect the cultural biases and insensitivity of the dominant culture. In the final phase, students then examine the question of whether persons could change in their attitudes toward culture.

To foster an awareness of cultural differences, I have students write about how their family, school, gender, or ethnic background shapes their lives and self-concept (Gorrell). Students then compare their perceptions in terms of background cultural differences. They then reflect on how their responses to a text portraying a nondominant culture would differ if they changed one aspect of their background, for example, if they responded as a female rather than as a male.

Once students are aware of how cultural differences shape their lives, they experiment with alternative cultural perspectives. By adopting speakers' or characters' perspectives or roles and role-playing or writing monologues, letters, journal entries, or narratives from those perspectives, students explore what it means to experience alternative culture perspectives (Karolides and Gerster). For example, in describing their own experience through the eyes of Rayona, the 17-year-old Native American female in Michael Dorris's *Yellow Raft in Blue Water*, students may recognize the ways in which alternative backgrounds shape perceptions.

I also have students compare their responses to a range of other students' or writers' published responses. Having defined the differences between their own and others' responses, they then consider possible reasons for those differences, reasons having to do with their stance or ideological orientation. For example, in his college writing class, Joseph Harris asked his students to write about the same specific scene in the Spike Lee movie, *Do the Right Thing;* in their writing they were to define a problem or issue posed by that scene. The students then shared their writing as well as their reading of a range of different published comments about the film. In comparing their different perceptions, the students then revised their perceptions in further discussions and writings. In writing their second drafts, students had to discuss the responses of at least two other viewers and "to show how these other viewers added to or contested their own readings of the movie" (38). Harris found that initially some students had difficulty doing more than simply agreeing or disagreeing with peers. They were reluctant to critically assess the limitations of their own perspective relative to other competing perspectives. However, through sharing and discussing their responses, students became increasingly aware of how their responses reflected their ideological orientation. Similarly, Pete Fraser recommends having students study the different discourses used to talk about readers' or viewers' responses. For example, given the range of different public commentary about the influence of television on adolescents, he suggests having students collect this material from newspapers and magazines, or interview parents and teachers. Students could then "discuss reasons why particular discourses are so dominant" (78).

At the same time, given their cultural egocentricity, students may be reluctant to grapple with the diversity and complexities in their own lives and society because they subscribe to simplistic, hegemonic cultural perspectives. I therefore try to challenge these perspectives by highlighting points of tension between the students' attitudes and the cultural perspectives portrayed in texts. For example, in having students respond to the portrayal of poverty in *Roll of Thunder, Hear My Cry*, I focus on the tension between students' own middle-class consumer attitudes and the family's own attitudes toward material goods. Or, in responding to *Their Eyes Were Watching God,* I focus on the tension between students' patriarchal attitudes and their perceptions of Janie or their perceptions of the mushrooms as powerful women.

In terms of long-range planning, I assume that with enough experience in grappling with these points of tension, students may ultimately reflect on the limitations of their own and others' cultural perspectives. As part of portfolio assessment, I therefore have the students reflect on changes in their cultural attitudes and particular points of tensions that may have precipitated those changes.

## Teacher Reflection/Research

In planning these activities, I also draw on the different response theories to reflect on what happens in classrooms, noting dissatisfactions with the nature and quality of the students' responses. In order to reflect systematically on their teaching, teachers may also conduct research on their own or others' teaching (Cochran-Smith and Lytle). For example, I audiotape my classroom discussion; write a narrative about the discussion; interview some students about their perceptions of the discussions; and then analyze the extent to which they or the students talked, the kinds of responses or thinking processes employed, and reasons for positive and negative student involvement/interest. An essential part of such research is the written narrative as a useful prerequisite for reflection and self-monitoring (Kondo; Kilbourn; Polkinghorne; Witherell and Noddings). In writing the narrative, I am constructing a dramatic literacy event featuring specific responses, student and teacher behaviors, the classroom context, other related events, or impinging aspects of the larger community. For example, I may dramatize an instance in which a student refused to participate in the discussion, exploring possible reasons for his refusal.

Teachers could also use the five theoretical perspectives to generate research questions, e.g., How do students' responses differ between two different texts? (textual); How do students A and B differ in their degree of engagement with a text? (experiential); To what degree do students define their own difficulties in understanding texts? (psychological); How do students' responses differ in small-group versus large-group discussion? (social); and, What are reasons that students resist alternative cultural perspectives?

In analyzing students' responses, teachers need to reflect on the limitation of their own theoretical perspectives (Prawat). Teachers who rely exclusively on a particular theoretical perspective—a Madeline

Hunter approach, feminist criticism, etc.—could contrast that perspective against some of the perspectives outlined in this book, creating a healthy, dialectical self-examination. At the same time, teachers also need to go beyond a self-sacrificing "making-do" attitude regarding their working conditions to ask the question, "What resources and support do I need, *as a professional*, to be successful in my work?" (Prawat, 750–51). In asking such questions, a teacher may recognize the impossibility of conducting meaningful discussions with thirty-six students in her class, while, acting as a professional, seeking to remedy the situation.

In conclusion, the theories of response described in this book not only broaden our understanding of how readers construct meaning in their experience with text, but may also serve to help teachers devise activities that will enhance the quality of students' classroom experiences.

# Glossary

**Aesthetic versus efferent stance:** As formulated by Louise Rosenblatt, in adopting an "aesthetic" stance, readers respond in terms of their "living through" engagement with a text. In adopting an "efferent" stance, readers read primarily for the information provided. Rosenblatt argues that much of literature instruction employing "correct answer" worksheet, test, and textbook questions requires students to adopt an efferent rather than aesthetic stance.

**Constructivist:** A theory of knowledge that posits that people formulate knowledge by actively constructing that knowledge within specific social contexts or discourse communities, this theory challenges the idea that knowledge exists as an autonomous, objective entity. Constructivists posit that by actively formulating their own knowledge through talk and writing, students truly understand that knowledge. By formulating their own interpretation of a text, students are more likely to understand the meaning of that interpretation than if they restate their teacher's or a critic's interpretation.

**Dialogic:** As articulated by Mikhail Bakhtin, it is the idea that the meaning of discourse derives from the interaction between differing, competing points of view of the speaker and audience in a social context. Speakers' acts invite others' reciprocal reactions. Teachers attuned to dialogic discourse attend to the multitude of competing voices and value assumptions in the classroom; monologic instruction limits the expression of multiple, competing voices.

**Hypertext:** In the context of literature instruction, it refers to a software database that contains related information about a text's author, topics portrayed, literary period, historical/cultural context, other texts, etc., and/or responses by other readers. Readers may use hypertext to explore and create intertextual links to a range of different yet related phenomena.

**Interpretive community:** As proposed by Stanley Fish, it is the notion that the meaning of responses is relative to the shared conventions, attitudes, and discourse practices of a particular community. Interpretive communities may adopt a religious, feminist, Marxist, or legalistic orientation. For example, members of a botany class might apply a scientific analysis to "Mushrooms," while members of a poetry writing class might attend to the poet's techniques. Critics of this notion charge that it is difficult to clearly distinguish between interpretive communities—that readers' responses may reflect membership in, or allegiances toward, a range of different interpretive communities.

163

**Intertextuality:** From a textual-theory perspective, it means an interest in not only authors' own references to other texts, but also readers' use of other related texts and genre conventions to respond to the current text. As Roland Barthes argues, for a reader, each text contains multiple texts. From a social-theory perspective, as suggested by David Bloome, the meaning of intertextuality is constituted by social motives and agendas, i.e., a reader refers to a related text in order to build a social bond with another reader.

**New Criticism:** This is a critical approach beginning in the 1940s that emphasizes a quasi-"scientific," close-reading of the text's language. Contrary to transactional response theorists, advocates of this approach assume that the meaning of a text is "in" the language of the text. The reader's task is to carefully explicate that use of techniques such as figurative language, point of view, meter, and rhyme; New Critics therefore privilege the teaching of poetry. They reject the idea that meaning varies according to the unique transactions between individual readers and text in particular contexts. They are therefore critical of attempts to locate meaning in the reader's own feelings (the affective fallacy) or in attempts to impute authorial intentions (the intentional fallacy).

**"Point-driven" stance:** As defined by Russell Hunt and Douglas Vipond, it is the idea that, in contrast to an "information-driven" or "story-driven" stance, readers are reading primarily to infer a text's point. In adopting a "point-driven" stance, readers attend to meanings most likely to contribute to inferring a larger symbolic meaning. In their more recent theory, Hunt and Vipond argue that the meaning of a text's point is constituted through readers' social, dialogic exchange.

**Poststructuralist Criticism:** This is a recent critical approach that questions the structuralists' insistence on a one-to-one correspondence between sign and signified. Its practitioners posit that the meanings of all language categories are suspect and slippery, suggesting the need for readers to reflect critically on the limitations of categories and assumptions shaping their responses.

**Schema:** These are cognitive frames, scripts, or scenarios representing prior knowledge that readers use to selectively attend to or recall particular aspects of a text. Readers applying a home-buyer schema to a description of a house may attend to aspects having to do with the value of the house, while readers applying a burglar schema may attend to aspects having to do with ways of breaking into the house.

**Stance:** This is defined as a reader's orientation or frame for responding to a text that reflects a certain set of attitudes or critical strategies. A reader may adopt a "male-gaze" stance in responding to a description of a female character, perceiving that character primarily in terms of her physical appearance.

**Reading formations/subject positions:** These are stances or orientations readers acquire from their socialization as members of certain cultural groups or communities. Members of a fundamentalist Bible reading group adopt the reading formation or subject position of one who reads the Bible as the absolute truth (Forstop). As Bennett and Woollacott document, in the 1960s, readers were socialized to respond to James Bond novels and movies in terms of reading formation or subject position associated with an anti-Communist, pro-Western, chauvinistic set of attitudes.

**Transactional theory:** As formulated by Louise Rosenblatt, this theory posits that the meaning of a text derives from a *transaction* between the text and reader within a specific context. Because each individual reader extracts his or her own unique, subjective meanings, this theory calls into question the New Critical assumption that the meaning resides solely "in" the text, accessible only to the trained eye of the critic/teacher. Rather than emphasize formalist analysis of a text, the primary goal of instruction from a transactional perspective is to foster students' trust in the expression of their own unique experience with a text.

# Bibliography

Adams, Bonnie Sue, Winifred Pardo, and Nancy Schneidwind. "Changing 'The Way Things Are Done Around Here.'" *Educational Leadership* 49 (1991): 37–42.

Adams, Jon. *Pragmatics and Fiction*. Philadelphia: Benjamins, 1985.

Adams, Peter. "Writing from Reading: 'Dependent Authorship' as a Response." *Readers, Texts, Teachers*. Eds. Bill Corcoran and Emrys Evans. Upper Montclair, NJ: Boynton/Cook, 1987. 119–52.

Alba, Richard. *Ethnic Identity*. New Haven: Yale UP, 1990.

Alcorn, Marshall, and Michael Brancher. "Literature, Psychoanalysis and the Re-Formation of the Self: A New Direction for Reader-Response Theory." *PMLA* 100.3 (1985): 342–54.

Alexander, Patricia, Diane Schallert, and Victoria Hare. "Coming to Terms: How Researchers in Learning and Literacy Talk about Knowledge." *Review of Educational Research* 61.3 (1991): 315–44.

Allen, Carolyn. "Louise Rosenblatt and Theories of Reader-Response." *Reader: Essays in Reader-Oriented Theory, Criticism, and Pedagogy* 20 (Fall 1988): 32–39.

———. "Louise Rosenblatt and Theories of Reader-Response." *The Experience of Reading: Louise Rosenblatt and Reader-Response Criticism*. Ed. John Clifford. Portsmouth, NH: Boynton/Cook, 1990. 18–29.

Althusser, Louis. *"Lenin and Philosophy" and Other Essays*, trans. Ben Brewster. London: Verso, 1971.

Anderson, Philip M., and Gregory Rubano. *Enhancing Aesthetic Reading and Response*. Urbana: NCTE, 1991.

Ang, Ien. *Desperately Seeking the Audience*. New York: Routledge, 1991.

Applebee, Arthur. *The Child's Concept of Story: Ages Two to Seventeen*. Chicago: U of Chicago P, 1978.

———. *A Study of Book-Length Works Taught in High School English Courses*. Albany, NY: Center for the Learning and Teaching of Literature, 1989.

———. *The Teaching of Literature in Programs with Reputations for Excellence in English*. Albany, NY: Center for the Learning and Teaching of Literature, 1989.

Applebee, Arthur, et al. *Contexts for Learning to Write*. Norwood, NJ: Ablex, 1984.

Appleyard, J. A. *Becoming a Reader: The Experience of Fiction from Adolescence to Adulthood*. New York: Cambridge UP, 1990.

Aronowitz, Stanley, and Henry Giroux. *Postmodern Education*. Minneapolis: U of Minnesota P, 1991.

Atkins, G. Douglas, and Laura Morrow, eds. *Contemporary Literary Theory.* Amherst: U of Massachusetts P, 1989.

Atwell, Nancie. *In the Middle.* Upper Montclair, NJ: Boynton/Cook, 1987.

Austin, J. L. *How to Do Things with Words.* 2nd ed. Cambridge, MA: Harvard UP, 1975.

Baker, Linda, and Anne Brown. "Metacognitive Skills and Reading." *Handbook of Reading Research.* Vol. 1. Eds. P. David Pearson, Michael Kamil, Rebecca Barr, and Peter Mosenthal. New York: Longman, 1984. 353–94.

Bakhtin, Mikhail. *The Dialogic Imagination: Four Essays by M. M. Bakhtin.* Trans. Caryl Emerson and Michael Holquist. Ed. Michael Holquist. Austin: U of Texas P, 1981.

———. *Speech Genres and Other Late Essays.* Trans. Vern W. McGee. Eds. Caryl Emerson and Michael Holquist. Austin: U of Texas P, 1986.

Barnes, Dorothy, et al. *Versions of English.* London: Heinemann, 1984.

Barnes, Douglas, and Dorothy Barnes. *Images, Music, Text.* New York: Hill, 1977.

Barnes, Douglas, James Britton, and Mike Torbe. *Language, the Learner, and the School.* 4th ed. Portsmouth, NH: Boynton/Cook, 1989.

Barthes, Roland. *S/Z.* Trans. Richard Miller. New York: Hill & Wang, 1974.

———. *The Pleasure of the Text.* Trans. Richard Miller. New York: Hill & Wang, 1975.

———. *Roland Barthes.* New York: Hill & Wang, 1977.

———. "From Work to Text." *Textual Strategies: Perspectives in Post-Structuralist Criticism.* Ed. Josue Harari. Ithaca, NY: Cornell UP, 1979. 73–81.

Bartholomae, David. "Inventing the University." *When a Writer Can't Write: Studies in Writer's Block and Other Composing-Process Problems.* Ed. Mike Rose. New York: Guilford, 1985. 134–65.

Barton, Bob, and David Booth. *Stories in the Classroom.* Portsmouth, NH: Heinemann, 1990.

Baudrillard, Jean. *The Evil Demon of Images.* Sydney, Australia: Power Institute of Fine Arts, 1987.

———. *Selected Writings.* Ed. Mark Poster. Stanford: Stanford UP, 1988.

Baym, Nina. *Novels, Readers, and Reviewers: Responses to Fiction in Antebellum America.* Ithaca, NY: Cornell UP, 1984.

Beach, Richard. "Issues of Censorship and Research on Effects of and Response to Reading." *Dealing with Censorship.* Ed. James Davis. Urbana: NCTE, 1979. 131–59.

———. "Discourse Conventions and Researching Response to Literary Dialogue." *Researching Response to Literature and the Teaching of Literature.* Ed. Charles Cooper. Norwood, NJ: Ablex, 1985. 103–27.

———. "The Creative Development of Meaning: Using Autobiographical Experiences to Interpret Literature." *Beyond Communication.* Eds. Deanne Bogdan and Stanley Straw. Portsmouth, NH: Boynton/Cook, 1990. 211–36.

———. "Evaluating Writing to Learn: Responding to Journals." *Encountering Student Texts.* Eds. Bruce Lawson, Susan Sterr Ryan, and W. Ross Winterowd. Urbana: NCTE, 1990. 183–98.

———. "Complexities of Adolescents' Responses to Literature." Annual meeting of the American Educational Research Association. Chicago, May, 1991.

Beach, Richard, and Chris Anson. "Using Peer Dialogue Journals to Foster Literary Response." *Writing and Literature.* Eds. George Nowell and Russel Durst. Norwood, MA: Christopher-Gordon, in press.

Beach, Richard, Deborah Appleman, and Sharon Dorsey. "Adolescents' Use of Intertextual Links to Understand Literature." *Developing Discourse Practices in Adolescence and Adulthood.* Eds. Richard Beach and Susan Hynds. Norwood, NJ: Ablex, 1990. 224–45.

Beach, Richard, and Robert Brown. "Discourse Conventions and Literary Inference." *Understanding Readers' Understanding.* Eds. Robert Tierney, Patricia Anders, and Judy Nichols Mitchell. Hillsdale, NJ: Erlbaum, 1986. 147–74.

Beach, Richard, and Kerry Freedman. "Responding as a Cultural Act: Adolescents' Responses to Magazine Ads and Short Stories." *Reader Stance and Literary Understanding.* Eds. Joyce Many and Carole Cox. Norwood, NJ: Ablex., 1992. 162–88.

Beach, Richard, and Susan Hynds, eds. *Developing Discourse Practices in Adolescence and Adulthood.* Norwood, NJ: Ablex, 1990.

Beach, Richard, and Susan Hynds. "Research on Response to Literature." *Transactions with Literature.* Eds. Edmund Farrell and James Squire. Urbana: NCTE, 1990. 131–205.

Beach, Richard. "Research on Response to Literature." *Handbook of Reading Research.* Vol. 2. Eds. Rebecca Barr, Michael Kamil, Peter Mosenthal, and P. David Pearson. New York: Longman, 1991. 453–91.

Beach, Richard, and James Marshall. *Teaching Literature in the Secondary School.* San Diego: Harcourt, 1990.

Beach, Richard, and Linda Wendler. "Developmental Differences in Response to a Story." *Research in the Teaching of English* 21.3 (1987): 286–97.

Beale, Walter. *A Pragmatic Theory of Rhetoric.* Carbondale: Southern Illinois UP, 1987.

Beers, Terry. "Reading Reading Constraints: Conventions, Schemata, and Literary Interpretation." *Diacritics* 18.4 (1988): 82–93.

Beidler, Phil. "Bad Business: Vietnam and Recent Mass-Market Fiction." *College English* 54 (1992): 64–75.

Belenky, Mary, Blythe Clinchy, Nancy Goldberger, and Jill Tarule. *Women's Ways of Knowing: The Development of Self, Voice, and Mind.* New York: Basic, 1986.

Belsey, Catherine. *Critical Practice.* London: Methuen, 1980.

Bennett, Susan G. *The Relationship Between Adolescents' Levels of Moral Development and Their Responses to Short Stories.* Diss. U of California, Berkeley, 1978.

Bennett, Tony. "Text, Readers, Reading Formations." *Literature and History* 9.2 (1983): 214–27.

Bennett, Tony, and Janet Woollacott. *Bond and Beyond: The Political Career of a Popular Hero.* New York: Methuen, 1987.

Benton, Michael, John Teasey, Ray Bell, and Keith Hurst. *Young Readers Responding to Poems*. London: Routledge, 1988.

Berger, John. *Ways of Seeing*. New York: Penguin, 1972.

Berman, Art. *From the New Criticism to Deconstruction*. Urbana: U of Illinois P, 1988.

Bettelheim, Bruno. *The Uses of Enchantment: The Meaning and Importance of Fairy Tales*. London: Thames & Hudson, 1976.

Bialostosky, Don. "Dialogic Criticism." *Contemporary Literary Theory*. Eds. G. Douglas Atkins and Laura Morrow. Amherst: U of Massachusetts P, 1989. 214–28.

Biddle, Arthur, and Toby Fulwiler, eds. *Angles of Visions: Reading, Writing, and the Study of Literature*. New York: McGraw-Hill, 1992.

Bird, S. Elizabeth. *For Enquiring Minds: A Cultural Study of Supermarket Tabloids*. Knoxville: U of Tennessee P, 1992.

Bishop, Wendy. " 'Traveling through the Dark': Teachers and Students Reading and Writing Together." *Reader: Essays in Reader-Oriented Theory, Criticism, and Pedagogy* 24 (1990): 1–20.

Bizzell, Patricia. "What Happens When Basic Writers Come to College?" *College Composition and Communication* 37 (1986): 294–301.

Black, John B., and Collen M. Seifert. "The Psychological Study of Story Understanding." *Researching Response to Literature and the Teaching of Literature: Points of Departure*. Ed. Charles Cooper. Norwood, NJ: Ablex, 1985. 190–211.

Bleich, David. *Readings and Feelings: An Introduction to Subjective Criticism*. Urbana: NCTE, 1975.

——. *Subjective Criticism*. Baltimore: Johns Hopkins UP, 1978.

——. "The Identity of Pedagogy and Research in the Study of Response to Literature." *College English* 42 (1980): 350–66.

——. *The Double Perspective: Language, Literacy, and Social Relations*. New York: Oxford UP, 1988.

Bloome, David. "Reading as a Social Process." *Language Arts* 62.2 (Feb. 1985): 134–42.

——. "The Social Construction of Intertextuality in Classroom Literacy Learning." Annual meeting of the American Educational Research Association. San Francisco, 1989.

——. "Anthropology and Research on Teaching the English Language Arts." *Handbook of Research on Teaching the English Language Arts*. Eds. James Flood, Julie Jensen, Diane Lapp, and James Squire. New York: Macmillan, 1991. 46–56.

——, ed. "Reading and Writing as a Social Process in a Middle School Classroom." *Literacy and Schooling*. Norwood, NJ: Ablex, 123–49.

Bloome, David, and Francis Bailey. "From Linguistics and Education: A Direction for the Study of Language and Literacy." *Multidisciplinary Perspectives on Literacy Research*. Eds. Richard Beach, Judith Green, Michael Kamil, and Timothy Shanahan. Urbana: NCRE/NCTE, 1992.

Bogdan, Deanne. *Re-Educating the Imagination: Toward a Poetics, Politics, and Pedagogy of Literary Engagement*. Portsmouth, NH: Boynton/Cook, 1992.

Bogdan, Deanne, and Stanley Straw, eds. *Beyond Communication*. Portsmouth, NH: Boynton/Cook, 1990.

Bolter, Jay David. *The Writing Space: The Computer, Hypertext, and the History of Writing*. Hillsdale, NJ: Erlbaum, 1991.

Bond, Guy, and Robert Dykstra. "The Co-Operative Research Program in First-Grade Reading Instruction." *Reading Research Quarterly* 2 (1962).

Booth, Wayne. *The Rhetoric of Fiction*. 2nd ed. Chicago: U of Chicago P, 1982.

———. *The Company We Keep*. Berkeley: U of California P, 1988.

Bormann, Ernest. "Fantasy and Rhetorical Vision: The Rhetorical Criticism of Social Reality." *Methods of Rhetorical Criticism*. 3rd ed. Eds. Bernard L. Brock, Robert L. Scott, and James W. Chesebro. Detroit: Wayne State UP, 1990. 210–22.

Boud, David, Rosemary Keogh, and David Walker, eds. "Promoting Reflection in Learning: A Model." *Reflection: Turning Experience into Learning*. London: Kogan Page, 1985. 18–40.

Bower, Gordon, and Daniel Morrow. "Mental Models in Narrative Comprehension." *Science* 247 (1990): 44–48.

Brandt, Deborah. *Literacy as Involvement: The Acts of Writers, Readers, and Texts*. Carbondale: Southern Illinois UP, 1990.

Britton, James. *Language and Learning*. Harmondsworth, England: Penguin, 1970.

———. "Viewpoints: The Distinction between Participant and Spectator Role Language in Research and Practice." *Research in the Teaching of English* 18.3 (1984): 320–31.

———. "The Spectator as Theorist: A Reply." *English Education* 21.1 (1989): 53–60.

Britzman, Deborah. *Practice Makes Practice: A Critical Study of Learning to Teach*. Albany: State U of New York P, 1991.

———. "The Terrible Problem of Knowing Thyself: Towards a Poststructuralist View of Teacher Identity." *Teacher Thinking, Teacher Knowledge*. Ed. Tim Shanahan. Urbana: National Conference on Research in English/NCTE, in press.

Brock, Bernard L., Robert L. Scott, and James W. Chesebro, eds. *Methods of Rhetorical Criticism*. 3rd ed. Detroit: Wayne State UP, 1990.

Brodkey, Linda. "Postmodern Pedagogy for Progressive Educators." *Journal of Education* 169.3 (1987): 138–43.

———. "On the Subjects of Class and Gender in 'The Literacy Letters.'" *College English* 51 (1989): 125–41.

Brooke, Robert E. *Writing and Sense of Self: Identity Negotiation in Writing Workshops*. Urbana: NCTE, 1991.

Brooks, Peter. *Reading for the Plot: Design and Intention in Narrative*. New York: Knopf, 1984.

Broudy, Harry, and Alan Purves. "Report on Case Studies on Uses of Knowledge." *ERIC Document* #224 016, 1982.

Brown, Penelope, and Stephen Levinson. *Politeness: Some Universals in Language Usage*. New York: Cambridge UP, 1987.

Brown, Rexford. "Schooling and Thoughtfulness." *The Journal of Basic Writing* 10.1 (1991): 3–15.

Bruce, Bertram C. "A Social Interaction Model of Reading." *Discourse Processes* 4 (1981): 273–311.

Bruffee, Kenneth A. "Social Construction, Language, and the Authority of Knowledge: A Bibliographical Essay." *College English* 48.8 (1986): 773–90.

Bruner, Jerome. *Actual Minds, Possible Worlds.* Cambridge, MA: Harvard UP, 1986.

———. *Acts of Meaning.* Cambridge, MA: Harvard UP, 1990.

Buchbinder, David. *Contemporary Literary Theory and the Reading of Poetry.* South Melbourne, Australia: Macmillan, 1991.

Buckingham, David. *Public Secrets: "Eastenders" and Its Audience.* London: BFI, 1987.

———, ed. *Watching Media Learning.* Philadelphia: Falmer, 1992.

Buckler, Patricia Prandini. "Combining Personal and Textual Experience: A Reader-Response Approach to Teaching American Literature." *Practicing Theory in Introductory College Literature Courses.* Eds. James Cahalan and David Downing. Urbana: NCTE, 1991. 36–46.

Burke, Kenneth. *Counter-Statement.* Berkeley: U of California P, 1931.

———. *Language as Symbolic Action: Essays on Life, Literature, and Method.* Berkeley: U of California P, 1966.

———. *A Rhetoric of Motives.* Berkeley: U of California P, 1969.

Buzzard, Sharon. "The Mirror of the Text: Reading Gilbert Sorrentino's *Mulligan Stew.*" *Reader: Essays in Reader-Oriented Theory, Criticism and Pedagogy* 26 (1991): 65–77.

Cahalan, James, and David Downing, eds. *Practicing Theory in Introductory College Literature Courses.* Urbana: NCTE, 1991.

———, eds. "Selected Further Resources for Theory and Pedagogy: A Bibliographic Essay." *Practicing Theory in Introductory College Literature Courses.* Urbana: NCTE, 1991. 293–333.

Cain, William. *The Crisis in Criticism: Theory, Literature, and Reform in English Studies.* Baltimore: Johns Hopkins UP, 1984.

Callender, Christine and Deborah Cameron. "Responsive Listening as a Part of Religious Rhetoric: The Case of Black Pentecostal Preaching." *Reception and Response: Hearer Creativity and the Analysis of Spoken and Written Texts.* Eds. Graham MacGregor and R. S. White. London: Routledge, 1990. 160–78.

Carlson, G. Robert. *Books and the Teenage Reader.* 2nd ed. New York: Harper and Row, 1980.

Carlson, Susan. "Readers Reading Green Reading Readers: Discovering Henry Green through Reader Response Criticism." *Language and Style* 17.2 (1984): 175–89.

Cawelti, John. *Adventure, Mystery, and Romance.* Chicago: U of Chicago P, 1976.

Cawelti, Scott, and Nancy Williams, eds. "Literary Theory in the Classroom," *The Iowa English Bulletin* 37 (1989).

Cazden, Courtney. *Classroom Discourse.* Portsmouth, NH: Heinemann, 1988.

Chatman, Seymour. *Story and Discourse: Narrative Structure in Fiction and Film.* Ithaca, NY: Cornell UP, 1978.

Cherryholmes, Cleo. *Power and Criticism: Poststructural Investigations in Education.* New York: Teachers College, 1988.

Christian-Smith, Linda. *Becoming a Woman through Romance.* New York: Routledge, 1990.

Clark, Gregory. *Dialogue, Dialectic, and Conversation.* Carbondale: Southern Illinois UP, 1990.

Clifford, John. "Introduction: On First Reading Rosenblatt." *Reader: Essays in Reader-Oriented Theory, Criticism, and Pedagogy* 20 (1988): 1–6.

———, ed. *The Experience of Reading: Louise Rosenblatt and Reader-Response Theory.* Portsmouth, NH: Boynton/Cook, 1990.

Cochran-Smith, Marilyn. *The Making of a Reader.* Norwood, NJ: Ablex, 1984.

Cohen, Philip, Jerry Morgan, and Martha Pollack, eds. *Intentions in Communication.* Cambridge, MA: MIT P, 1990.

Coles, Nicholas, and Susan V. Wall. "Conflict and Power in the Reader-Responses of Adult Basic Writers." *College English* 49.3 (1987): 298–312.

Coles, Robert. *The Call of Stories: Teaching and the Moral Imagination.* Boston: Houghton Mifflin, 1989.

Collins, Allan, John Seeley Brown, and Kathy M. Larkin. "Inference in Text Understanding." *Theoretical Issues in Reading Comprehension.* Eds. Rand Spiro, Bertram Bruce, and William Brewer. Hillsdale, NJ: Erlbaum, 1980. 385–407.

Collins, Christopher. *The Poetics of the Mind's Eye: Literature and the Psychology of Imagination.* Philadelphia: U of Pennsylvania P, 1991.

Cooper, Charles, ed. *Researching Response to Literature and the Teaching of Literature.* Norwood, NJ: Ablex, 1985.

Cooper, Marilyn, and Michael Holzman. *Writing as Social Action.* Portsmouth, NH: Boynton/Cook, 1989.

Corcoran, Bill. "Teachers Creating Readers." *Readers, Texts, Teachers.* Eds. Bill Corcoran and Emrys Evans. Upper Montclair, NJ: Boynton/Cook, 1987. 41–74.

Corcoran, Bill, and Emrys Evans, eds. *Readers, Texts, Teachers.* Upper Montclair, NJ: Boynton/Cook, 1987.

Cox, Carole, and Joyce Many. "Toward an Understanding of the Aesthetic Response to Literature." *Language Arts* 69.1 (1992): 28–33.

Crowley, Sharon. *A Teacher's Introduction to Deconstruction.* Urbana: NCTE, 1989.

Culler, Jonathan. *Structuralist Poetics: Structuralism, Linguistics and the Study of Literature.* Ithaca, NY: Cornell UP, 1975.

———. "Prolegomena to a Theory of Reading." *The Reader in the Text: Essays on Audience and Interpretation.* Eds. Susan Suleiman and Inge Crosman. Princeton: Princeton UP, 1980. 46–66.

———. *The Pursuit of Signs: Semiotics, Literature, Deconstruction.* Ithaca, NY: Cornell UP, 1981.

————. *The Pursuit of Signs: Semiotics, Literature, Deconstruction.* London: Routledge, 1981.

————. *On Deconstruction: Theory and Criticism After Structuralism.* Ithaca: Cornell UP, 1982.

————. "The Identity of the Literary Text." Eds. Mario J. Valdes and Owen Miller. Toronto: U of Toronto P, 1985. 3–15.

Culley, Margo, and Catherine Portuges, eds. *Gendered Subjects: The Dynamics of Feminist Teaching.* Boston: Routledge, 1985.

Cullinan, Bernice E., Kathy T. Harwood, and Lee Galda. "The Reader and the Story: Comprehension and Response." *Journal of Research and Development in Education* 16.3 (1983): 29–38.

Dasenbrock, Reed Way. "Do We Write the Text We Read?" *College English* 53 (1991): 7–18.

Davis, Lennard. *Resisting Novels: Ideology and Fiction.* London: Methuen, 1987.

Davis, Robert Con. "A Manifesto for Oppositional Pedagogy: Freire, Bourdieu, Merod, and Graff." *Reorientations: Critical Theories and Pedagogies.* Eds. Bruce Henricksen and Thais Morgan. Urbana: U of Illinois P, 1990. 248–67.

Davis, Steven, ed. *Pragmatics: A Reader.* New York: Oxford UP, 1991.

Davison, Mark L., Patricia M. King, and Karen Strohm Kitchener. "Developing Reflective Thinking and Writing." *Developing Discourse Practices in Adolescence and Adulthood.* Eds. Richard Beach and Susan Hynds. Norwood, NJ: Ablex, 1990. 265–86.

De Beaugrande, Robert. *Critical Discourse: A Survey of Literary Theorists.* Norwood, NJ: Ablex, 1988.

DeMott, Benjamin. "In Hollywood, Class Doesn't Put Up Much of a Struggle." *The New York Times* (Jan. 20, 1991): 1,22.

Dewey, John. *Art as Experience.* New York: Putnam, 1958.

Dias, Patrick. "Literary Reading and Classroom Constraints: Aligning Practice with Theory." *Literature Instruction: A Focus on Student Response.* Ed. Judith Langer. Urbana: NCTE, 1992. 131–62.

Dias, Patrick, and Michael Hayhoe. *Developing Response to Poetry.* Milton Keynes, England: Open UP, 1988.

Dickinson, Emily. *Letters.* Cambridge, MA: Harvard UP, 1958.

Dillon, David, and Dennis Searle. "The Role of Language in One First-Grade Classroom." *Research in the Teaching of English* 15 (1981): 311–28.

Donahue, Patricia. "Teaching Common Sense: Barthes and the Rhetoric of Culture." *Reclaiming Pedagogy: The Rhetoric of the Classroom.* Eds. Patricia Donahue and Ellen Quandahl. Carbondale: Southern Illinois UP, 1989. 72–82.

Donahue, Patricia, and Ellen Quandahl, eds. *Reclaiming Pedagogy: The Rhetoric of the Classroom.* Carbondale: Southern Illinois UP, 1989.

Donaldson, Margaret. *Children's Minds.* New York: Norton, 1978.

Downing, David, ed. *Changing Classroom Practices: Resources for Literary and Cultural Studies.* Urbana: U of Illinois P, 1992.

Durant, Alan, and Nigel Fabb. *Literary Studies in Action.* New York: Routledge, 1990.

Durrant, Cal, Lynne Goodwin, and Ken Watson. "Encouraging Young Readers to Reflect on Their Processes of Response: Can It Be Done, Is It Worth Doing?" *English Education* 22 (1990): 211–19.

Dyson, Anne Haas. *Multiple Worlds of Child Writers.* New York: Teachers College, 1989.

———. "The Case of the Singing Scientist: A Performance Perspective on the 'Stages' of School Literacy." *Written Communication* 9.1 (1992): 3–47.

Eagleton, Mary, ed. *Feminist Literary Theory.* Oxford: Blackwell, 1986.

Eagleton, Terry. *Literary Theory.* Minneapolis: U of Minnesota P, 1983.

———. *Against the Grain.* London: Verso, 1986.

Easthope, Antony. *Literary into Cultural Studies.* New York: Routledge, 1991.

Ebert, Karen. "Research Conceptions of Adult and College Reader Response to Literature." Diss., U of British Columbia, 1990.

Ebert, Teresa L. "The Romance of Patriarchy: Ideology, Subjectivity, and Postmodern Feminist Cultural Theory." *Cultural Critique* 10 (1988): 19–58.

Eckert, Penelope. *Jocks and Burnouts.* New York: Teachers College, 1989.

Eco, Umberto. *The Role of the Reader: Explorations in the Semiotics of the Text.* Bloomington: Indiana UP, 1978.

———. *Travels in Hyperreality.* Orlando: Harcourt, Brace, Jovanovich, 1986.

———. *The Limits of Interpretation.* Bloomington: Indiana UP, 1990.

Edminston, Patricia. "Engagement and Drama." NCTE annual meeting. Seattle, 1991.

Eeds, Maryann, and Deborah Wells. "Grand Conversations: An Exploration of Meaning Construction in Literature Study Groups." *Research in the Teaching of English* 23.1 (1989): 4–29.

Elbow, Peter. *Writing with Power.* New York: Oxford UP, 1981.

Elkind, David. *The Hurried Child: Growing Up Too Fast Too Soon.* Reading, MA: Addison-Wesley, 1981.

Erikson, Erik. *Identity: Youth and Crisis.* New York: Norton, 1976.

Evans, Emrys. "Readers Re-Creating Texts." *Readers, Texts, Teachers.* Eds. Bill Corcoran and Emrys Evans. Upper Montclair, NJ: Boynton/Cook, 1987. 22–40.

Ewen, Stuart. *All Consuming Images.* New York: Basic, 1990.

Farrell, Edmund, and James Squire, eds. *Transactions with Literature.* Urbana: NCTE, 1990.

Felman, Shoshana. *The Literary Speech Act.* Trans. Catherine Porter. Ithaca, NY: Cornell UP, 1983.

Ferdman, Bernardo. "Literacy and Cultural Identity." *Harvard Educational Review* 60.2 (1990): 181–204.

Fetterley, Judith. *The Resisting Reader: A Feminist Approach to American Fiction.* Bloomington: Indiana UP, 1978.

Fish, Stanley. "Literature in the Reader: Affective Stylistics." *New Literary History* 2 (1970): 123–62.

———. *Self-Consuming Artifacts: The Experience of Seventeenth-Century Literature.* Berkeley: U of California P, 1972.

————. *Is There a Text in This Class? The Authority of Interpretive Communities.* Cambridge, MA: Harvard UP, 1980.

Fiske, John. *Television Culture.* London: Metheun, 1987.

————. *Reading the Popular.* Boston: Hyman, 1989.

Flitterman-Lewis, Sandy. "Psychoanalysis, Film, and Television." *Channels of Discourse: Television and Contemporary Criticism.* Ed. Robert Allen. Chapel Hill: U of North Carolina P, 1987. 172–210.

Flynn, Elizabeth. "Composing Responses to Literary Texts: A Process Approach." *College Composition and Communication* 34 (1983): 342–48.

————. "Gender and Reading." *College English* 45 (1983): 236–53.

Forstop, Per-Anders. "Receiving and Responding: Ways of Taking from the Bible." *Bible Reading in Sweden.* Ed. Gunnar Hansson. Stockholm: Almqvist & Wiksell, 1990. 149–69.

Foucault, Michel. *Power/Knowlege.* Trans. Colin Gordon. New York: Pantheon, 1980.

————. *The Archaeology of Knowledge.* Trans. A. M. Sheridan-Smith. New York: Pantheon, 1982.

————. *The Use of Pleasure.* Trans. Robert Hurley. New York: Pantheon, 1985.

Fox, Thomas. *The Social Uses of Writing: Politics and Pedagogy.* Norwood, NJ: Ablex, 1990.

Frankovits, Andre. *Seduced and Abandoned: The Baudrillard Scene.* London: Stonemoss, 1984.

Fraser, Pete. "How Do Teachers and Students Talk about Television?" *Watching Media Learning.* Ed. David Buckingham. Bristol, PA: Falmer, 1990. 60–80.

Fredericks, Casey. *The Future of Eternity: Mythologies of Science Fiction and Fantasy.* Bloomington: Indiana UP, 1982.

Freedberg, David. *The Power of Images: Studies in the History and Theory of Response.* Chicago: U of Chicago P, 1989.

Freud, Sigmund. *The Standard Edition of the Complete Psychological Works.* London: Hogarth Press, 1951.

Freund, Elizabeth. *The Return of the Reader: Reader-Response Criticism.* New York: Methuen, 1987.

Frey, Olivia. "Beyond Literary Darwinism: Women's Voices and Critical Discourse." *College English* 52.5 (1990): 507–26.

Fry, Donald. *Children Talk about Books: Seeing Themselves as Readers.* Milton Keynes, England: Open UP, 1985.

Frye, Northrop. *Anatomy of Criticism: Four Essays.* Princeton: Princeton UP, 1957.

Gabriel, Susan, and Isaiah Smithson. *Gender in the Classroom: Power and Pedagogy.* Urbana: U of Illinois P, 1990.

Galda, Lee. "A Longitudinal Study of the Spectator Stance as a Function of Age and Genre." *Research in the Teaching of English* 24.3 (1990): 261–78.

Garrison, Brigitte, and Susan Hynds. "Evocation and Reflection in the Reading Transaction: A Comparison of Proficient and Less Proficient Readers." *Journal of Reading Behavior* 23 (1991): 259–80.

Gass, William H. *Fiction and the Figures of Life.* New York: Knopf, 1970.

Gee, James Paul. "The Legacies of Literacy: From Plato to Freire through Harvey Graff." *Harvard Educational Review* 58 (1988): 195–213.

Geertz, Clifford. *The Interpretation of Cultures.* New York: Basic, 1973.

Geisler, Cheryl. "The Artful Conversation: Characterizing the Development of Advanced Literacy." *Developing Discourse Practices in Adolescence and Adulthood.* Eds. Richard Beach and Susan Hynds. Norwood, NJ: Ablex, 1990. 93–109.

———. "Reader, Parent, Coach: Defining the Profession by Our Practice of Response." *Reader: Essays in Reader-Oriented Theory, Criticism, and Pedagogy* 25 (1991): 17–33.

Gergen, Kenneth. *The Saturated Self: Dilemmas of Identity in Contemporary Life.* New York: Basic, 1991.

Gianetti, Louis. *Understanding Movies.* 4th ed. Englewood Cliffs, NJ: Prentice-Hall, 1987.

Gilbert, Pam. "Post Reader-Response: The Deconstructive Critique." *Readers, Texts, Teachers.* Eds. Bill Corcoran and Emrys Evans. Upper Montclair, NJ: Boynton/Cook, 1987. 234–50.

Gilligan, Carol. *In a Different Voice: Psychological Theory and Women's Development.* Cambridge, MA: Harvard UP, 1982.

Gilligan, Carol, Nona Lyons, Trudy Hanmer, eds. *Making Connections: The Relational Worlds of Adolescent Girls at Emma Willard School.* Cambridge, MA: Harvard UP, 1990.

Gilmore, Perry. " 'Gimme Room': School Resistance, Attitude, and Access to Literacy." *Journal of Education* 167.1 (1985): 111–28.

Giroux, Henry A., and Roger Simon. "Popular Culture and Critical Pedagogy: Everyday Life as a Basis for Curriculum Knowledge." *Critical Pedagogy, the State, and Cultural Struggle.* Eds. Henry A. Giroux and Peter McLaren. Albany: State U of New York P, 1989. 236–52.

Glesne, Corrine, and Alan Peshkin. *Becoming Qualitative Researchers: An Introduction.* White Plains, NY: Longman, 1992.

Goffman, Erving. *Strategic Interaction.* Philadelphia: U of Pennsylvania P, 1969.

———. *Gender Advertisements.* Cambridge, MA: Harvard UP, 1976.

Goldman, Irene. "Feminism, Deconstruction, and the Universal: A Case Study on Walden." *Conversations: Contemporary Critical Theory and the Teaching of Literature.* Eds. Charles Moran and Elizabeth F. Penfield. Urbana: NCTE, 1990. 120–31.

Goldstein, Philip. *The Politics of Literary Theory.* Tallahassee: Florida State UP, 1990.

Goodheart, Eugene. *The Skeptic Disposition in Contemporary Criticism.* Princeton: Princeton UP, 1984.

Goodlad, John. *A Place Called School.* New York: McGraw-Hill, 1984.

Gorrell, Donna. "The Rhetoric of Cultural Diversity." *Minnesota English Journal* 22 (1991): 1–10.

Graff, Gerald. *Professing Literature: An Institutional History.* Chicago: U of Chicago P, 1987.

Green, Georgia M. *Pragmatics and Natural Language Understanding.* Hillsdale, NJ: Erlbaum, 1989.

Greenberg, Robert. *The Power of the Image.* Princeton: Princeton UP, 1989.

Greenblatt, Stephen. "Culture." *Critical Terms for Literary Study.* Eds. Frank Lentricchia and Thomas McLaughlin. Chicago: U of Chicago P, 1990. 225–32.

Greene, Gayle, and Coppelia Kahn, eds. *Making a Difference: Feminist Literary Criticism.* London: Methuen, 1985.

Greenfield, Carol. "On Readers, Readerships, and Reading Practices." *Southern Review* 16 (1983): 121–42.

Grice, H. Paul. *Studies in the Way of Words.* Cambridge, MA: Harvard UP, 1989.

Griffin, Peg, and Michael Cole. "New Technologies, Basic Skills, and the Underside of Education." *Language, Literacy, and Culture.* Ed. Judith A. Langer. Norwood, NJ: Ablex, 1987. 199–231.

Griffith, Peter. *Literary Theory and English Teaching.* Philadelphia: Open UP, 1987.

Grossman, Pamela. *The Making of a Teacher.* New York: Teachers College, 1990.

Habermas, Jurgen. *The Philosophical Discourse of Modernity.* Trans. Frederick G. Lawrence. Cambridge, MA: MIT P, 1987.

Hancher, Michael. "What Kind of Speech Act Is Interpretation?" *Poetics* 10.2–3 (1981): 263–81.

———. "Pragmatics in Wonderland." *Rhetoric, Literature, and Interpretation.* Ed. Harry R. Garvin. Lewisburg, PA: Bucknell UP, 1983. 165–84.

Hansson, Gunnar. *Readers' Reading—And Then?* Albany, NY: Center for the Study of Teaching and Learning of Literature, 1992.

———. "Verbal Scales in Research on Response to Literature." *Researching Response to Literature and the Teaching of Literature.* Ed. Charles Cooper. Norwood, NJ: Ablex, 1985. 212–32.

Harding, D. W. "Psychological Processes in the Reading of Fiction." *British Journal of Aesthetics* 2 (1962): 133–47.

Harris, Joseph. "The Resistance to Teaching: A Review of *Reclaiming Pedagogy: The Rhetoric of the Classroom,* ed. by Patricia Donahue and Ellen Quandahl, and *Popular Culture, Schooling, and Everyday Life,* ed. by Henry A. Giroux and Roger I. Simon." *Journal of Teaching Writing* 8.2 (1989): 169–178.

———. "Reading the Right Thing." *Reader* 27 (1992): 29–47.

Harris, Wendell. *Interpretive Acts: In Search of Meaning.* New York: Oxford UP, 1988.

Hartley, John. "Invisible Fictions: Television Audiences, Paedocracy, Pleasure." *Textual Practice* 1.2 (1987): 121–38.

Hartman, Douglas. "8 Readers Reading: The Intertextual Links of Able Readers Using Multiple Passages." Diss. U of Illinois, Urbana, 1990.

Hassan, Ihab. *The Dismemberment of Orpheus: Toward a Postmodern Literature.* Madison, WI: U of Wisconsin P, 1982.

———. *The Postmodern Turn: Essays in Postmodern Theory and Culture.* Columbus: Ohio State UP, 1987.

Haswell, Richard. "Beyond Forms in Freewriting: The Issue of Organization." *Nothing Begins with N: New Investigations of Freewriting.* Eds. Pat Belanoff, Peter Elbow, and Sheryl Fontaine. Carbondale: Southern Illinois UP, 1991. 32–70.

Hawthorn, Jeremy. *Unlocking the Text: Fundamental Problems in Literary Theory.* London: Arnold, 1987.

Hayhoe, Mike, and Stephen Parker, eds. *Reading and Response.* Philadelphia: Open UP, 1990.

Heathcote, Dorothy. *Dorothy Heathcote: Collected Writings on Education and Drama.* Eds. Liz Johnson and Cecily O'Neill. Portsmouth, NH: Heinemann, 1984.

Hebdige, Dick. *Hiding in the Light: On Images and Things.* London: Routledge, 1988.

———. "The Bottom Line on Planet One." *Modern Literary Theory: A Reader.* Eds. Philip Rice and Patricia Waugh. London: Arnold, 1989. 260–81.

Henricksen, Bruce, and Thais Morgan, eds. *Reorientations: Critical Theories and Pedagogies.* Urbana: U of Illinois P, 1990.

Hickman, Janice. "Everything Considered: Response to Literature in an Elementary Classroom." *Journal of Research and Development in Education* 16 (1983): 8–13.

Hobson, Dorothy. *Crossroads: The Drama of a Soap Opera.* London: Methuen, 1982.

Hoesterey, Ingeborg. "The Intertextual Loop: Kafka, Robbe-Grillet, Kafka." *Poetics Today* 8 (1987): 373–92.

Hoffner, Cynthia, and Joanne Cantor. "Perceiving and Responding to Mass Media Characters." *Responding to the Screen: Reception and Reaction Processes.* Eds. Jennings Bryant and Dolf Zillmann. Hillsdale, NJ: Erlbaum, 1991. 63–102.

Hoffstaedter, Petra. "Poetic Text Processing and Its Empirical Investigation." *Poetics* 16 (1987): 75–91.

Holland, Norman. *The Dynamics of Literary Response.* New York: Oxford UP, 1968.

———. *Poems in Persons: An Introduction to the Psychoanalysis of Literature.* New York: Norton, 1973.

———. *5 Readers Reading.* New Haven: Yale UP, 1975.

———. "Unity Identity Text Self." *PMLA* 90 (1975): 813–22.

———. *The Brain of Robert Frost.* London: Routledge, 1988.

———. *Holland's Guide to Psychoanalytic Psychology and Literature-and-Psychology.* New York: Oxford UP, 1990.

———. *The Critical I.* New York: Columbia UP, 1992.

Holquist, Michael. *Dialogism: Bakhtin and His World.* New York: Routledge, 1990.

Holub, Robert C. *Reception Theory: A Critical Introduction.* New York: Methuen, 1984.

Hooks, Bell. *Yearning: Race, Gender, and Cultural Politics.* Boston: South End, 1990.

Hubert, Karen. *Teaching and Writing Popular Fiction.* New York: Teachers and Writers Collaborative, 1976.

Hull, Glynda, and Mike Rose. " 'This Wooden Shack Place': The Logic of an Unconventional Reading." *College Composition and Communication* 41 (1990): 287–98.

Hunt, Russell, and Douglas Vipond, "Crash-Testing a Transactional Model of Literary Learning." *Reader: Essays in Reader-Oriented Theory, Criticism and Pedagogy* 14 (1985): 23–39.

———. "First, Catch the Rabbit: Methodological Imperative and the Dramatization of Dialogic Reading." *Multidisciplinary Perspectives on Literary Research.* Eds. Richard Beach, Judith Green, Michael Kamil, and Timothy Shanahan. Urbana: NCRE/NCTE, 1992. 69–90.

Hurst, Keith. "Group Discussions of Poetry." *Young Readers Responding to Poems.* Eds. Michael Benton, John Teasey, Ray Bell, and Keith Hurst. London: Routledge, 1988. 157–201.

Hynds, Susan. "Interpersonal Cognitive Complexity and the Literary Response Processes of Adolescent Readers." *Research in the Teaching of English* 19.4 (1985): 386–402.

———. "Bringing Life to Literature and Literature to Life: Social Constructs and Contexts of Four Adolescent Readers." *Research in the Teaching of English* 23.1 (1989): 30–61.

———. "Reading as a Social Event: Comprehension and Response in the Text, Classroom, and World." *Beyond Communication.* Eds. Deanne Bogdan and Stanley Straw. Portsmouth, NH: Boynton/Cook, 1990. 237–58.

———. "Challenging Questions in the Literature Classroom." *New Directions in the Teaching of Literature.* Ed. Judith Langer. Urbana: NCTE, in press.

Ianni, Francis A. J. *The Search for Structure: A Report on American Youth Today.* New York: Free P, 1989.

Ingarden, Roman. *The Cognition of the Literary Work of Art.* Trans. Ruth Ann Crowley and Kenneth R. Olson. Evanston: Northwestern UP, 1973.

Iran-Nejad, Asghar. "The Schema: A Long-Term Memory Structure or a Transient Structural Phenomena." *Understanding Readers Understanding.* Eds. Robert Tierney, Patricia Anders, and Judy Nichols Mitchell. Hillsdale, NJ: Erlbaum, 1986. 109–28.

Iser, Wolfgang. *The Implied Reader: Patterns of Communication in Prose Fiction from Bunyan to Beckett.* Baltimore: Johns Hopkins UP, 1974.

———. *The Act of Reading: A Theory of Aesthetic Response.* Baltimore: Johns Hopkins UP, 1978.

———. "Texts and Readers." *Discourse Processes* 3.4 (1980): 327–43.

———. *Prospecting: From Reader Response to Literary Anthropology.* Baltimore: Johns Hopkins UP, 1989.

———. "Towards a Literary Anthropology." *The Future of Literary Theory.* Ed. Ralph Cohen. London: Routledge, 1989. 208–28.

Jack, Ian Robert James. *The Poet and His Audience.* Cambridge; New York: Cambridge UP, 1984.

Jameson, Fredric. *The Political Unconscious: Narrative as a Socially Symbolic Act.* Ithaca: Cornell UP, 1981.

———. "Postmodernism and Consumer Society." *The Anti-Aesthetic: Essays on Postmodern Culture.* Ed. Hal Foster. London: Macmillan, 1985. 53–66.

Jauss, Hans Robert. "Literary History as a Challenge to Literary Theory." *New Literary History* 2.1 (1970): 7–37.

———. *Toward an Aesthetic of Reception.* Trans. Timothy Bahti. Minneapolis: U of Minnesota P, 1982.

Jefferson, Ann, and David Robey, eds. *Modern Literary Theory: A Comparative Introduction.* London: Batsford, 1986.

Jehlen, Myra. "Gender." *Critical Terms for Literary Study.* Eds. Frank Lentricchia and Thomas McLaughlin. Chicago: U of Chicago P, 1990. 263–73.

Johnson, Barbara. *The Critical Difference: Essays in the Contemporary Rhetoric of Reading.* Baltimore: Johns Hopkins UP, 1980.

———. *Reading "Piers Plowman" and "The Pilgrim's Progress": Reception and the Protestant Reader.* Carbondale: Southern Illinois UP, 1992.

Johnson, Mark. *The Body in the Mind.* Chicago: U of Chicago P, 1987.

Kaivola, Karen. "Becoming Woman: Identification and Desire in *The Sound and the Fury.*" *Reader: Essays in Reader-Oriented Theory, Criticism, and Pedagogy* 17 (Spring 1987): 29–43.

Karen, Robert. "Shame." *The Atlantic* 269.2 (1992): 40–70.

Karolides, Nicholas, ed. *Reader Response in the Classroom.* New York: Longman, 1992.

Karolides, Nicholas, and Carole Gerster. "Ethnic Literature in the Secondary School Curriculum." *Minnesota English Journal* 22 (1991): 26–31.

Kecht, Maria-Regina, ed. *Pedagogy Is Politics: Literary Theory and Critical Teaching.* Urbana: U of Illinois P, 1992.

Kelly, George. *The Psychology of Personal Constructs.* New York: Norton, 1955.

Keroes, Jo. "Half Someone Else's: Theories, Stories, and the Conversation of Literature." *Reader: Essays in Reader-Oriented Theory, Criticism, and Pedagogy* 25 (1991): 1–16.

Kiell, Norman. *Psychoanalysis, Psychology, and Literature: A Bibliography.* 2nd ed. Metuchen, NJ: Scarecrow, 1982.

Kilbourn, Brent. *Constructive Feedback: Learning the Art.* Cambridge: Brookline, 1990.

Kintgen, Eugene. "The Perception of Poetry." *Style* 14 (1980): 22–40.

———. "Expectations and Processes in Reading Poetic Narratives." *Empirical Studies of the Arts* 4.1 (1986): 79–95.

Kintgen, Eugene, and Norman N. Holland. "Carlos Reads a Poem." *College English* 46.5 (1984): 478–91.

Klancher, Jon. "Bakhtin's Rhetoric." *Reclaiming Pedagogy: The Rhetoric of the Classroom.* Eds. Patricia Donahue and Ellen Quandahl. Carbondale: Southern Illinois UP, 1989. 83–96.

Kohlberg, Lawrence. *The Philosophy of Moral Development: Moral Stages and the Idea of Justice.* San Francisco: Harper, 1981.

Kolodny, Annette. "Dancing through the Minefield: Some Observations on the Theory, Practice, and Politics of a Feminist Literary Criticism." *The New*

*Feminist Criticism: Essays on Women, Literature, and Theory.* Ed. Elaine Showalter. New York: Pantheon, 1986. 147–61.

Kondo, Dorrine K. *Crafting Selves.* Chicago: U of Chicago P, 1990.

Kristeva, Julia. *The Kristeva Reader.* Ed. Toril Moi. Oxford: Blackwell, 1986.

Kroger, Jane. *Identity in Adolescence.* London: Routledge, 1989.

Kuhn, Thomas S. *The Structure of Scientific Revolutions.* 2nd ed. Chicago: U of Chicago P, 1970.

Labov, William. *Language in the Inner City.* Philadelphia: U of Pennsylvania P, 1972.

Lacan, Jacques. *The Four Fundamental Concepts of Psychoanalysis.* New York: Norton, 1978.

Lakoff, George. *Women, Fire, and Dangerous Things: What Categories Reveal about the Mind.* Chicago: U of Chicago P, 1987.

Lakoff, George, and Mark Johnson. *Metaphors We Live By.* Chicago: U of Chicago P, 1980.

Lakoff, George, and Mark Turner. *More than Cool Reason: A Field Guide to Poetic Metaphor.* Chicago: U of Chicago P, 1989.

Lamb, Catherine. "Beyond Argument in Feminist Composition." *College Composition and Communication* 42.1 (1991): 11–24.

Landow, George. "Changing Texts, Changing Readers: Hypertext in Literary Education, Criticism, and Scholarship." *Reorientations: Critical Theories and Pedagogies.* Eds. Bruce Henricksen and Thais Morgan. Urbana: U of Illinois P, 1990. 133–61.

———. *Hypertext: The Convergence of Contemporary Critical Theory and Technology.* Baltimore: Johns Hopkins UP, 1992.

Langer, Judith. *The Process of Understanding Literature.* Albany, NY: Center for the Learning and Teaching of Literature, 1989.

———. "The Process of Understanding: Reading for Literary and Informative Purposes." *Research in the Teaching of English* 24.3 (1990): 229–60.

———, ed. *Literature Instruction: A Focus on Student Response.* Urbana: NCTE, 1992.

Lee, Valerie. "Responses of White Students to Ethnic Literature: One Teacher's Experience." *Reader: Essays in Reader-Oriented Theory, Criticism, and Pedagogy* 15 (1986): 24–33.

Leech, Geoffrey N. *Principles of Pragmatics.* New York: Longman, 1983.

Lehr, Susan. *The Child's Developing Sense of Theme.* New York: Teachers College, 1991.

Leibman-Kleine, JoAnne. "Reading Thomas Hardy's *The Mayor of Casterbridge:* Towards a Problem-Solving Theory of Reading Literature." *Reader: Essays in Reader-Oriented Theory, Criticism, and Pedagogy* 17 (1987): 13–28.

Leitch, Vincent. *American Literary Criticism from the Thirties to the Eighties.* New York: Columbia UP, 1988.

Lentricchia, Frank. *After the New Criticism.* Chicago: U of Chicago P, 1980.

Lentricchia, Frank, and Thomas McLaughlin, eds. *Critical Terms for Literary Study.* Chicago: U of Chicago P, 1990.

Levinson, Stephen C. *Pragmatics.* New York: Cambridge UP, 1983.

Lodge, David, ed. *Modern Criticism and Theory: A Reader.* London: Longman, 1988.

Long, Elizabeth. "Women, Reading, and Cultural Authority: Some Implications of the Audience Perspective in Cultural Studies." *American Quarterly* 38.4 (1986): 591–612.

Lundberg, Patricia Lorimer. "Dialogically Feminized Reading: A Critique of Reader-Response Criticism." *Reader: Essays in Reader-Oriented Theory, Criticism, and Pedagogy* 22 (1989): 9–37.

Lyotard, Jean-Francois. *The Postmodern Condition: A Report on Knowledge.* Minneapolis: U of Minnesota P, 1984.

Lytle, Susan. *Exploring Comprehension Style: A Study of Twelfth-Grade Readers' Transactions with Text.* Diss. Stanford U, 1982.

MacGregor, Graham, and R. S. White, eds. *Reception and Response: Hearer Creativity and the Analysis of Spoken and Written Texts.* London: Routledge, 1990.

Machet, Myrna. "The Effect of Sociocultural Values on Adolescents' Response to Literature." *Journal of Reading* 35.5 (1992): 356–62.

Machor, James. "Poetics as Ideological Hermeneutics: American Fiction and the Historicized Reader of the Early Nineteenth Century." *Reader: Essays in Reader-Oriented Theory, Criticism, and Pedagogy* 25 (1991): 49–64.

Maill, David. "The Structure of Response: A Repertory Grid Study of a Poem." *Research in the Teaching of English* 19.3 (1989): 254–68.

Mailloux, Steven. *Interpretive Conventions: The Reader in the Study of American Fiction.* Ithaca, NY: Cornell UP, 1982.

———. *Rhetorical Power.* Ithaca, NY: Cornell UP, 1989.

———. "The Turns of Reader-Response Criticism." *Conversations: Contemporary Critical Theory and the Teaching of Literature.* Eds. Charles Moran and Elizabeth F. Penfield. Urbana: NCTE, 1990. 38–54.

Mandler, Jean. *Stories, Scripts, and Scenes: Aspects of Schema Theory.* Hillsdale, NJ: Erlbaum, 1984.

Manlove, Colin. *Critical Thinking: A Guide to Interpreting Literary Texts.* New York: St. Martin's, 1989.

Marshall, Brenda. *Teaching the Postmodern.* New York: Routledge, 1991.

Marshall, James. *Patterns of Discourse in Classroom Discussions of Literature.* Albany, NY: Center for the Learning and Teaching of Literature, 1989.

———. "Writing and Reasoning about Literature." *Developing Discourse Practices in Adolescence and Adulthood.* Eds. Richard Beach and Susan Hynds. Norwood, NJ: Ablex, 1990. 161–82.

Martin, Bruce K. "Teaching Literature as Experience." *College English* 51 (1989): 377–85.

Martinez, Miriam, and Nancy Roser. "Children's Responses to Literature." *Handbook of Research on Teaching the English Language Arts.* Eds. James Flood, Julie Jensen, Diane Lapp, and James Squire. New York: Macmillan, 1991. 643–54.

Marzano, Robert J. *Cultivating Thinking in English and the Language Arts.* Urbana: NCTE, 1991.

Masterman, Len. *Teaching About Television.* London: Macmillan, 1980.

Mayher, John Sawyer. *Uncommon Sense.* Portsmouth, NH: Boynton/Cook, 1990.

McAleese, Ray. *Hypertext.* Norwood, NJ: Ablex, 1989.

McCormick, Kathleen. "Theory in the Reader: Bleich, Holland, and Beyond." *College English* 47.8 (1985): 836–50.

McCormick, Kathleen, Gary Waller, and Linda Flower. *Reading Texts: Reading, Responding, Writing.* Lexington, MA: Heath, 1987.

McNamara, Timothy P., Diana L. Miller, and John D. Bransford. "Mental Models and Reading Comprehension." *Handbook of Reading Research.* Vol. 2. Eds. Rebecca Barr, Michael Kamil, Peter Mosenthal, and P. David Pearson. New York: Longman, 1991. 490–511.

McRobbie, Angela. *Feminism and Youth Culture.* Cambridge, MA: Hyman, 1990.

Means, Barbara, and Michael Knapp. "Cognitive Approaches to Teaching Advanced Skills to Educationally Disadvantaged Students." *Phi Delta Kappan* 73.4 (1991): 282–89.

Merod, Jim. *The Political Responsibility of the Critic.* Ithaca, NY: Cornell UP, 1987.

Messer-Davidow, Ellen. "The Philosophical Bases of Feminist Literary Criticisms." *Gender and Theory.* Ed. Linda Kauffman. New York: Blackwell, 1989. 63–106.

Miall, David. "The Structure of Response: A Repertory Grid Study of a Poem." *Research in the Teaching of English* 19.3 (1985): 254–68.

Miller, Mark. "Prime Time." *Watching Television.* Ed. Todd Gitlin. New York: Pantheon, 1986. 183–228.

Modleski, Tania. *Feminism without Women: Culture and Criticism in a "Post-Feminist" Age.* New York: Routledge, 1991.

Moffett, James. *Storm in the Mountains: A Case Study of Censorship, Conflict, and Consciousness.* Carbondale: Southern Illinois UP, 1988.

Montgomery, Robert Langford. *Terms of Response: Language and Audience in Seventeenth- and Eighteenth-Century Theory.* University Park: Pennsylvania State UP, 1991.

Moran, Charles, and Elizabeth F. Penfield, eds. *Conversations: Contemporary Critical Theory and the Teaching of Literature.* Urbana: NCTE, 1990.

Morgan, Robert. "Reading as Discursive Practice: The Politics and History of Reading." *Beyond Communication.* Eds. Deanne Bogdan and Stanley Straw. Portsmouth, NH: Boynton/Cook, 1990. 319–36.

Morgan, Thais. "Is There an Intertext in This Text." *American Journal of Semiotics* 3 (1985): 1–40.

———. "The Space of Intertextuality." *Identity of the Literary Text.* Eds. Mario J. Valdes and Owen Miller. Toronto: U of Toronto P, 1985. 209–47.

Mortensen, Peter. "Reading Authority, Writing Authority." *Reader: Essays in Reader-Oriented Theory, Criticism, and Pedagogy* 21 (1989): 35–55.

Morton, Donald, and Mas'ud Zavarzadeh, eds. *Theory/Pedagogy/Politics: Texts for Change.* Urbana: U of Illinois P, 1991.

Mosenthal, Peter, and Michael Kamil. "Understanding Progress in Reading

Research." *Handbook of Reading Research.* Vol. 2. Eds. Rebecca Barr, Michael Kamil, Peter Mosenthal, and P. David Pearson. White Plains, NY: Longman, 1991. 1013–46.

Moss, Gemma. *Un/popular fictions.* London: Virago, 1989.

Mulvey, Laura. "Visual Pleasure and Narrative Cinema." *Screen* 16 (1975): 6–18.

———. *Visual and Other Pleasures.* Bloomington: Indiana UP, 1989.

Murray, Donald. *A Writer Teaches Writing.* Boston: Houghton-Mifflin, 1985.

Natoli, Joseph, ed. *Tracing Literary Theory.* Urbana: U of Illinois P, 1987.

Natoli, Joseph, and Frederik Rusch. *Psychocriticism: An Annotated Bibliography.* Westport, CT: Greenwood, 1984.

Neilsen, Allan. *Critical Thinking and Reading: Empowering Learners to Think and Act.* Urbana: NCTE, 1989.

Nell, Victor. *Lost in a Book: The Psychology of Reading for Pleasure.* New Haven: Yale UP, 1988.

Nelms, Ben, ed. *Literature in the Classroom: Readers, Texts, and Contexts.* Urbana: NCTE, 1988.

Newell, George, Peter MacAdams, and Linda Spears-Burton. "Process Approaches to Writing about Literary Texts: Case Studies of Three Classrooms." NCTE annual meeting. Los Angeles, 1987.

Newkirk, Thomas. "Looking for Trouble: A Way to Unmask Our Readings." *College English* 46.8 (1984): 756–66.

Nix, Don, and Rand Spiro. *Cognition, Education, and Multimedia: Exploring Ideas in High Technology.* Hillsdale, NJ: Erlbaum, 1990.

Noble, Grant. *Children in Front of the Small Screen.* Beverly Hills: Sage, 1975.

Nystrand, Martin. "A Social-Interactive Model of Writing." *Written Communication* 6.1 (1989): 66–85.

Nystrand, Martin, and Adam Gamoran. "Instructional Discourse, Student Engagement, and Literature Achievement." *Research in the Teaching of English* 25.3 (1991): 261–90.

O'Donnell, Patrick, and Robert Con Davis, eds. *Intertextuality and Contemporary American Fiction.* Baltimore: Johns Hopkins UP, 1989.

O'Neill, Cecily, and Alan Lambert. *Drama Structures.* Portsmouth, NH: Heinemann, 1982.

Odell, Lee. "Students' Thinking Processes in Reading and Writing Tasks." NCTE annual meeting. Seattle, 1991.

Ogbu, John. "Minority Status and Literacy in Comparative Perspective." *Daedalus* 119.2 (1990): 141–68.

Ohmann, Richard. "Teaching Historically." *Pedagogy Is Politics: Literary Theory and Critical Teaching.* Ed. Maria-Regina Kecht. Urbana: U of Illinois P, 173–92.

———. *English in America: A Radical View of the Profession.* New York: Oxford UP, 1976.

———. *Politics of Letters.* Middletown: Wesleyan UP, 1987.

———. "History and Literary History: The Case of Mass Culture." *The Rhetoric of Interpretation and the Interpretation of Rhetoric.* Ed. Paul Hernadi. Durham, NC: Duke UP, 1989. 105–24.

Orr, Leonard. "Intertextuality and the Cultural Text in Recent Semiotics." *College English* 48.8 (1986): 811–23.

Paivio, Allan. *Mental Representations: A Dual Coding Approach.* New York: Oxford UP, 1986.

Paris, Mark S. "From Clinic to Classroom while Uncovering the Evil Dead in *Dracula*: A Psychoanalytic Pedagogy." *Practicing Theory in Introductory College Literature Courses.* Eds. James Cahalan and David Downing. Urbana: NCTE, 1991. 47–56.

Peck, Richard. "I Go Along." *Connections.* Ed. Don Gallo. New York: Delacorte, 1990. 184–90.

Peel, Ernest. *The Nature of Adolescent Judgment.* London: Staples P, 1971.

Perl, Sondra, and Nancy Wilson. *Through Teachers' Eyes.* Portsmouth, NH: Heinemann, 1986.

Perry, William. *Forms of Intellectual and Ethical Development in the College Years.* New York: Holt, 1970.

Peterson, Carla L. *The Determined Reader: Gender and Culture in the Novel from Napoleon to Victoria.* New Brunswick, NJ: Rutgers UP, 1986.

Petrey, Sandy. *Speech Acts and Literary Theory.* New York: Routledge, 1990.

Petrosky, Anthony R. "Genetic Epistemology and Psychoanalytic Ego Psychology: Clinical Support for the Study of Response to Literature." *Research in the Teaching of English* 11.1 (1977): 28–38.

———. "From Story to Essay: Reading and Writing." *College Composition and Communication* 33 (1982): 19–36.

Phelps, Louise Wetherbee. *Composition as a Human Science.* New York: Oxford UP, 1988.

Philips, Susan Urmston. *The Invisible Culture: Communication in Classroom and Community on the Warm Spring Indian Reservation.* New York: Longman, 1982.

Piaget, Jean. *The Language and Thought of the Child.* Cleveland: World Publishing, 1955.

Pichert, James, and Richard C. Anderson. "Taking Different Perspectives on a Story." *Journal of Educational Psychology* (1977): 309–15.

Pikulski, John. "The Transition Years: Middle School." *Handbook of Research on Teaching the English Language Arts.* Eds. James Flood, Julie Jensen, Diane Lapp, and James Squire. New York: Macmillan, 1991. 303–19.

Polkinghorne, Donald. *Narrative Knowing and the Human Sciences.* Albany: State U of New York P, 1988.

Porter, James E. *Audience and Rhetoric: An Archaeological Composition of the Discourse Community.* Englewood Cliffs, NJ: Prentice-Hall, 1992.

Porter, Joseph. "Pragmatics for Criticism: Two Generations of Speech Act Theory." *Poetics* 15 (1986): 243–57.

Porter, Sue. *Play It Again: Suggestions for Drama.* Portsmouth, NH: Boynton/ Cook, 1989.

Poulet, Georges. "Phenomenology of Reading." *New Literary History* 1 (1969): 53–68.

Powell, Arthur G., Eleanor Farrar, and David K. Cohen. *The Shopping Mall High School: Winners and Losers in the Educational Marketplace.* Boston: Houghton Mifflin, 1985.

Pratt, Mary Louise. *Toward a Speech Act Theory of Literary Discourse.* Bloomington: Indiana UP, 1977.

Pratt, Mary Louise. "Interpretive Strategies/Strategic Interpretations: On Anglo-American Reader-Response Criticism." *Boundary* 2 (1982–83): 201–31.

Prawat, Richard. "Conversations with Self and Settings: A Framework for Thinking about Teacher Empowerment." *American Educational Research Journal* 28.4 (1991): 737–57.

Press, Andrea L. *Women Watching Television: Gender, Class, and Generation in the American Television Experience.* Philadelphia: U of Pennsylvania P, 1991.

Price, Marian. *Reader-Response Criticism: A Test of Its Usefulness in a First-Year College Course in Writing about Literature.* New York: Lang, 1990.

Pritchard, Robert. "The Effects of Cultural Schemata on Reading Processing Strategies." *Reading Research Quarterly* 25.4 (1990): 273–95.

Probst, Robert. *Response and Analysis.* Portsmouth, NH: Boynton/ Cook, 1987.

———. "*Literature as Exploration* and the Classroom." *Transactions with Literature: A Fifty-Year Perspective.* Eds. Edmund J. Farrell and James R. Squire. Urbana: NCTE, 1990. 27–37.

———. "Response to Literature." *Handbook of Research on Teaching the English Language Arts.* Eds. James Flood, Julie Jensen, Diane Lapp, and James Squire. New York: Macmillan, 1991. 655–63.

Protherough, Robert. *Developing Response to Fiction.* Milton Keynes, England: Open UP, 1983.

———. "The Stories that Readers Tell." *Readers, Texts, Teachers.* Eds. Bill Corcoran and Emrys Evans. Upper Montclair, NJ: Boynton/Cook, 1987. 75–92.

Pugh, Sharon, Jean Wolph Hicks, Marcia Davis, and Tonya Venstra. *Bridging: A Teacher's Guide to Metaphorical Thinking.* Urbana: NCTE, 1992.

Purves, Alan C. *Literature Education in Ten Countries: An Empirical Study.* New York: John Wiley, 1973.

———. *Reading and Literature: American Achievement in International Perspective.* Urbana: NCTE, 1981.

———. "The Aesthetic Mind of Louise Rosenblatt." *Reader: Essays in Reader-Oriented Theory, Criticism, and Pedagogy* 20 (1988): 68–76.

———. "Can Literature Be Rescued from Reading?" *Transactions with Literature: A Fifty-Year Perspective.* Eds. Edmund J. Farrell and James R. Squire. Urbana: NCTE, 1990. 79–93.

Purves, Alan C., and Richard Beach. *Literature and the Reader: Research on Response to Literature, Reading Interests, and the Teaching of Literature.* Urbana: NCTE, 1972.

Purves, Alan C., Terry Rogers, and Anna Soter. *How Porcupines Make Love, No. Two.* White Plains, NY: Longman, 1990.

Purves, Alan C., and Sharon Silkey. "What Happens When We Read a Poem." *Journal of Aesthetic Education* 7.3 (1973): 63–72.

Rabinowitz, Peter. *Before Reading: Narrative Conventions and the Politics of Interpretation.* Ithaca, NY: Cornell UP, 1987.

———. "End Sinister: Neat Closure as Disruptive Force." *Reading Narrative.* Ed. James Phelan. Columbus: Ohio State UP, 1989. 120–31.

———. "A Thousand Times and Never Like: Re-Reading for Class." NCTE Assembly on Research Conference. Chicago, 1991.

Radway, Janice A. *Reading the Romance.* Chapel Hill: U of North Carolina P, 1984.

———. "Introduction: Reading *Reading the Romance.*" *Reading the Romance.* London: Verso, 1987. 1–18.

———. "The Book-of-the-Month Club and the General Reader: On the Uses of 'Serious' Fiction." *Critical Inquiry* 14 (1988): 516–38.

Railton, Stephen. *Authorship and Audience: Literary Performance in the American Renaissance.* Princeton: Princeton UP, 1991.

Rank, Hugh. *The Pitch.* Park Forest, IL: Counter-Propaganda, 1991.

Ransom, John Crowe. *The New Criticism.* Norfolk, CT: New Directions, 1941.

Raphael, Taffy, et al. "Literature and Discusssion in the Reading Program." *Language Arts* 69.1 (1992): 54–61.

Ray, William. *Literary Meaning: From Phenomenology to Deconstruction.* Oxford: Blackwell, 1984.

Reynolds, Kimberley. *Girls Only? Gender and Popular Children's Fiction in Britain, 1880-1910.* Philadelphia: Temple UP, 1990.

Rice, Philip, and Patricia Waugh, eds. *Modern Literary Theory: A Reader.* London: Arnold, 1989.

Richards, I.A. *Practical Criticism.* New York: Harcourt, 1929.

Rico, Gabriele Lusser. "Daedalus and Icarus Within: The Literature/Art/Writing Connection." *English Journal* 78.3 (1989): 14–23.

Ricoeur, Paul. *Time and Narrative.* Chicago: U of Chicago P, 1984.

Rief, Linda. *Seeking Diversity.* Portsmouth, NH: Boynton/Cook, 1992.

Ringer, Benjamin B., and Elinor R. Lawless. *Race-Ethnicity and Society.* New York: Routledge, 1989.

Robinson, Jeffrey. *Radical Literary Education: A Classroom Experiment with Wordsworth's "Ode."* Madison: U of Wisconsin P, 1987.

Roemer, Marjorie Godlin. "Which Reader's Response?" *College English* 49.8 (1987): 911–21.

Rogers, Mary F. *Novels, Novelists, and Readers: Toward a Phenomenological Sociology of Literature.* Albany: State U of New York P, 1991.

Rogers, Theresa. "Exploring a Socio-Cognitive Perspective on the Interpretive Processes of Junior High School Students." *English Quarterly* 20.3 (1987): 218–30.

Rogers, Theresa, Judith Green, and Nancy Nussbaum. "Asking Questions about Questions." *Perspectives on Talk and Learning.* Eds. Susan Hynds and Don Rubin. Urbana: NCTE, 1990. 73–90.

Rosenblatt, Louise M. *The Reader, The Text, The Poem: The Transactional Theory of the Literary Work.* Carbondale: Southern Illinois UP, 1978.

———. *Literature as Exploration.* 1938. 4th ed. New York: MLA, 1983.

———. "Writing and Reading: The Transactional Theory." *Reader: Essays in Reader-Oriented Theory, Criticism, and Pedagogy* 20 (1988): 7–31.

———. "Literary Theory." *Handbook of Research on Teaching the English Language Arts*. Eds. James Flood, Julie Jensen, Diane Lapp, and James Squire. New York: Macmillan, 1991. 57–62.

Roser, Nancy, and Miriam Martinez. "Roles Adults Play in Preschoolers' Response to Literature." *Language Arts* 61 (1985): 485–90.

Rylance, Rick, ed. *Debating Texts: Readings in Twentieth-Century Literary Theory and Method*. Toronto: U of Toronto P, 1987.

Ryle, Gilbert. *The Concept of Mind*. London: Hutchison, 1966.

Sadoski, Mark, Ernest Goetz, and Suzanne Kangiser. "Imagination in Story Response: Relationships Between Imagery, Affect, and Structural Importance." *Reading Research Quarterly* 23.3 (1988): 320–36.

Sadoski, Mark, Allan Paivio, and Ernest Goetz. "A Critique of Schema Theory in Reading and A Dual Coding Alternative." *Reading Research Quarterly* 26.4 (1991): 463–84.

Sadoski, Mark, and Zeba Quast. "Reader Response and Long-Term Recall for Journalistic Text: The Roles of Imagery, Affect, and Importance." *Reading Research Quarterly* 25 (1990): 256–72.

Salvatori, Mariolina. "Reading and Writing a Text: Correlations Between Reading and Writing Patterns." *College English* 45.7 (1983): 657–66.

———. "Pedagogy: From the Periphery to the Center." *Reclaiming Pedagogy*. Eds. Patricia Donahue and Ellen Quandahl. Carbondale: Southern Illinois UP, 1989. 17–34.

Sarland, Charles. *Young People Reading: Culture and Response*. Philadelphia: Milton Keynes, 1991.

Scafe, Suzanne. *Teaching Black Literature*. London: Virago, 1989.

Schatzburg-Smith, Kathie. *Dialogue Journal Writing and the Study Habits and Attitudes of Underprepared College Students*. Diss. Hofstra U, 1988.

Schein, Edgar. "How Culture Forms, Develops, and Changes." *Gaining Control of the Corporate Culture*. Eds. Ralph H. Kilmann et al. San Francisco: Jossey-Bass, 1985. 17–43.

Schilb, John. "Canonical Theories and Noncanonical Literature: Steps Toward a Pedagogy." *Reader* 15 (1986): 3–23.

Scholes, Robert. *Structuralism in Literature: An Introduction*. New Haven: Yale UP, 1974.

———. *Textual Power*. New Haven: Yale UP, 1985.

———. *Protocols of Reading*. New Haven: Yale UP, 1989.

Scholes, Robert, Nancy R. Comley, and Gregory L. Ulmer. *Text Book: An Introduction to Literary Language*. New York: St. Martin's Press, 1988.

Schon, Donald A. *The Reflective Practitioner*. New York: Basic, 1983.

———. *Educating the Reflective Practitioner*. San Francisco: Jossey-Bass, 1987.

Schuster, Charles. "Mikhail Bakhtin as Rhetorical Theorist." *College English* 47.6 (1985): 594–607.

Schweickart, Patrocinio. "Reading Ourselves: Toward a Feminist Theory of Reading." *Gender and Reading: Essays on Readers, Texts, and Contexts*. Eds.

Elizabeth A. Flynn and Patrocinio Schweickart. Baltimore: Johns Hopkins UP, 1986. 31–62.

Schwenger, Peter. "The Masculine Mode." *Speaking of Gender.* Ed. Elaine Showalter. New York: Routledge, 1989. 101–12.

Searle, John R. *Speech Acts.* London: Cambridge UP, 1969.

———. *Expression and Meaning.* New York: Cambridge UP, 1979.

Searle, John R., and Daniel Vanderveken. *Foundations of Illocutionary Logic.* New York: Cambridge UP, 1985.

Seiter, Ellen. "Semiotics and Television." *Channels of Discourse.* Ed. Robert Allen. Chapel Hill: U of North Carolina P, 1987. 17–42.

Selden, Raman. *A Reader's Guide to Contemporary Literary Theory.* Lexington: UP of Kentucky, 1985.

———. *Practicing Theory and Reading Literature.* Lexington: UP of Kentucky, 1989.

———. *A Reader's Guide to Contemporary Literary Theory.* Lexington: UP of Kentucky, 1989.

Shank, Roger. *The Dynamics of Memory.* Cambridge: Cambridge UP, 1982.

Sharpe, Patricia, F. E. Mascia-Lees, and C. B. Cohen. "White Women and Black Men: Differential Responses to Reading Black Women's Texts." *College English* 52.2 (1990): 142–53.

Shneiderman, Ben, and Greg Kearsley. *Hypertext Hands-On!: An Introduction to a New Way of Organizing and Accessing Information.* Reading, MA: Addison-Wesley, 1989.

Short, Kathy, and Kathryn Pierce, eds. *Talking About Books.* Portsmouth, NH: Heinemann, 1990.

Showalter, Elaine, ed. *The New Feminist Criticism: Essays on Women, Literature, and Theory.* New York: Pantheon, 1985.

Sicherman, Barbara. "Sense and Sensibility: A Case Study of Women's Reading in Late-Victorian America." *Reading in America.* Eds. Kathy Davidson and John Unger. Baltimore: Johns Hopkins UP, 1989. 201–31.

Simpkins, Scott. "Telling the Reader What to Do: Wordsworth and the Fenwick Notes." *Reader: Essays in Reader-Oriented Theory, Criticism and Pedagogy* 26 (1991): 39–64.

Sizer, Theodore R. *Horace's Compromise: The Dilemma of the American High School.* Boston: Houghton, 1984.

Slatin, John M. "Reading Hypertext: Order and Coherence in a New Medium." *College English* 52.8 (1990): 870–83.

Slatoff, Walter J. *With Respect to Readers: Dimensions of Literary Response.* Ithaca, NY: Cornell UP, 1970.

Sleeter, Christine. "The White Ethnic Experience in America: To Whom Does It Generalize?" *Educational Researcher* 21.1 (1992): 33–36.

Smith, Barbara Herrnstein. *Poetic Closure: A Study of How Poems End.* Chicago: U of Chicago P, 1968.

———. *On the Margins of Discourse: The Relation of Literature to Language.* Chicago: U of Chicago P, 1978.

Smith, Michael W. *Understanding Unreliable Narrators.* Urbana: NCTE, 1991.

Smith, Michael W., and James Marshall. "Toward an Understanding of the Culture of Practice in the Discussion of Literature: An Analysis of Adult Reading Groups." AERA annual meeting. Chicago, 1991.

Smith, Michael W., and Brian White. " 'That reminds me of the time . . .': Using Autobiographical Writing Before Reading." *Constructive Reading: Teaching Beyond Communication*. Eds. Deanne Bogdan and Stanley Straw. Portsmouth, NH: Boynton/Cook, in press.

Solomon, Robert. "Literacy and the Education of the Emotions." *Literacy, Society, and Schooling*. Eds. Suzanne deCastell, Allan Luke, and Kieran Egan. New York: Cambridge UP, 1986. 37–58.

———. "Literacy and the Education of the Emotions." *Education and the Arts*. Ed. Linda Reed. St. Louis: CEMREL, 1984. 37–58.

Sontag, Susan. "The Imagination of Disaster." *Film Theory and Criticism*. Eds. Gerald Mast and Marshall Cohen. New York: Oxford UP, 1974. 422–37.

Sosnoski, James J. "Students as Theorists: Collaborative Hypertextbooks." *Practicing Theory in Introductory College Literature Courses*. Eds. James Cahalan and David Downing. Urbana: NCTE, 1991. 271–90.

Spellmeyer, Kurt. "Foucault and the Freshman Writer: Considering the Self in Discourse." *College English* 51 (1989): 715–29.

Sperber, Dan, and Deirdre Wilson. *Relevance: Communication and Cognition*. Cambridge, MA: Harvard UP, 1986.

Spiro, Rand. *Schema Theory and Reading Comprehension: New Directions*. Technical Report No. 191. Urbana: Center for the Study of Reading, U of Illinois, 1980.

Spurlin, William. "Theorizing Signifyin(g) and the Role of the Reader: Possible Directions for African-American Literary Criticism." *College English* 52 (1990): 732–42.

Squire, James, ed. *Response to Literature*. Urbana: NCTE, 1968.

Steig, Michael. *Stories of Reading*. Baltimore: Johns Hopkins UP, 1989.

———. "Stories of Reading Pedagogy: Problems and Possibilities." *Reader: Essays in Reader-Oriented Theory, Criticism, and Pedagogy* 26 (1991): 27–38.

Stein, Nancy L., and Christine Glenn. "An Analysis of Story Comprehension in Elementary School Children." *New Directions in Discourse Processing*. Ed. Roy Freedle. Norwood, NJ: Ablex, 1979. 53–121.

Stone, Robert. "We Are Not Excused." *Paths of Resistance: The Art and Craft of the Political Novel*. Ed. William Zinsser. Boston: Houghton, 1989. 18–37.

Straus, Barrie Ruth. "Influencing Theory: Speech Acts." *Tracing Literary Theory*. Ed. Joseph Natoli. Urbana: U of Illinois P, 1987. 213–47.

Suleiman, Susan. "Introduction." *The Reader in the Text: Essays on Audience and Interpretation*. Princeton: Princeton UP, 1980. 3.

Suleiman, Susan, and Inge Crosman, eds. *The Reader in the Text: Essays on Audience and Interpretation*. Princeton: Princeton UP, 1980.

Sutton-Smith, Brian. *The Folkstories of Children*. Philadelphia: U of Pennsylvania P, 1980.

Svenson, Cai. *The Construction of Poetic Meaning: A Cultural-Developmental*

*Study of Symbolic and Non-Symbolic Strategies in the Interpretation of Contemporary Poetry.* Vasterik, Sweden: Liber Forlag, 1985.

Tannen, Deborah. *You Just Don't Understand: Women and Men in Conversation.* New York: Morrow, 1990.

Thomson, Jack. *Understanding Teenagers' Reading: Reading Processes and the Teaching of Literature.* Melbourne: Methuen, 1987.

Thurber, Barton, Gary Macy, and Jack Pope. "The Book, the Computer, and the Humanities." *Technical Horizons in Education Journal* 19 (1991): 57–61.

Tierney, Robert, and Patricia Edminston. "The Relationships Between Readers' Involvement in and Comprehension of a Fictional Short Story." American Educational Research Association. Chicago, April 2–7, 1991.

Todorov, Tzvetan. *The Fantastic: A Structural Approach to a Literary Genre.* Trans. Richard Howard. Ithaca, NY: Cornell UP, 1975.

Tompkins, Jane P. "The Reader in History." *Reader-Response Criticism: From Formalism to Post-Structuralism.* Ed. Jane P. Tompkins. Baltimore: Johns Hopkins UP, 1980. 201–32.

———, ed. *Reader-Response Criticism: From Formalism to Post-Structuralism.* Baltimore: Johns Hopkins UP, 1980.

———. *Sensational Designs: The Cultural Work of American Fiction, 1790-1860.* New York: Oxford UP, 1985.

———. "Me and My Shadow." *Gender and Theory.* Ed. Linda Kauffman. New York: Blackwell, 1989. 121–39.

———. "Comment and Response." *College English* 53.5 (1991): 601–04.

Trillin, Calvin. "The Life and Times of Joe Bob Briggs, So Far." *American Stories.* New York: Ticknort Fields, 1991. 41–72.

Turner, Graeme. *British Cultural Studies: An Introduction.* Boston: Hyman, 1990.

Turner, Mark. *Death Is the Mother of Beauty.* Chicago: U of Chicago P, 1987.

———. *Reading Minds.* Princeton: Princeton UP, 1991.

Valdes, Mario J., and Owen Miller, eds. *Identity of the Literary Text.* Toronto: U of Toronto P, 1985.

van den Broek, Paul. "The Causal Inference Maker: Towards a Process Model of Inference Generation in Text Comprehension." *Comprehension Processes in Reading.* Eds. David A. Balota, G. B. Flores d'Arcais, and Keith Rayner. Hillsdale, NJ: Erlbaum, 1990. 423–36.

VanDeWeghe, Richard. "Making and Remaking Meaning: Developing Literary Responses through Purposeful, Informal Writing." *English Quarterly* 20.1 (1987): 38–51.

Varsava, Jerry. *Contingent Meanings: Postmodern Fiction, Mimesis, and the Reader.* Tallahassee: The Florida State UP, 1990.

Viehoff, Reinhold. "How to Construct a Literary Poem?" *Poetics* 1.5 (1986) 287–306.

Vipond, Douglas, Russell Hunt, James Jewett, and James Reither. "Making Sense of Reading." *Developing Discourse Processes in Adolescence and Adulthood.* Eds. Richard Beach and Susan Hynds. Norwood, NJ: Ablex, 1990. 110–35.

Vygotsky, Lev. *Mind in Society.* Cambridge: Harvard UP, 1978.

Wallace, Michele. *Black Macho and the Myth of the Superwoman.* New York: Dial, 1979.

Wardhaugh, Ronald. *How Conversation Works.* New York: Blackwell, 1985.

Webb, Edwin. *Literature in Education: Encounter and Experience.* Philadelphia: Farmer, 1992.

Webster, Roger. *Studying Literary Theory: An Introduction.* London: Arnold, 1990.

Weedon, Chris. *Feminist Practice and Poststructuralist Theory.* New York: Blackwell, 1987.

Welleck, Rene, and Austin Warren. *Theory of Literature.* New York: Harcourt, 1949.

White, Brian. *The Effects of Pre-Discussion Writing on Students' Discussion Responses to Literature.* Diss. U of Wisconsin, 1990.

White, Hayden. "The Fictions of Factual Representation." *The Literature of Fact.* Ed. Angus Fletcher. New York: Columbia UP, 1976, 156–83.

Willbern, David. "Reading after Freud." *Contemporary Literary Theory.* Eds. G. Douglas Atkins and Laura Morrow. Amherst: U of Massachusetts P, 1989. 158–79.

Williams, Raymond. *Marxism and Literature.* New York: Oxford UP, 1977.

Williamson, Judith. *Decoding Advertisements.* London: Boyars, 1978.

Willinsky, John. *The Triumph of Literature/The Fate of Literacy.* New York: Teachers College, 1991.

Willinsky, John, and R. M. Hunniford. "Reading the Romance Younger: The Mirrors and Fears of a Preparatory Literature." *Reading-Canada-Lecture* 4 (1986): 16–31.

Willis, Meredith Sue. *Personal Fiction Writing.* New York: Teachers and Writers Collaborative, 1984.

Wilson, W. Daniel. "Readers in Texts." *PMLA* 96.5 (1981): 848–63.

Wimmers, Inge Crosman. *Poetics of Reading: Approaches to the Novel.* Princeton: Princeton UP, 1988.

Wimsatt, William K., and Monroe C. Beardsley. "The Affective Fallacy." *The Verbal Icon: Studies in the Meaning of Poetry.* W. K. Wimsatt. Lexington: U of Kentucky P, 1954. 21–39.

Winnett, Susan. "Coming Unstrung: Women, Men, Narrative, and Principles of Pleasure." *PMLA* 105 (1990): 505–19.

Witherell, Carol, and Nel Noddings, eds. *Stories Lives Tell: Narrative and Dialogue in Education.* New York: Teachers College P, 1991.

Wolf, Dennie Palmer. *Reading—Reconsidered.* New York: College Entrance Examination Board, 1988.

Worton, Michael, and Judith Still, eds. *Intertextuality: Theories and Practice.* Manchester, England: Manchester UP, 1990.

Wright, Elizabeth. *Psychoanalytic Criticism.* New York: Methuen, 1984.

Zancanella, Don. "Teachers Reading/Readers Teaching: Five Teachers' Personal Approaches to Literature and Their Teaching of Literature." *Research in the Teaching of English* 25 (1991): 5–32.

## Additional Readings

Ady, Paul. "Reading as a Communal Act of Discovery: *Finnegan's Wake* in the Classroom." *Reader: Essays in Reader-Oriented Theory, Criticism, and Pedagogy* 16 (1986): 50–62.

Allen, Robert, ed. *Channels of Discourse: Television and Contemporary Criticism.* London: Methuen, 1987.

Andrasick, Kathleen. *Opening Texts.* Portsmouth, NH: Heinemann, 1990.

Ang, Ien. *Watching "Dallas": Soap Opera and the Melodramatic Imagination.* London: Methuen, 1985.

Apple, Michael. *Teachers and Texts.* New York: Routledge, 1988.

Armstrong, Paul. *Conflicting Readings: Variety and Validity in Interpretation.* Chapel Hill: U of North Carolina P, 1990.

Bennett, Susan. *Theatre Audiences: A Theory of Production and Reception.* New York: Routledge, 1990.

Bennett, Tony, Colin Mercer, and Janet Woollacott, eds. *Popular Culture and Social Relations.* Milton Keynes: Open UP, 1986.

Benton, Michael. "Secondary Worlds." *Journal of Research and Development in Education* 16.3 (1983): 68–75.

Berg, Temma F. "Psychologies of Reading." *Tracing Literary Theory.* Ed. Joseph Natoli. Urbana: U of Illinois P, 1987. 248–77.

Berman, Art. *From the New Criticism to Deconstruction: The Reception of Structuralism and Post-Structuralism.* Urbana: U of Illinois P, 1988.

Black, John B., and Collen M. Seifert. "The Psychological Study of Story Understanding." *Researching Response to Literature and the Teaching of Literature: Points of Departure.* Ed. Charles R. Cooper. Norwood, New Jersey: Ablex, 1985. 190–211.

Blake, Robert, and A. Lumm. "Responding to Poetry: High School Students Read Poetry." *English Journal* 75 (1986): 68–73.

Bloome, David. "Reading as a Social Process." *Language Arts* 62.2 (1985): 134–42.

Bortine, David. *Reading, Criticism, and Culture: Theory and Teaching in the United States and England, 1820–1950.* Columbia: U of South Carolina P, 1992.

Brooke, Robert. "Three Models of Narrative Comprehension in William Stafford's 'Traveling through the Dark': Some Relations between Schemata and Interpretive Context." *Empirical Studies of the Arts* 2.2 (1984): 173–93.

Brower, Sue. "Inside Stories: Gossip and Television Audiences." *Culture and Communication* 4. Eds. Sari Thomas and William A. Evans. Norwood, NJ: Ablex.

Buckley, William. *Senses' Tender: Recovering the Novel for the Reader.* New York: Lang, 1989.

Butler, Christopher. "The Future of Theory: Saving the Reader." *The Future of Literary Theory.* Ed. Ralph Cohen. London: Routledge, 1989. 229–49.

Callahan, John F. *In the African-American Grain: Call-and-Response in Twentieth-Century Black Fiction.* Middletown, CT: Wesleyan UP, 1990.

Carlson, Susan. "Readers Reading Green Reading Readers: Discovering Henry Green through Reader-Response Criticism." *Language and Style* 17 (1984): 175–89.

Christian, Barbara. *Black Feminist Criticism*. New York: Pergamon, 1985.

Clifford, John, ed. *The Experience of Reading: Louise Rosenblatt and Reader-Response Theory*. Portsmouth, NH: Boynton/Cook, 1990.

Collins, James, ed. *Vital Signs 1: Bringing Together Reading and Writing*. Portsmouth, NH: Boynton/Cook, 1989.

———, ed. *Vital Signs 2: Teaching and Learning Cooperatively*. Portsmouth, NH: Boynton/Cook, 1990.

Comley, Nancy R. "Reading and Writing Genders." *Reorientations: Critical Theories and Pedagogies*. Eds. Bruce Henricksen and Thais Morgan. Urbana: U of Illinois P, 1990. 179–92.

Culler, Jonathan. *Framing the Sign: Criticism and Its Institutions*. Norman: U of Oklahoma P, 1988.

Curtis, Jared. "Reading *Lyrical Ballads*: Teaching by Response." *Reader: Essays in Reader-Oriented Theory, Criticism, and Pedagogy* 16 (1986): 50–62.

Davis, Leonard. *Resisting Novels*. New York: Methuen, 1987.

de Lauretis, Teresa. *Alice Doesn't: Feminism, Semiotics, Cinema*. London: Macmillan, 1984.

De Beaugrande, Robert. "Poetry and the Ordinary Reader: A Study of Immediate Responses." *Empirical Studies of the Arts* 3 (1985): 1–21.

Dias, Patrick. *Making Sense of Poetry: Patterns in the Process*. Ottawa: Canadian Council of Teachers of English, 1987.

Dillon, George L. *Language Processing and the Reading of Literature: Toward a Model of Comprehension*. Bloomington: Indiana UP, 1978.

Donahue, Patricia, and Ellen Quandahl, eds. *Reclaiming Pedagogy: The Rhetoric of the Classroom*. Carbondale: Southern Illinois UP, 1989.

Flynn, Elizabeth, and Patrocinio P. Schweickart, eds. *Gender and Reading: Essays on Readers, Texts, and Contexts*. Baltimore: Johns Hopkins UP, 1986.

Fowler, Bridget. *The Alienated Reader: Women and Romantic Literature in the Twentieth Century*. New York: Harvester Wheatsheaf, 1991.

Fowler, Robert. *Let the Reader Understand: Reader-Response Criticism and the Gospel of Mark*. Minneapolis: Fortress Press, 1991.

Fry, Donald. *Children Talk about Books: Seeing Themselves as Readers*. Milton Keynes: Open UP, 1985.

Galda, Lee. "Readers, Texts, and Contexts: A Response-Based View of Literature in the Classroom." *New Advocate* 1 (1988): 92–102.

Gates, Henry Louis, Jr. *Figures in Black: Words, Signs, and the "Racial" Self*. New York: Oxford UP, 1987.

Giddings, Robert. *The Author, the Book, and the Reader*. London: Greenwich Exchange, 1991.

Gilbert, Pam. "Post Reader-Response: The Deconstructive Critique." *Readers, Texts, Teachers*. Eds. Bill Corcoran and Emrys Evans. Upper Montclair, NJ: Boynton/Cook, 1987. 234–50.

Giroux, Henry, and Roger Simon, eds. *Popular Culture, Schooling, and Everyday Life*. Granby, MA: Bergin and Garvey, 1989.

Goffman, Erving. *Gender Advertisements.* New York: Harper and Row, 1979.

Goldstein, Philip. *The Politics of Literary Theory: An Introduction to Marxist Criticism.* Tallahassee: Florida State UP, 1990.

Graesser, Arthur, Jonathan Golding, and Debra Long. "Narrative Representation and Comprehension." *Handbook of Reading Research,* Vol 2. Eds. Rebecca Barr, Michael Kamil, Peter Mosenthal, and P. David Pearson. White Plains, NY: Longman, 1991. 171–205.

Grossberg, Lawrence, Tony Fry, Ann Curthoys, and Paul Patton, eds. *It's a Sin: Essays on Postmodernism, Politics, and Culture.* Sydney: Power, 1988.

Hade, Daniel. "Children, Stories, and Narrative Transformations." *Research in the Teaching of English* 22 (1988): 310–25.

Harker, W. John. "Information Processing and the Reading of Literary Texts." *New Literary History* 20 (1989). 465–81.

Hebdige, Dick. *Hiding in the Light: On Images and Things.* London: Routledge, 1988.

Henricksen, Bruce, and Thais Morgan, eds. *Reorientations: Criticial Theories and Pedagogies.* Urbana: U of Illinois P, 1990.

Hernadi, Paul, ed. *The Rhetoric of Interpretation and the Interpretation of Rhetoric.* Durham, NC: Duke UP, 1989.

Horton, Susan. *The Reader in the Dickens World: Style and Response.* Pittsburgh, PA: U of Pittsburgh P, 1981.

Hunt, Russell, and Douglas Vipond. "The Parallel Socialization of Reading Comprehension Research and Literary Theory." *Beyond Communication: Reading Comprehension and Criticism.* Eds. Stanley B. Straw and Deanne Bogdan. Portsmouth, NH: Boynton/Cook, 1990. 91–108.

Hynds, Susan. "Reading as a Social Event." *Beyond Communication: Reading Comprehension and Criticism.* Eds. Stanley B. Straw and Deanne Bogdan. Portsmouth, NH: Boynton/Cook, 1990. 237–58.

Hynds, Susan, and Donald Rubin, eds. *Perspectives on Talk and Learning.* Urbana: NCTE, 1990.

Jacobsen, Mary. "Looking for Literary Space: The Willing Suspension of Disbelief." *Research in the Teaching of English* 16 (1982): 21–38.

Jay, Gregory S. "The Subject of Pedagogy: Lessons in Psychoanalysis and Politics." *College English* 49.7 (1987): 785–800.

Kantz, Margaret. "Toward a Pedagogically Useful Theory of Literary Reading." *Poetics* 16 (1987): 155–68.

Kecht, Maria-Regina, ed. *Pedagogy Is Politics: Literary Theory and Critical Teaching.* Urbana: U of Illinois P, 1991.

Keymer, Tom. *Richardson's Clarissa and the Eighteenth-Century Reader.* New York: Cambridge UP, 1992.

Kintgen, Eugene R. *The Perception of Poetry.* Bloomington: Indiana UP, 1983.

Klancher, Jon. *The Making of English Reader Audiences, 1790–1832.* Madison: U of Wisconsin P, 1987.

Lakoff, George. *Women, Fire, and Dangerous Things: What Categories Reveal About the Mind.* Chicago: U of Chicago P, 1987.

Larsen, Steen F., and Uffe Seilman. "Personal Remindings While Reading Literature." *TEXT* 8 (1988): 411–29.

Lehr, Susan. "The Child's Developing Sense of Theme as a Response to Literature." *Reading Research Quarterly* 23.3 (1988). 337–57.

Lewis, Lisa. "Consumer Girl Culture: How Music Video Appeals to Girls." *Television and Women's Culture.* Ed. Mary Ellen Brown. Newbury Park, CA: Sage, 1990. 89–101.

———, ed. *The Adoring Audience.* Boston: Unwin Hyman, 1990.

Liebes, Tamar. "Cultural Differences in the Retelling of Television Fiction." *Methods of Rhetorical Criticism.* Eds. Bernard Brock, Robert Scott, and James W. Chesebro. Detroit: Wayne State UP, 1989. 461–76.

MacKenzie, Nancy. "Subjective Criticism in Literature Courses: Learning through Writing." *Teaching English in the Two-Year College* 12 (1985): 228–33.

Many, Joyce. "The Effects of Stance and Age Level on Children's Literary Responses." *Journal of Reading Behavior* 23 (1991): 61–86.

Martin, Bruce. "Teaching Literature as Experience." *College English* 51 (1989): 377–85.

McClure, Amy, and Connie Zitlow. "Not Just the Facts: Aesthetic Responses in Elementary Content Area Studies." *Language Arts* 68 (1991): 27–33.

McCormick, Kathleen. "Theory in the Reader: Bleich, Holland, and Beyond." *College English* 47.8 (1985): 836–50.

McCormick, Katherine. "Psychological Realism: A New Epistemology for Reader-Response Criticism. *Reader: Essays in Reader-Oriented Theory, Criticism, and Pedagogy* 14 (1985): 40–53.

Meutsch, Dietrich, and Reinhold Viehoff, eds. *Comprehension of Literary Discourse: Results and Problems of Interdisciplinary Approaches.* Berlin: De Gruyter, 1990.

Miall, David S. "Affect and Narrative: A Model of Response to Stories." *Poetics* 17 (1988): 259–72.

Miner, Madonne. "Gender, Reading, and Misreading." *Reader: Essays in Reader-Oriented Theory, Criticism, and Pedagogy* 13(1985): 10–18.

Modleski, Tania. *Loving with a Vengeance: Mass-Produced Fantasies for Women.* Hamden, CT: Archon, 1982.

———, ed. *Studies in Entertainment: Critical Approaches to Mass Culture.* Bloomington, IN: Indiana UP, 1986.

Morgan, Nicholas H. *Secret Journeys: Theory and Practice in Reading Dickens.* Rutherford, NJ: Fairleigh Dickinson UP, 1992.

Morgan, Norah, and Juliana Saxton. *Teaching Drama.* London: Hutchison, 1987.

Morley, David. *Family Television: Cultural Power and Domestic Leisure.* London: Comedia, 1986.

Morrow, Lesley Mandel. "Young Children's Responses to One-to-One Story Readings in School Settings." *Reading Research Quarterly* 22.1 (1988): 89–107.

Natoli, Joseph, ed. *Psychological Perspectives on Literature: Freudian Dissidents and Non-Freudians.* Hamden, CT: Shoe String, 1984.

Neaman, Mimi, and Mary Strong. *Literature Circles: Cooperative Learning for Grades 3–8.* Englewood, CO: Teachers Ideas, 1992.

Nord, David Paul. "Working-Class Readers: Family, Community and Reading in Later Nineteenth-Century America." *Communication Research* 13 (1986): 156–81.

O'Neill, Cecily and Alan Lambert. *Drama Structures.* Portsmouth, NH: Heinemann, 1982.

Oster, Judith. *Toward Robert Frost: The Reader and the Poet.* Athens: U of Georgia P, 1991.

Peterson, Carla. *The Determined Reader: Gender and Culture in the Novel from Napoleon to Victoria.* New Brunswick, NJ: Rutgers UP, 1987.

Phelan, James, ed. *Reading Narrative: Form, Ethics, Ideology.* Columbus: Ohio State UP, 1989.

Porter, James. "The Reasonable Reader: Knowledge and Inquiry in Freshman English." *College English* 49 (1987): 332–44.

———. *Audience and Rhetoric.* Englewood Cliffs, NJ: Prentice-Hall, 1992.

Potter, Jonathan, Peter Stringer, and Margaret Witherell. *Social Texts and Context: Literature and Social Psychology.* London: Routledge and Kegan Paul, 1984.

Pratt, Mary Louise. "Interpretative Strategies/Strategic Interpretations: On Anglo-American Reader Response Criticism." *Boundary* 2 (1981/82): 201–31.

Probst, Robert E. "Mom, Wolfgang, and Me: Adolescent Literature, Critical Theory, and the English Classroom." *English Journal* 75 (1986): 33–39.

———. "Transactional Theory and Response to Student Writing." *Writing and Response: Theory, Practice, and Research.* Ed. Chris M. Anson. Urbana: NCTE, 1989. 68–79.

Purves, Alan, ed. *The Idea of Difficulty in Literature.* Albany, NY: State UP of New York, 1991.

Rabinowitz, Peter J. "Whirl Without End: Audience-Oriented Criticism." *Contemporary Literary Theory.* Ed. G. Douglas Atkins and Laura Morrow. Amherst: U of Massachusetts P, 1989. 81–100.

Railton, Stephen. *Authorship and Audience: Literary Performance in the American Renaissance.* Princeton: Princeton UP, 1991.

Rosenblatt, Louise M. "Transaction versus Interaction: A Terminological Rescue Operation." *Research in the Teaching of English* 19 (1985): 96–107.

———. "Retrospect." *Transactions with Literature: A Fifty-Year Perspective.* Eds. Edmund J. Farrell and James R. Squire. Urbana: NCTE, 1990. 97–107.

Sadoski, Mark, Ernest T. Goetz, and Suzanne Kangiser. "Imagination in Story Response: Relationships Between Imagery, Affect, and Structural Importance." *Reading Research Quarterly* 23.3 (1988): 320–36.

Said, Edward. *The World, the Text, and the Critic.* Cambridge, MA: Harvard UP, 1983.

Schallert, Diane. "The Contribution of Psychology to Teaching the Language Arts." *Handbook of Research on Teaching the English Language Arts.* Eds. James Flood, Julie Jensen, Diane Lapp, and James Squire. New York: Macmillan, 1990. 30–39.

Schilb, John. "Canonical Theories and Noncanonical Literature: Steps Toward a Pedagogy." *Reader: Essays in Reader-Oriented Theory, Criticism, and Pedagogy* 15 (1986): 3–23.

Short, Kathy, and Kathryn Pierce, eds. *Talking about Books.* Portsmouth, NH: Heinemann, 1990.

Showalter, Elaine, ed. *Speaking of Gender.* New York: Routledge, 1989.

Spiro, Rand, Bertrum Bruce, and William Brewer. *Theoretical Issues in Reading Comprehension: Perspectives from Cognitive Psychology, Linguistics, Artificial Intelligence, and Education.* Hillsdale, NJ: Erlbaum, 1980.

Spolsky, Ellen, ed. *The Uses of Adversity: Failure and Accommodation in Reader Response.* Lewisburg: Bucknell UP; Cranbury, NY: Associated University Presses, 1990.

Spurlin, William. "Theorizing Signifyin(g) and the Role of the Reader: Possible Directions for African-American Literary Criticism." *College English* 52 (1990): 732–42.

Straw, Stanley B. "Reading and Response to Literature: Transactionalizing Instruction." *Perspectives on Talk and Learning.* Eds. Susan Hynds and Donald L. Rubin. Urbana: NCTE, 1990. 129–48.

Swartz, Larry. *Dramathemes: A Practical Guide for Teaching Drama.* Portsmouth, NH: Heinemann, 1988.

Thomson, Jack. *Understanding Teenagers Reading: Reading Processes and the Teaching of Literature.* New York: Nichols, 1986.

Tierney, Robert, Patricia Anders, and Judith Mitchell. *Understanding Readers Understanding.* Hillsdale, NJ: Erlbaum, 1987.

Tomlinson, Alan, ed. *Consumption, Identity, Style.* New York: Routledge, 1991.

Trimmer, Joseph. "Reading and Writing Culture: A Group Memoir." *Reader: Essays in Reader-Oriented Theory, Criticism, and Pedagogy* 27 (1992): 21–28.

Vipond, Douglas, and Russell A. Hunt. "Literary Processing and Response as Transaction: Evidence for the Contribution of Readers, Texts, and Situations." *Comprehension of Literary Discourse: Results and Problems of Interdisciplinary Approaches.* Eds. Dietrich Meutsch and Reinhold Viehoff. Berlin: De Gruyter, 1988. 155–74.

Williamson, Judith. *Consuming Passions.* London: Marion Boyars, 1987.

Winnett, Susan. "Coming Unstrung: Women, Men, Narrative, and Principles of Pleasure." *PMLA* 105 (1990): 505–19.

# Index

Abrams, M. H., 1
Abstract thinking, 76
*Act of Reading, The,* 20
Act/trait/belief/goal/plan relationships, 86–87
Actual reader, 25
Advertisements, response to, 32–33, 138, 142–143
Aesthetic response, 46, 50, 69, 163
Affective fallacy, 15, 17, 53, 164
Alcorn, Marshall, 97–98
Analogizers, 92
Ang, Ien, 127
Anxiety, 54
Applebee, Arthur, 75, 76
Appleyard, J. A., 72–75
Artifacts, 126
Assertion, 90
Associationists, 91
Assumptions, 126
Atwell, Nancie, 121, 123
Audience identification, 33
Authorial audience, 24–25, 27
Autobiographical experiences, 64–65, 82

Bakhtin, Mikhail, 111–112, 113, 163
Barthes, Roland, 37, 38, 43, 58, 129, 164
Bartholomae, David, 109
Baudrillard, Jean, 44, 124
Baym, Nina, 137
Beardsley, Monroe, 17
*Becoming a Reader,* 72
Beers, Terry, 90
*Before Reading,* 24, 25
Beidler, Phil, 65
Bettelheim, Bruno, 72
Bishop, Wendy, 58
Bleich, David, 53, 97, 132
Bloome, David, 105–106, 120, 164
Body of knowledge, 46
Bolter, Jay David, 40
Book clubs, 9, 114, 120–121, 122, 145–146
Book-of-the-Month Club, 146

Booth, Wayne, 61
Bormann, Ernest, 34
*Brain of Robert Frost,* The, 96
Brancher, Michael, 97–98
Britzman, Deborah, 41–42
Brooks, Peter, 95
Broudy, Harry, 91
Brown, Rexford, 118
Bruner, Jerome, 27, 100–101
Burke, Kenneth, 32, 33

*Call of Stories, The,* 61
Causal links, defining, 84–85
Cause-and-effect relationships, 110
Censorship, 110–111
Characterized audience, 25
Characterized reader, 25
*Child's Concept of Story, The,* 75
Clark, Gregory, 111–112
Class, 145–148
Classics, 7
Classroom as social community, 117–123
Clifford, John, 51, 54
Close reading, 2
Closure, 29, 43, 51
Cognitive development, 75–77
Cognitive linguistic theory of response, 92–94
Cognitive processing models of response, 82–92
    defining causal links, 84–85
    hypothesis making/problem finding, 83–84
    individual differences in use of cognitive strategies, 91–92
    inference, 86–87
    prediction, 85
    schema, readers' use of, 87–91
Cognitive strategies, 91–92
Coherence, 26, 29–30
Coles, Nicholas, 147
Coles, Robert, 61
Collins, Christopher, 90
*Company We Keep, The,* 61

Competent reader, 6, 43, 51
Complexity, 158
Composing process, influence of theories on, 3, 69
Computer graphics, 63
Conceptual metaphors, 92–93
Concretizations, 20
Configuration, 26, 29
Connected knowing, 113–114, 142
Connecting, 52, 64–65
Connotation, 36
Consistency-building, 21, 23
Constance School of Reception Theory, 20
Constructed knowledge, 81
Constructing, 52, 59–60
Constructivist theory, 163
Construers, 91
Context, 7, 9, 35, 47–48, 87, 97, 100, 115, 136–139
*Contingent Meanings: Postmodern Fiction, Mimesis, and the Reader,* 43
Controlled literary events, 123–124
Cooperative Principle, theory of, 115
Corcoron, Bill, 62
Correct answers, 50, 51, 80, 83, 87, 118, 120, 157
Correct predictions, 85
Critical interpretation, 31
*Critical I, The,* 94
Critical reader, 35
Cruising, 44
Culler, Jonathan, 19, 43, 46, 96
Cultural consciousness, 159
Cultural context, 47, 100
Cultural differences, 108, 128, 159
Cultural psychology, 100–101
Cultural socialization, 69
Cultural theories of response, 14, 125–152
  applying, 159–161
  class, 145–148
  common cultural practices, 125–126
  defined, 9
  ethnographic exploration of cultural worlds, 148–150
  gender roles and attitudes, 139–144
  limitations of, 150–152
  poststructuralist theories, 126–139
  reading formations, 129–130, 136–139
  teachers', 148
Cycles of utterances, 121


Dasenbrock, Reed Way, 107
Davidson, Donald, 107

DEFT (defense, expectation, fantasy, transformation), 94
DeMott, Benjamin, 146–147
Denotation, 36
Describer perspective, 76
Developmental psychological theories, 71–82
  reader roles and, 72–75
Dialogic theory, 111–114, 163
Dias, Patrick, 52, 54, 104
Disbelief, suspension of, 27, 28
Discourses, 127–128
Discursive practices, 127–128
Dominant specularity, 126–127
Donahue, Patricia, 130
*Double Perspective, The,* 97
Drama activities, 122
Dualism, 19, 112
Dualist stage of development, 74–75, 80, 82
Dynamic memory, 88–89


Eagleton, Terry, 1, 46
Easthope, Anthony, 152
Ebert, Teresa, 125
Eckert, Penelope, 109, 133, 148
Eco, Umberto, 30–31, 35
Efferent response, 50–51, 163
Emotional response, 53–54
Empathizing, 60–61
Encoded reader, 6
Engaging, 52–55
*Enhancing Aesthetic Reading and Response,* 62
Envisionments, 49, 59–60, 83, 157
Ethnographic exploration, 148–150
Evaluating, 52, 64–65
Ewen, Stuart, 138
Expectations, 90
Experiential theories of response, 14, 49–70
  applying, 156–157
  connecting, 64–65
  constructing an imagined world, 59–60
  defined, 8, 49
  engaging, 52–55
  experiencing the language of emotions, 55–59
  identifying/empathizing, 60–61
  judging the quality of one's experience with texts, 65–66
  limitations of, 68–70
  processes of, 52–66
  reflecting on one's responses to texts, 66–68

and textual theories compared, 51–52
visualizing, 62–63
Exploratory talk, 118, 120

Fantasy theme, 34
Fantasy vision, 34
Feedback loop, 96
Felt-sense experience, 52
Feminist criticism, 132, 139
Feminist theories, 9, 113
Film, 37, 98
Fish, Stanley, 22, 106–108, 151, 163
Fiske, John, 130–131
Flitterman-Lewis, Sandy, 98, 99
Formalist approach, 2
Forstrop, Per-Anders, 131–132
Forum, 128–129
Foucault, Michel, 127, 128, 150
Fox, Thomas, 141–142
Free-association response, 96
Freewriting, 24, 33, 38, 112, 121, 157
Freund, Elizabeth, 5, 22, 46, 96

Galda, Lee, 77
Gass, William, 62
Gee, James Paul, 104
Gender differences, 114
Gender identity, 131
Gender roles, 131, 135, 139–144
Genre(s), 7, 17, 30–32
Gergen, Kenneth, 100
Gilligan, Carol, 79
Goffman, Erving, 115, 117
Goldman, Irene, 144
Green, Henry, 42
Grice, H. Paul, 115–116
Griffith, Peter, 22–23
Grossman, Pamela, 5
Group membership, 34, 131, 132–135
Group visions, 34

Habermas, Jurgen, 41
Hansson, Gunnar, 23–24
Harris, Joseph, 4, 160
Haswell, Richard, 33
Hebdige, Dick, 44
Heteroglossia, 112, 113
Historical context, 23–24, 136–139
Historical writing, 7
Historical-empirical approach, 23
Hobson, Dorothy, 108–109
Holland, Norman, 47, 94–97
Horizon(s), 21

of expectations, 23
of possibilities, 60
Hull, Glynda, 147
Hunt, Russell, 27, 28, 92, 164
Hurst, Kenneth, 121
Hyperreality, 124
Hypertext, 39–41, 163
Hynds, Susan, 86–87, 120
Hypothesis making, 83–84

Ideal ego, 97, 98
Idealistic approach, 23
Identifying, 60–61
Identity style, 95, 99
Ideology, 47
Illusion of regularity, 129
Images, meaning of, 138
Imaginative reconstruction, 60
Imagined world, constructing, 59–60
Implied reader, 5–6, 25
*Implied Reader, The*, 20
Inference, 86–87
Information-driven stance, 27–28, 92,
    164
Information-processing approach, 100
Informed reader, 6
Ingarden, Roman, 19, 20, 22, 24
Inscribed reader, 6
Intellectual development, 80–82
Intended reader, 25
Intentional fallacy, 15, 164
Interactive essays, 39–40
Internal dialogue, 111–112
Interpretive community, 6, 106–108, 118,
    151, 163
*Interpretive Conventions*, 21
Intertextual loop, 38
Intertextuality, 37–41, 65, 105, 131, 164
Introspection, 90
Iran-Nejad, Asghar, 88
Iser, Wolfgang, 20, 21, 22–23, 24
I-Test, 95

Jauss, Hans Robert, 23, 24
Journal writing, 57–58, 68, 121, 158
Judgment, 90

Kaivola, Karen, 144
Keroes, Jo, 28
Knowing, perspectives on, 81
Knowing-how knowledge, 17–18, 24, 25,
    44–45
Knowing-that knowledge, 18, 44–45

Knowledge-transmission model, 4
Kohlberg, Lawrence, 77, 78–79
Kuhn, Thomas, 105

Labov, William, 26
Lacan, Jacques, 97
Lamb, Catherine, 113
Landow, George, 40
Langer, Judith, 59–60, 66, 83
Language of reflection, 56–57, 68
Language of the emotions, experiencing, 55–59
Large-group discussions, 119–120
Learned cultural practice, 132
Lehr, Susan, 87
Literacy events, 123–124
Literal recall questions, 51
Literalists, 91
Literary canon, 7
Literary criticism, 1, 128
Literary theory, traditional, 7
Literate reader, 6
*Literature as Exploration*, 49
Long, Elizabeth, 145–146
Loop, 31
*Lost in a Book: The Psychology of Reading for Pleasure*, 55

Machor, James, 137
Mailloux, Steven, 2, 15, 21–22, 23, 136
Marshall, James, 119–120
Mass media, 35–37
Meaning-making, 1, 9, 22
Media forms, response to, 7, 37
Mental models, 89–90
Mock reader, 5
Modeling, 58
Model reader, 6, 31, 35
Modleski, Tania, 132
Monologic perspective, 112
Moore, Michael, 149
Moral messages, 51
Moral reasoning, 77–80
Moral relativism, 79
*Mulligan Stew*, 42–43
Multiplicity, 80, 148

Naive moves, 117
Narratee/reader, 6
Narrative audience, 27–28
Narrative conventions, knowledge of, 24–30
Nell, Victor, 55, 75, 99

*NewBook Editor*, 39
New Criticism, 1–2, 15, 128, 164
   challenges to, 17
   influence of on practice, 2–3
Notice, 25, 26–27

Objective paradigm, 53
Obtuse meanings, 129–130
Ohmann, Richard, 145, 150
Old Criticism, 15
Open culture, 126
Organization, reader-based definition of, 33–34
Other-shoe rule, 29

Paper icon cutouts, 63
Paradigms, 126
Passing theory, 107–108
Peer evaluation, 3
Perception, 90
Perry, William, 80
Phenomenological response theories, 19–24
Plurality, 43
*Poetic Closure*, 29
Point-driven stance, 28, 92, 106, 164
Porter, James, 128–129
Postmodernism, 42–45
Poststructuralist theory, 6, 9, 69, 126–139, 164
   critique of textual theory, 41–45, 47
   group membership, 132–135
   institutional socialization of response, 130–132
   and postmodern literature, 42–45
   reading formations, 129–130, 136–139
Poulet, Georges, 19–20
Pratt, Mary Louise, 148
Predicting, 85
Preferred response, 120
Presentational talk, 118, 120
Press, Andrea, 146
Price, Marian, 157
Prior knowledge, 20, 38, 84–85, 121, 156
Problem-solving process, 83–84
Probst, Robert, 52, 54
Procedural display, 120
Procedural knowledge, 81
Process-centered approach, 3
Psychoanalytical theories of response, 94–99
Psychological theories of response, 14, 71–101
   applying, 157–158

cognitive development, 75–77
cognitive linguistic theory, 92–94
cognitive-processing models, 82–92
  defined, 8
developmental theories, 71–82
intellectual development, levels of, 80–82
limitations of, 99–101
moral reasoning and response, 77–80
psychoanalytical theories, 94–99
Psychological-symbolic approach, 24
Purves, Alan, 51, 91, 108

Rabinowitz, Peter, 24–25, 26, 27, 29–30, 31, 85
Radway, Janice, 140, 146, 149
Ransom, John Crowe, 15
Ray, William, 107
Reader(s)
  differing interpretations of, 5–6
  as hero and heroine, 72–73
  as interpreter, 74–75
  as player, 72
  as pragmatic user of texts, 75
  response of, 6
  rules to assist, 25–26
  as thinker, 73–74
  types of, 25
*Reader in the Text, The,* 1
*Reader, The Text, The Poem, The,* 50, 52
Reader-based theory of reading, 5, 57
Reader-response critics, 1–2, 132
Reader-response theory
  and New Criticism compared, 1–2, 15
  conceptions of roles, purposes, texts, and contexts, 5–7
  five perspectives on, overview of, 7–14
  growing influence of, 1
Reading for character, 137–138
Reading formations, 145, 164
  acquiring, 129–130
  in historical contexts, 136–139
  teachers', 148
*Reading Minds,* 93
Reading the culture, 127
*Reading the Romance,* 140
Real reader, 25
Received knowledge, 81
Reflection process, three phases of, 67–68
Relativist/committed relativist stage of development, 80–81
Response
  as an event, 50
  planning activities for, 153–154

Response media, 6
Response statement, 57
Retrospection, 90
Revision, 3
*Rhetorical Power,* 15
Rhetorical response theories, 32–35
  responding to form, 33–35
Rich, Adrienne, 114, 143–144
Richards, I. A., 16
Roemer, Marjorie Godlin, 128
*Roger and Me,* 149
Rogers, Mary, 117
*Roland Barthes,* 38
Romance novels, 140–141
Rose, Mike, 147
Rosenblatt, Louise, 46, 49–52, 59, 68, 163, 165
Rule of conclusive endings, 29
Rules of balance, 29
Rules of coherence, 26, 29–30
Rules of configuration, 26, 29
Rules of contingencies, 30, 85
Rules of notice, 25, 26–27
Rules of rupture, 26
Rules of significance, 25, 27–29

Saturated self, 100
Saussure, Ferdinand de, 35, 126
Schein, Edgar, 125–126
Schema, 164
  readers' use of, 20, 87–91
Scholes, Robert, 32, 127
Schweickart, Patricinio, 59, 114, 139
Schwenger, Peter, 141
Scientific approach, 15, 47
Searle, John, 115
Selden, Raman, 43
Self, 96–97, 100–101, 104
Self-definition, 68
Semantic differential scales, 63
Semantic interpretation, 30
Semiotic response theories, 35–41
  intertextuality in, 37–41
Sicherman, Barbara, 114
Significance, 25, 27–29
Signifier/signified, 126
Slatoff, William, 53
Small-group discussions, 67, 120
Smith, Barbara Herrnstein, 29, 47
Smith, Michael, 28, 120
Social constructivist theory, 9, 105–111
  interpretive community, 106–108
  social roles, 108–111
Social context, 35, 48, 87, 97, 100
Social interactionalists, 114–115

Social negotiation, 87, 109–110
Social roles, 108–111, 118, 122–123
Social theories of response, 14, 103–124
   applying, 158–159
   classroom as social community, 117–
      123
   defined, 8–9
   dialogic theory, 111–114, 163
   limitations of, 123–124
   social constructivist theory, 105–111
   speech-act and sociological theories,
      114–117
Solomon, Robert, 55–56
Sorrentino, Gilbert, 42–43
Sosnoski, James, 40–41
Spectator's perspective, 56, 68, 77
Speech-act theory, 17, 105, 114–117, 132
Speech communities, 127
Spiro, Rand, 90–91
Spurlin, William, 23
Stance, 164
Steig, Michael, 54–55, 64–65
*Stories of Reading*, 54
Story-driven stance, 28, 92, 164
Strategic interaction, 117
Stream-of-consciousness response, exam-
   ples of, 11–14
Structuralist linguistics, 17, 19, 46
*Structuralist Poetics: Structuralism, Lin-
   guistics and the Study of Literature*, 19
Student(s)
   social roles of, 109–110, 118, 122
*Subjective Criticism*, 53
Subjective knowledge, 81
Subjective paradigm, 53
Subjective positions, 129. *See also* Read-
   ing formations
Subjective tense, 26, 27
Subjective voice, 81, 82
Sufficiency, maxim of, 116
Suleiman, Susan, 1
Super reader, 6
Svensson, Cai, 45, 77


Tannen, Deborah, 114, 144
Teacher(s)
   reading formations, 148
   reflection/research, 161–162
   social roles of, 109, 110, 118, 122–123
Teacher-controlled classroom, 119–120
Television, 37, 98–99, 127, 146, 160
Tellability, 26–27
Text(s)
   as autonomous entities, 38

effect of on readers, 16
   links between, 38–39
   total view of, 21
Textual shifters, 129, 131
Textual theories of response, 14, 15–48
   applying, 155–156
   defined, 8
   evolution of, 15–19
   genre conventions, knowledge of, 30–
      32
   intertextuality, 37–41
   limitations of, 45–48
   narrative conventions, knowledge of,
      24–30
   phenomenological theories, 19–24
   poststructuralist critique of, 41–45, 47
   rhetorical theories, 32–35
   semiotic theories, 35–41
Text-centered theory of reading, 4–5, 16,
   57
Thematic analysis, 103
Theory
   application of, 3–4, 153–162
   influence of on practice, 2–5
Think-aloud responses, 24, 45, 52, 58,
   85, 95, 157
Tompkins, Jane, 123, 142
Total view, 21
Transactional theory, 5, 52, 165
Transmission/testing model of teaching,
   46
Trillin, Calvin, 133–134
Turner, Graeme, 151
Turner, Mark, 93


Unconventional responses, 147–148
*Uses of Enchantment, The*, 72


Values, 126
Varsava, Jerry, 43
Vipond, Douglas, 27, 28, 92, 164
Visualizing, 62–63
Visual perception, 90
Vygotsky, Lev, 105


Wall, Susan, 147
Wandering viewpoint, 20–21
Whole Language Movement, 44
Willbern, David, 94–95
Williams, Raymond, 104
Willinsky, John, 52, 69
Wilson, W. Daniel, 25
Wimsatt, William, 17

Winnett, Susan, 95
Winning over metaphor, 113
*With Respect to Readers*, 53
*Women's Ways of Knowing*, 81
Wordsworth, William, 24
Wright, Elizabeth, 47

Writing instruction, 3, 118
*Writing Space, The*, 40
Writing workshop approach, 3, 110


Zancanella, Don, 4

# Author

**Richard Beach** is professor of English education at the University of Minnesota. He has served as treasurer and is currently president of NCRE. He coedited *New Directions in Composition Research, Developing Discourse Practices in Adolescence and Adulthood,* and *Multidisciplinary Perspectives on Literacy Research,* and is coauthor of *Teaching Literature in the Secondary School.* He has chaired the Board of Trustees for the NCTE Research Foundation and is currently a member of the National Board for Professional Teaching Standards.